graphis annual 76|77

Edited by Walter Herdeg

This is the 25th annual edition of a work that has been consistently called "a visual feast." This year's collection, from all over the world, continues its survey of graphics in advertisements, annual reports, booklets, book jackets and magazine covers, trade marks, letterheads, packaging, record covers, film and television and editorial design—selecting and beautifully reproducing what is happening in all design fields. Here is an endless source of ideas and a perfect "swipe file" for art directors, illustrators and designers, keeping them up-to-date as well as offering new ideas and solutions to graphic arts problems.

The Two Companion Annuals, Edited by Walter Herdeg:

GRAPHIS POSTERS

The International Annual of Poster Art

"The contemporary poster in its diverse usage for art, the stage, trade and industry and political propaganda, fills the need for many purposes," reports *Creative Signs & Displays*. "Technical advances have added to the richness and multiformity of the modern poster, which has risen to the position of an evolving art form." This new third edition offers visual evidence arranged in four major categories: *Advertising* posters, *Cultural* posters, *Social* posters, *Decorative* posters.
Published each year in early Spring.

PHOTOGRAPHIS

The International Annual of Advertising, Editorial and Television Photography

Here presented are outstanding photographic achievements from some 30 countries around the world in Advertising (magazines, newspapers, films); Annual Reports; Book Jackets; Editorial Photography; Magazine Covers; Record Covers; Packaging; Calendars; House Organs; Booklets; Television. "A 'must have' for anyone who wants to keep up-to-date in the visual communications business."—*Art Direction Magazine*.
Published each year in late Spring.

Other Graphis Books, Edited by Walter Herdeg:

A new series in "Square Books" format (9-½" × 9-⅜") :

GRAPHIS / RECORD COVERS

GRAPHIS / DIAGRAMS

The Graphic Visualization of Abstract Data

FILM AND TV GRAPHICS 2

introduction by John Halas

In 9-½" × 12" format :

GRAPHIS / ANNUAL REPORTS

Text by Richard A. Lewis

GRAPHIS / PACKAGING 2

GRAPHIS / PACKAGING 3 (In Preparation)

Write for a complete catalogue :

VISUAL COMMUNICATION BOOKS

Hastings House, Publishers, Inc., 10 East 40th Street, New York, N.Y. 10016

graphis annual

76|77 graphis annual

The International Annual of Advertising and
Editorial Graphics

Das internationale Jahrbuch der Werbe-
graphik und der redaktionellen Graphik

Le répertoire international de l'art graphique
publicitaire et rédactionnel

Edited by: / Herausgegeben von: / Réalisé par:

Walter Herdeg

Walter Herdeg, The Graphis Press, Zurich

Distributed in the United States by

Hastings House

Publishers

10 East 40th Street, New York, N.Y. 10016

PUBLICATION No. 145   [ISBN   0-8038-2682-6]

Contents

Inhalt

Sommaire

Abbreviations

Argentina . . . . ARG
Australia . . . . AUL
Belgium . . . . BEL
Brazil . . . . BRA
Canada . . . . CAN
Cuba . . . . CUB
Czechoslovakia . . . . CSR
Finland . . . . FIN
France . . . . FRA
Germany (East) . . . . GDR
Germany (West) . . . . GER
Great Britain . . . . GBR
Hawaii . . . . HAW
Hong Kong . . . . HKG
Hungary . . . . HUN
India . . . . IND
Israel . . . . ISR
Italy . . . . ITA
Japan . . . . JPN
Mexico . . . . MEX
Monte Carlo . . . . MON
Netherlands . . . . NLD
Norway . . . . NOR
Poland . . . . POL
South Africa . . . . SAF
Spain . . . . SPA
Sweden . . . . SWE
Switzerland . . . . SWI
USA . . . . USA
Yugoslavia . . . . YUG

Abkürzungen

Argentinien . . . . ARG
Australien . . . . AUL
Belgien . . . . BEL
Brasilien . . . . BRA
Deutschland (Ost) . . . . . . GDR
Deutschland (West) . . . . . GER
Finnland . . . . FIN
Frankreich . . . . FRA
Grossbritannien . . . . GBR
Hawaii . . . . HAW
Hongkong . . . . HKG
Indien . . . . IND
Israel . . . . ISR
Italien . . . . ITA
Japan . . . . JPN
Jugoslawien . . . . YUG
Kanada . . . . CAN
Kuba . . . . CUB
Mexiko . . . . MEX
Monte Carlo . . . . MON
Niederlande . . . . NLD
Norwegen . . . . NOR
Polen . . . . POL
Schweden . . . . SWE
Schweiz . . . . SWI
Spanien . . . . SPA
Südafrika . . . . SAF
Tschechoslowakei . . . . . . CSR
Ungarn . . . . HUN
USA . . . . USA

Abréviations

Afrique du Sud . . . . SAF
Allemagne occidentale . . . . GER
Allemagne orientale . . . . . GDR
Argentine . . . . ARG
Australie . . . . AUL
Belgique . . . . BEL
Brésil . . . . BRA
Canada . . . . CAN
Cuba . . . . CUB
Espagne . . . . SPA
Etats-Unis . . . . USA
Finlande . . . . FIN
France . . . . FRA
Grande-Bretagne . . . . . . GBR
Hawaii . . . . HAW
Hongkong . . . . HKG
Hongrie . . . . HUN
Inde . . . . IND
Israël . . . . ISR
Italie . . . . ITA
Japon . . . . JPN
Mexique . . . . MEX
Monte Carlo . . . . MON
Norvège . . . . NOR
Pays-Bas . . . . NLD
Pologne . . . . POL
Suède . . . . SWE
Suisse . . . . SWI
Tchécoslovaquie . . . . CSR
Yougoslavie . . . . YUG

■ ARNOLD SAKS has designed the cover of this issue and has succeeded in suggesting something of the excitement of opening a new book. Born in New York in 1931, he studied at Syracuse University and the Yale School of Design before setting up his own design studio in 1967. Since then he has worked for some of the leading American companies and has gained a considerable international reputation.

HELMUT SCHMITZ has distinguished himself as a Creative Director of the German Doyle Dane Bernbach agency in Düsseldorf, for instance in his work on Volkswagen advertising in Germany. He is also a partner in the Hildmann, Simon, Rempen & Schmitz agency. He recently attracted attention with a plea for more creativity in a publication of the Art Directors Club of West Germany, and we therefore invited him to summarize here views which, though inspired primarily by the German scene, are equally applicable in most other countries.

■ ARNOLD SAKS, der den Umschlag dieser Ausgabe gestaltet hat, drückt damit die Erwartung und Neugierde beim Öffnen eines neuen Buches aus. Er wurde 1931 in New York geboren und studierte an der Syracuse Universität und der Yale School of Design, bevor er 1967 sein eigenes Design-Studio eröffnete. Zu seinen Kunden zählt er führende amerikanische Unternehmen. Durch seine Arbeiten errang er grosse internationale Anerkennung.

HELMUT SCHMITZ machte sich vor allem als Kreativer Direktor von Doyle Dane Bernbach in Düsseldorf einen Namen, zum Beispiel durch die VW-Werbung in Deutschland. Er ist Mitinhaber der Agentur Hildmann, Simon, Rempen & Schmitz. Kürzlich zog er die Aufmerksamkeit der Werbebranche auf sich durch einen fundierten Aufruf nach mehr Kreativität, der in einer Publikation des westdeutschen Art Director Clubs erschien. Wir haben ihn deshalb eingeladen, hier seine Ansichten in gekürzter Form darzulegen. Obwohl er sich natürlich hauptsächlich an der deutschen Werbeszene orientiert, gelten seine Aussagen weitgehend auch für andere Länder.

■ ARNOLD SAKS, qui a réalisé l'illustration de couverture, a réussi à exprimer l'excitation et la curiosité dont le lecteur est piqué en ouvrant un nouveau livre. Né en 1931 à New York, Arnold Saks a fait ses études à l'Université de Syracuse et à la Yale School of Design, avant de fonder son propre studio de design. Depuis lors il travaille pour des compagnies américaines importantes et ses créations lui ont valu une réputation internationale.

HELMUT SCHMITZ s'est fait un nom en tant que directeur créatif de Doyle Dane Bernbach à Dusseldorf, p. ex. par les campagnes publicitaires pour la VW en Allemagne. Il est l'un des associés de l'agence Hildmann, Simon, Rempen & Schmitz. Récemment il a retenu l'attention des publicitaires allemands par l'appel qu'il a lancé dans une publication du Club des directeurs artistiques de l'Allemagne occidentale en faveur d'un retour à la créativité. Nous l'avons invité à exposer ses idées dans ces pages. Nous sommes bien conscients qu'il s'oriente à la situation de la publicité en Allemagne, mais ses déclarations sont également valables pour nombre d'autres pays.

Although the graphic design profession has felt the pinch of the recession, the contents of this volume seem to show that the quality of its productions has not suffered, at least not in the higher performance ranges. Once again our sincere thanks go to all our contributors for the trouble taken in submitting their work, whether it has been retained in this final selection or not.

Obwohl auf dem Gebiet des Graphik-Designs der durch die Rezession bedingte Rückschlag deutlich spürbar war, zeigt doch der Inhalt dieses Bandes, dass die Qualität der Arbeiten nicht darunter gelitten hat, zumindest nicht, was die niveaumässig hochstehenden Arbeiten betrifft. Auch dieses Jahr möchten wir wieder allen Mitarbeitern für Ihre Bemühungen danken, ob ihre Arbeiten reproduziert werden konnten oder nicht.

Bien que le recul dû à la récession ait touché avant tout les professions graphiques, il est manifeste — en voilà la preuve — que la qualité des créations graphiques n'en a pas souffert, du moins des créations d'un niveau élevé. Nous tenons à adresser nos sincères remerciements à tous ceux qui ont contribué à la réalisation de cet ouvrage, que leurs travaux aient été reproduits ou non.

Competition improves business. Competition improves the quality of advertising.

There's little or no competition in the Eastern Bloc countries. Hence there has never been any advertising worthy of mention. And surely none at all that could compare with the advertising of the highly industrialized, consumption-minded Western world as we see it day by day. A simple case? An extreme one? Of course. But one that can help us to understand why and when advertising has been and is important.

Why is it that for about seventy years now the essential impulses for innovative, attention-getting, creative, human, convincing and artistically outstanding advertising have come from the USA?

Why is it that good advertising was done in Europe before World War I? In the Golden Twenties? But not in the fifties?

Before World War I, when the idea of product brands was born, competition and the pressure of competition grew rapidly. This also applies to the Golden Twenties, but competition and the pressure of competition in those days increased even more.

During both wars there was hardly any advertising because there was nothing to be advertised. In simple words: goods were rationed. And very few companies advertised their products with patriotic or other goodwill advertisements just to be sure that the consumer would remember them. Not many companies realized in those days that advertising is a long-term investment.

As far as the fifties are concerned, the demand then exceeded the supply in most countries. It is, however, curious and difficult to understand why in the mid-fifties most European countries failed to learn anything from the advertising being done in the USA. After all, there was outstanding advertising by Ogilvy, Bernbach, Y&R and others. Good campaigns of that period are still good in our period. Twenty years later these campaigns speak for themselves. They made, and now are advertising history.

Perhaps this phenomenon can be explained by the fact that marketing and advertising people did not think it necessary to win the consumer's confidence in new ways in the absence of pressure from competition. Another explanation might be that the higher advertising echelons of those days, the old gentlemen in general, continued to do advertising the way they had learned to do it in the pre-war years. Simple, primitive, boring, trivial and ugly advertising. For that's how their advertising looked, with very few exceptions.

A little bit of Swiss graphics, mostly badly copied, was the most advertising in Germany aspired to. And the few good posters were nearly all made by Swiss. They were—to name a few designers— by Looser, Bühler or Leupin. If one browses in old annuals of that period or in magazines and newspapers, this fact is very evident.

There was lack of discernment, of mobility, though not really of talent. The existence of talent soon became obvious in the advertising of the sixties and seventies.

Things really started in the early sixties when, for example, the "VW beetle" in Germany for the first time met with competition from the new "Opel Kadett" and the new "Ford Taunus". Then the American detergent giants and other powerful companies penetrated the preserves of European business with vigour and success.

Dozens of examples reveal that for the first time since the twenties the quality of European advertising now became comparable with the quality of American advertising.

Creativity was in.

Creativity was essential, for there was no other way to be different in advertising from the competition, which became more fierce as the market was saturated with products. A few years later, though, from about 1972 onwards until 1974, creativity was out again. The reason was the recession with its cult of playing safe. Fear of possible failure destroyed the first creative phase in the post-war period.

Marketing techniques, exaggerated ad-hoc sales promotion measures and an unreasonable belief in tests of all kinds destroyed creative work instead of supplying creative impulses, although the times would have needed them. Marketing and creative people regarded each other as enemies instead of partners.

Nowadays, and particularly in the past two years, creativity has ceased to be a dirty word and has again become a recognized means—perhaps the only one—of reaching people, of inspiring enthusiasm in them and convincing them. Mathematics and frequently debatable tests are again considered only as auxiliaries and are being replaced more and more by common sense, intuition and art.

The second creative wave, already predicted by a small group, is now under way. More and more advertising is called for that does not merely satisfy the ego of the salesman or the marketing strategist but puts the consumer first. Advertising which doesn't talk down to the consumer, but with him. That doesn't use a sledgehammer to make a point, but argument and persuasion. That doesn't employ appalling artwork, but modesty and understanding, disciplined creativity and art.

Art is not a science, nor is advertising, which is instead the art of presentation and demonstration, but also of persuasion. And anybody who tells you anything else deserves neither your confidence nor your money.

Helmut Schmitz

Konkurrenz belebt des Geschäft.
Konkurrenz hebt die Qualität der Werbung.

In den Ländern des Ostblocks gab es und gibt es kaum Konkurrenz. Gab und gibt es also auch kaum Werbung. Schon gar keine, die sich messen könnte mit dem, was heute in der hochindustrialisierten, konsumintensiven westlichen Welt tagtäglich erscheint. Ein einfaches Beispiel? Ein extremes? Sicherlich. Aber auch eines, das uns helfen kann, zu begreifen, warum wann Werbung wichtig war und ist.

Woran liegt es, dass seit gut 70 Jahren die wesentlichen Impulse für innovative, aufmerksamkeitsstarke, kreative, menschliche, überzeugende und ästhetisch hervorragende Werbung aus den USA kommen?

Woran liegt es, dass in Europa gute Werbung vor dem ersten Weltkrieg gemacht wurde? In den Goldenen 20igern? Aber nicht in den 50iger Jahren?

Vor dem ersten Weltkrieg, als die Idee des Markenartikels geboren wurde, entstand ziemlich schnell Wettbewerb und Konkurrenzdruck. In den Goldenen 20igern war es nicht anders, nur dass sich in diesen Jahren Konkurrenzdruck und Wettbewerb verschärften.

Während der beiden Kriege gab es fast keine Werbung, weil es fast nichts zu bewerben gab. Vereinfacht gesagt: Ware wurde zugeteilt. Und nur wenige Firmen warben mit patriotischen oder anderen Goodwill-Anzeigen für ihre Produkte, damit sie im Gedächtnis der Verbraucher blieben. Denn nur wenige Firmen hatten in dieser Zeit begriffen, dass Werbung langfristige Investition bedeutet.

Was die 50iger Jahre anbelangt, so existierte in den meisten Ländern viel Nachfrage und wenig Angebot. Warum man aber trotzdem in den mittleren 50iger Jahren in fast allen europäischen Ländern nichts von der Werbung gelernt hat, die in den USA erschien, bleibt ein Rätsel. Immerhin gab es dort die hervorragende Werbung von Ogilvy, von Bernbach, von Y & R und vielen anderen. Alles Kampagnen, die so gut waren zu ihrer Zeit, dass sie noch gut sind für unsere Zeit. Alles Kampagnen, die sich selbst nach 20 Jahren sehen lassen können. Alles Kampagnen, die Bestand haben und die Werbegeschichte gemacht haben.

Erklären kann man es vielleicht damit, dass man nicht eingesehen hat, dass man den Verbraucher umwerben muss mit neuen Möglichkeiten, auch wenn es nicht unbedingt nötig ist, sich gegen die Konkurrenz zu behaupten. Erklären kann man es auch damit, dass die früheren Werbegewaltigen, die alten Herren überhaupt und überall, Werbung weiter so machten, wie sie das vor dem Krieg gelernt hatten. Einfach, primitiv, langweilig, nichtssagend und hässlich. Denn so sah sie aus. Und so wirkte sie. Von wenigen Ausnahmen abgesehen.

Ein bisschen Schweizer Graphik — oberflächlich kopiert — war das Höchste, zu dem sich die Werbung besonders in Deutschland gelegentlich aufschwang. Und was es da an guten Plakaten gab, war meist von Schweizern gemacht. Von Looser etwa, von Bühler, von Leupin, um nur ein paar zu nennen. Wenn man in alten Jahrbüchern der Zeit oder in den Zeitschriften und Zeitungen der Zeit blättert, erkennt man das ganz deutlich.

Es hat also an der Einsicht gefehlt, an der Beweglichkeit, nicht aber unbedingt an Talent. Dass Talent vorhanden war, zeigte sich bald in der Werbung der 60iger und 70iger Jahre.

Richtig los ging es eigentlich erst in den frühen 60iger Jahren, als zum Beispiel in Deutschland der «VW-Käfer» zum ersten Mal Konkurrenz bekam durch den neuen «Opel-Kadett» und den neuen «Ford-Taunus». Als die amerikanischen Waschmittelriesen und andere potente Firmen in die Reservate europäischer Firmen mit Brisanz und Erfolg einbrachen.

Warum erst ab etwa 1962 die Qualität der europäischen Werbung zum ersten Mal seit den 20iger Jahren vergleichbar wurde mit der Qualität der amerikanischen lässt sich an Dutzenden von Beispielen erkennen.

Kreativität war in.

Weil Kreativität gebraucht wurde, denn sonst gab es keine Möglichkeit, sich durch Werbung von der Konkurrenz abzuheben, die immer stärker wurde, je besetzter die Märkte mit Produkten wurden. Doch ein paar Jahre später, etwa zwischen 1972 und 1974, war sie wieder out. Der Grund: Rezession, Angst, das Bestreben nach Sicherheit. Die Furcht vor einem Misserfolg zerstörte die erste kreative Phase der Nachkriegszeit.

Marketingtechniken, übertriebene, nur auf die Situation zugeschnittene Salespromotion-Massnahmen und eine unvernünftige Testgläubigkeit zerstörten kreative Arbeit, anstatt kreative Impulse zu geben. Obwohl das gerade in einer solchen Zeit besonders nötig gewesen wäre. Marketingleute und Kreative betrachteten einander als Feind anstatt als Partner.

Heute, besonders in den letzten zwei Jahren, ist Kreativität kein Schimpfwort mehr, sondern eine anerkannte Möglichkeit und wahrscheinlich sogar die einzige, Menschen zu erreichen, zu begeistern und zu überzeugen. Mathematik und oft höchst fragwürdige Tests aller Art werden wieder nur als Hilfsmittel angesehen und mehr und mehr durch Vernunft, Intuition und Kunst ersetzt.

Die zweite kreative Welle, die einige wenige unbeirrt von aller Hektik bereits vor gut zwei Jahren prophezeit haben, rollt. Mehr und mehr wird wieder Werbung verlangt, die nicht das Ego der Verkäufer, der Marketing-Strategen befriedigt, sondern die auf den Verbraucher eingeht. Die nicht auf ihn einredet, sondern mit ihm redet. Die nicht mit dem Holzhammer dummer und unglaubwürdiger Anbiederei und grauenhaftem Artwork arbeitet, sondern mit Bescheidenheit, Verständnis, gesteuerter Kreativität und Kunst.

Nun ist Kunst keine Wissenschaft. Werbung aber auch keine. Nicht nur als Kunst der Darbietung und der Darstellung, sondern auch als Kunst der Überzeugung. Und wenn Ihnen jemand etwas anderes vormacht, verdient er weder Ihr Vertrauen noch Ihr Geld.

Helmut Schmitz

Sans concurrence, pas d'affaires prospères.
Comment la concurrence profite à la qualité de la publicité.

Les pays socialistes de l'Est européen ne connaissent pratiquement pas la concurrence. Il ne faut donc pas s'étonner qu'il ne s'y soit jamais manifesté aucune publicité digne de ce nom. En tout cas pas une qui eût pu se comparer avec la publicité qui fleurit jour par jour dans les pays occidentaux fortement industrialisés où règne la société de consommation. Un exemple facile? trop exemplaire? Certes. Mais un exemple qui peut nous aider à saisir pourquoi et à quelle époque la publicité a eu et a encore de l'importance.

En effet, comment expliquer qu'il y a quelque soixante-dix ans, ce soient les Etats-Unis qui aient fourni l'essentiel des impulsions en faveur d'une publicité novatrice, accrochante, créatrice, humaine, convaincante et remarquable sur le plan artistique?

Comment expliquer que l'Europe ait connu une publicité de qualité avant la Première Guerre mondiale et au cours des «folles» années 1920, mais pas dans les années 50?

C'est dans les années précédant la Grande Guerre que fut lancée l'idée des produits de marque et que la concurrence se développa rapidement, et avec elle la pression commerciale. Le même phénomène se répéta avec une virulence accrue au cours des années 20.

En période de guerre – 14–18 et 39–45 –, la publicité fut à peu près nulle en raison de la pénurie de marchandises et du rationnement. Rares furent les entreprises qui veillèrent à maintenir vivante l'image de leurs produits en faisant une publicité aux accents patriotiques ou humanitaires. On peut compter sur les doigts les sociétés qui réalisaient alors que la publicité représente un investissement à long terme.

Quant au profil des années 50, il faut retenir que la demande excédait alors l'offre dans la plupart des pays du monde. Il paraît pourtant curieux et difficile à comprendre que, vers le milieu des années 50, la plupart des pays européens aient négligé de s'inspirer des expériences publicitaires américaines. Il existait pourtant d'excellentes agences telles qu'Ogilvy, Bernbach, Y & R, et d'autres. Les campagnes de qualité réalisées à cette époque ont gardé toute leur valeur. Vingt ans après, elles soutiennent parfaitement la comparaison. Elles ont modifié le cours de l'histoire de la publicité et en sont aujourd'hui des témoins capitaux.

Peut-être le phénomène sur lequel nous nous interrogeons peut-il s'expliquer par le fait que les spécialistes du marketing et les publicitaires de l'époque ne jugeaient pas nécessaire d'imaginer des voies nouvelles pour gagner la confiance du public en l'absence de la pression qu'exerce une concurrence acharnée. Une autre explication serait que les hommes occupant les échelons supérieurs de la profession se contentaient, l'âge venu, de faire la publicité de leur jeunesse, celle d'avant-guerre. Ne reculons pas devant les adjectifs simplet, primitif, insipide, trivial et laid pour caractériser ces productions, à quelques rares exceptions près.

En Allemagne par exemple, une faible dose de graphismes suisses, généralement mal copiés, constituait le sommet des aspirations créatrices. Les rares affiches de qualité étaient toutes l'œuvre d'artistes suisses, d'un Looser, d'un Bühler, d'un Leupin, pour ne nommer que ceux-là. C'est un fait qui saute aux yeux de qui se donne la peine de feuilleter les annuaires, magazines et journaux de l'époque.

Ce n'était pas tant le talent qui manquait que la faculté de discernement et la mobilité de l'esprit. Les talents n'attendaient pour s'affirmer et s'épanouir que l'atmosphère propice des années 60 et 70.

Le démarrage se fit au début des années 60 lorsque, pour prendre encore un exemple allemand, la Coccinelle VW se heurta à la concurrence des nouveaux modèles de Ford (Taunus) et d'Opel (Kadett). Puis quand les géants industriels américains, lessives en tête, s'attaquèrent avec vigueur et succès à la conquête des marchés européens.

Les exemples se comptent par douzaines où, pour la première fois depuis les années 1920, la qualité de la publicité européenne se haussa au niveau de l'américaine, autorisant la comparaison.

Le mot d'ordre de la créativité était désormais reconnu.

Ce souci de créativité était essentiel, car c'était bien là le seul moyen de se distinguer par rapport à la publicité de la concurrence, qui se fit de plus en plus vive dans la mesure où les marchés commencèrent à se saturer. Quelques années plus tard, pourtant, la créativité connut une éclipse passagère, d'environ

1972 à 1974. La raison en fut le climat de récession, qui incitait à la prudence. C'est ainsi que la crainte de l'échec commercial mit fin à la première phase créatrice de l'après-guerre.

Les techniques de marketing, les mesures exagérées de promotion des ventes décidées ad hoc et une propension à attacher une foi aveugle aux tests de tout genre eurent plus vite fait de tordre le cou à la créativité que de déclencher les impulsions créatrices pourtant indispensables au vu des circonstances. C'est ce qui amena la brouille entre gens du marketing et créateurs publicitaires, qui devraient rester tout naturellement étroitement associés dans toute entreprise de commercialisation.

Aujourd'hui, soit depuis deux ans, la créativité est ressortie des oubliettes et a de nouveau cours comme moyen — parmi d'autres, mais peut-être bien le seul — d'établir le contact avec le public, de susciter son enthousiasme et de le persuader. L'appel aux mathématiques et à la psychotechnique aux tests souvent discutés se fait de nouveau avec la discrétion qui sied à ces sciences purement auxili-aires. Ce qui prime à nouveau, c'est à juste titre le bon sens, l'intuition et l'art.

La seconde vague créatrice, annoncée par des efforts de groupes encore restreints, est en route. Les commandes publicitaires visent de plus en plus à satisfaire les besoins du consommateur aux dépens du prestige du vendeur ou de la satisfaction du stratège du marketing. Le résultat en est une publicité qui ne le prend pas de haut avec le consommateur, mais qui lui parle d'égal à égal. Il n'est alors plus question de frapper des grands coups de marteau, mais d'user d'une argumentation séduisante et de persuasion. Sur le plan artistique, cela signifie le renoncement aux grands effets souvent déplorables et le retour aux sources que sont la modestie, la compréhension, la créativité et l'art soumis à une discipline.

Si l'art n'est pas une science, la publicité l'est encore moins. C'est un art de présentation et de démonstration, mais aussi de persuasion. Ceux qui vous disent le contraire ne méritent ni votre confiance ni de se voir confier votre argent.

Helmut Schmitz

Index to Artists and Designers
Verzeichnis der Künstler und Gestalter
Index des artistes et maquettistes

15

Index to Art Directors
Verzeichnis der künstlerischen Leiter
Index des directeurs artistiques

Index to Agencies and Studios
Verzeichnis der Agenturen und Studios
Index des agences et studios

Index to Publishers
Verzeichnis der Verleger
Index des éditeurs

Index to Advertisers
Verzeichnis der Auftraggeber
Index des clients

■ Entry instructions will be mailed to anyone interested in submitting samples of outstanding graphics or photography for possible inclusion in our annuals. No fees involved. Closing dates for entries:
GRAPHIS ANNUAL (Advertising and editorial art): 15 December
PHOTOGRAPHIS (Advertising and editorial photography): 30 June
GRAPHIS POSTERS (International annual on poster art): 30 March
Write to: The Graphis Press, Dufourstr. 107, 8008 Zurich, Switzerland.

■ Einsendebedingungen können von jedermann angefordert werden, der uns Beispiele hervorragender Graphik oder Photographie zur Auswahl für unsere Jahrbücher unterbreiten möchte. Es werden keine Gebühren erhoben. Einsendetermine:
GRAPHIS ANNUAL (Werbe- und redaktionelle Graphik): 15. Dezember
PHOTOGRAPHIS (Werbe- und redaktionelle Photographie): 30. Juni
GRAPHIS POSTERS (Internationales Jahrbuch der Plakatkunst): 30. März
Adresse: Graphis Verlag, Dufourstr. 107, 8008 Zürich, Schweiz.

■ Tout intéressé à la soumission de travaux graphiques et photographiques est prié de nous demander les informations nécessaires. Sans charge de participation. Dates limites:
GRAPHIS ANNUAL (art graphique publicitaire et rédactionnel): 15 décembre
PHOTOGRAPHIS (photographie publicitaire et rédactionnelle): 30 juin
GRAPHIS POSTERS (répertoire international de l'art de l'affiche): 30 mars
S'adresser à: Editions Graphis, Dufourstr. 107, 8008 Zurich, Suisse.

Editor, Art Director, Designer: Walter Herdeg
Assistant Editor: Stanley Mason
Project Manager: Gabrielle Baumann
Art Assistants: Martin Byland, Ulrich Kemmner, René Sahli, Klaus Schröder, Otmar Staubli, Peter Wittwer

1

Magazine Advertisements

Newspaper Advertisements

Zeitschriften-Inserate

Zeitungs-Inserate

Annonces de revues

Annonces de presse

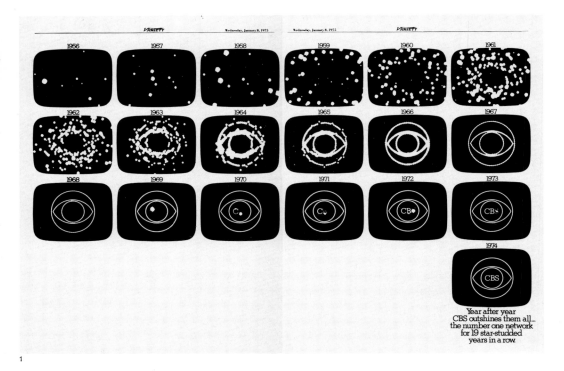

The hose you've waited for is now waiting for you.

New Synthecure™ from B.F.Goodrich. Available now. In a wide variety of types and sizes. And long lengths, up to 600'. Synthecure hose is tough and flexible. It's everything general purpose hose should be. And more. **BFGoodrich** Engineered Systems Company. The Moving Force Behind Your Business.

1 A titling sequence serves in this trade spread to celebrate the nineteen-year popularity lead of CBS Television. (USA)
2 Trade newspaper ad in full colour for a new type of hose made by B.F. Goodrich Co. (USA)
3 Ad for *Plessey* telecommunications urging people not to phone but to go and embrace friends personally at Christmas. (BRA)
4 Trade ad about *Grumman* systems of waste recovery. (USA)
5 Ad illustrating the preference of American concert pianists for *Steinway* pianos. Black and white. (USA)
6 Christmas greetings from Illinois Bell. Newspaper ad. (USA)
7, 8 Announcing the transmission of messages by RCA satellite—cheaper than by land. Magazine ad and artwork. (USA)

1 Inserat für CBS Television, das auf ihre 19jährige Führung in Zuschauerzahlen aufmerksam macht. (USA)
2 Zeitungs-Inserat für eine neue Sorte von Schläuchen, hergestellt von B.F. Goodrich Co. Mehrfarbig. (USA)
3 Inserat aus einer Kampagne für *Plessey*-Übermittlungssysteme, mit der Aufforderung, an Weihnachten nicht zu telefonieren, sondern die Wünsche persönlich zu überbringen. (USA)
4 Inserat für neue Systeme zur Wiederverwertung von Abfällen. (USA)
5 Inserat für *Steinway*-Klaviere, die von amerikanischen Konzert-Pianisten vorgezogen werden. Schwarzweiss. (USA)
6 Weihnachtswünsche einer Telefon-Gesellschaft, erschienen als Zeitungsinserat. (USA)
7, 8 Vollständiges Inserat und Detail, in welchem verkündet wird, dass Übermittlungen per Satellit billiger sind. (USA)

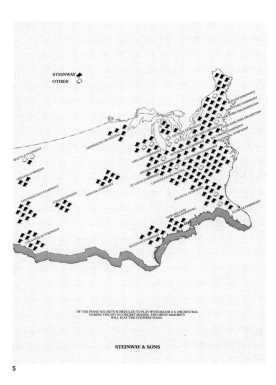

5

6

ARTIST / KÜNSTLER / ARTISTE:

1 George Mc Ginnis/Stan Beck
2 Elwyn Mehlman
3 Marguerita Bornstein
4 Don Ivan Punchatz
5 Catherine Campbell
6 John J. Asencio/Shawaluddin Anis (Photo)
7, 8 Richard Hess

DESIGNER / GESTALTER / MAQUETTISTE:

1 Lou Dorfsman/Ted Andresakes
2 Bob Kwait
4 Art Christy/Frank Perry
6 John J. Asencio
7, 8 Michael Sweret

ART DIRECTOR / DIRECTEUR ARTISTIQUE:

1 Lou Dorfsman
2 Bob Kwait
4 Frank Perry/Art Christy
5 Catherine Campbell
6 John J. Asencio
7, 8 Michael Sweret

1 Afin de célébrer les dix-neuf ans de prédominance CBS Tele-vision utilise une séquence extraite du générique. (USA)
2 Annonce de presse en couleurs pour une nouvelle sorte de tuyaux fabriqués par *Goodrich*. (USA)
3 Pour *Plessey*: message invitant le public à ne pas téléphoner à Noël, mais à exprimer ses vœux personnellement. (USA)
4 En faveur d'un système pour le recyclage de déchets. (USA)
5 Annonce illustrant que les pianistes américains ont leurs préférences: les pianos *Steinway*. Noir et blanc. (USA)
6 Vœux de bonne année d'une maison de communication. (USA)
7, 8 Annonce et illustration annonçant que la transmission de messages par satellite est meilleur marché que par bande. (USA)

AGENCY / AGENTUR / AGENCE – STUDIO:

1 CBS Broadcast Group
2 Griswold-Eshleman Co.
3 F.B. & Levy
4 Fuller & Smith & Ross, Inc.
5 Lord, Geller, Federico, Inc.
6 O.M.A.R., Inc.
7, 8 J. Walter Thompson Co.

7

10

10 Artwork of an advertisement in the trade press for *Helanca* textiles for women's fashions. (FRA)
11 Full-page magazine advertisement for *Scherk* eye make-up. Illustrations in full colour. (GER)
12, 13 From a campaign in the trade press for various lines of *Arrow* sports shirts. Shirts in full colour. (USA)
14 Ad in the trade press for *Quiana* fibre for fashions. Full page, shades of brown. (FRA)
15 For *Branded Lion* jeans and jackets. Black-and-white trade press advertisement. (USA)

10 Inserat für *Helanca*-Textilien, erschienen in einer Fachzeitschrift. (FRA)
11 Ganzseitiges Zeitschriften-Inserat für *Scherk*-Augen-Make-up. Illustrationen mehrfarbig. (GER)
12, 13 Aus einer Kampagne in Fachzeitschriften für Sporthemden von *Arrow*. Hemden mehrfarbig. (USA)
14 Fachzeitschriften-Inserat für die Faser *Quiana*, die vor allem in der Modebranche verwendet wird. Ganzseitig, Brauntöne. (FRA)
15 Schwarzweisses Fachzeitschriften-Inserat für Jeans und Jacken der Marke *Branded Lion*. (USA)

10 Illustration d'une annonce parue dans la presse professionnelle. Publicité en faveur des tissus *Helanca* préférés pour les vêtements de femmes. (FRA)
11 Annonce de magazine pleine page pour une marque de maquillage pour les yeux. Illustrations en couleurs. (GER)
12, 13 D'une campagne publicitaire parue dans la presse professionnelle pour divers modèles de chemises. Chemises en couleurs. (USA)
14 Annonce parue dans la presse professionnelle pour les fibres *Quiana* qu'on utilise pour la fabrication de vêtements en vogue. Page entière en tons bruns. (FRA)
15 Annonce de presse en noir et blanc pour une marque de jeans et de jaquettes. (USA)

11

ARTIST / KÜNSTLER / ARTISTE:

10, 14 Hélène Majera
11 Elisabeth von Janota-Bzowski
12, 13 Andy di Martino
15 Michael Morgan

DESIGNER / GESTALTER / MAQUETTISTE:

10, 14 Hélène Majera
12, 13 Andy di Martino
15 Jerry Berman

...a envoûté Harry Lans

95

14

Our star performer.

Scrambler, another All-Star, is our best-selling sports shirt. Just stock it and you'll
sell out. Fast. Because it's got a lot going for it. The Arrow name.
Arrow styling. Arrow advertising. And lots, lots more.

►Arrow►

It's got a lot more going for it than just good looks.

12

Our super star.

Another of our All-Stars, Ultressa.' It feels like silk. Sells like crazy. And you have a lot
more going for you when you stock and sell our Ultressa knit
line. The Arrow name. Arrow styling. Arrow advertising. And lots, lots more.

►Arrow►

It's got a lot more going for it than just good looks.

13

Branded new. From Branded Lion.

Branded Lion has a way of
staying ahead of the pack.
This time with a whole new
line of light weight, pre-washed
cotton jeans and jackets. Made
from our new 7-ounce 100%
cotton sheeting, these Euro-
pean-styled jeans and jackets have the same great styling and fit that has made
our denim jeans and jackets
so famous.
In Blue, Sand, Rust and
Light Green they'll provide all
sorts of excitement for your
store this Spring. They're ready
for you to see right now.
Just contact Branded Lion at
any of the locations listed below.
BRANDED LION SPORTSWEAR
Division of John Morris Co., Inc.
1401 16th Street
San Francisco, California 94103
(415) 621-8242

Showrooms: San Francisco
Los Angeles/Seattle/Chicago
New York/Atlanta/Denver
In Canada: Bottoms Up
Fashions, Montreal

ART DIRECTOR:

10 Christian Becque
11 Knut Schumacher
12, 13 Andy di Martino
14 Jean-Louis Dufour
15 Jerry Berman

AGENCY / AGENTUR:

10 G.A.P.
11 Adfortex
12, 13 Graphicsgroup Inc.
14 Dépêche-Mode
15 Jerry Berman & Associates, Inc.

Advertisements

Inserate

Annonces

15

29

16

Advertisements / Inserate / Annonces

16 From a campaign for *Knorr* food products. (ITA)
17 A further addition to the long series of great thoughts illustrated by artists which the Container Corporation has been running as corporate advertising for many years. The typography (white on red) symbolizes the advance of man's ideas. (USA)
18 Ad for *Cross Siclare* offering a sample of a new half-recycled offset paper. Red type, grey logo, black scissors. (USA)
19 Black-and-white newspaper ad about the *Swissair* line. (USA)
20 Ad from a trade campaign about the versatility of *Correx* containers. Bright colours on red. (AUL)
21, 22 Artwork and complete trade ad for *Benisone* cream for the treatment of dermatoses. (USA)

16 Aus einer Kampagne für *Knorr*-Lebensmittel. (ITA)
17 Ein Beispiel aus einer Werbe-Serie der Container Corp. über grosse Ideen, von berühmten Künstlern illustriert. Die Typographie (weiss auf Rot) symbolisiert den geistlichen Fortschritt des Menschen. (USA)
18 Inserat für ein Offsetpapier, welches teilweise aus wiederverwerteten Materialien hergestellt ist. (USA)
19 Schwarzweisses Inserat für die *Swissair*. (USA)
20 Inserat aus einer Kampagne über die vielseitige Verwendbarkeit von *Correx*-Containern. Mehrfarbig auf Rot. (AUL)
21, 22 Illustration und vollständiges Inserat für die Salbe *Benisone*, gegen Hautausschläge. (USA)

16 D'une campagne pour les produits alimentaires *Knorr*. (ITA)
17 Exemple de la série des grandes idées illustrée par différents artistes. Depuis des années cette série constitue une partie intégrante de la publicité de la Container Corp. La typographie symbolise l'évolution successive de la pensée. (USA)
18 Annonce pour *Cross Sinclare* qui offre un nouveau papier à moitié recyclé. Typo rouge, logo gris, ciseaux noirs. (USA)
19 Annonce de presse en noir et blanc pour *Swissair*. (USA)
20 D'une campagne vantant les récipients *Correx* et leur emploi pour de multiples applications. Couleurs vives sur rouge. (AUL)
21, 22 Illustration et annonce professionnelle où elle figure. Publicité pour un onguent des dermatoses. (USA)

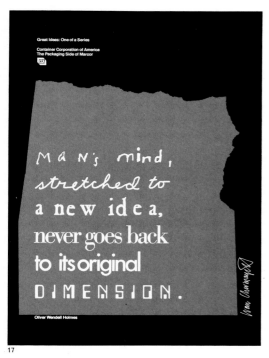

17

18

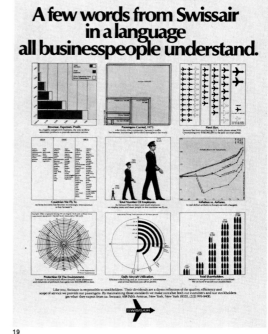

19

The aerotruck-trainship

20

21

22

ARTIST / KÜNSTLER / ARTISTE:

16 Adelchi Galloni
19 Push Pin Studios, Inc.
20 Jonathan Milne/Dennis Russell (Photo)
21, 22 Don Moss

DESIGNER / GESTALTER / MAQUETTISTE:

17 Ivan Chermayeff
19 Howard Title
20 John Ward/Jonathan Milne
21, 22 Tom Haynes

ART DIRECTOR / DIRECTEUR ARTISTIQUE:

16 Piero Mora
17 Ivan Chermayeff
19 Howard Title
20 John Ward
21, 22 Tom Haynes

AGENCY / AGENTUR / AGENCE – STUDIO:

16 Young & Rubicam Italia S.p.A.
17 Chermayeff & Geismar Associates, Inc.
19 Waring & LaRosa, Inc.
20 Carden Advertising Pty Ltd.
21, 22 Sudler & Hennessey, Inc.

23–28

This is all we want to do. But perfectly.

The engineering of high-fidelity turntables is a technical and controversial subject.

But the concept of a perfect turntable is perfectly simple.

Since a perfect turntable is what we at Garrard have been striving to make, we'd like to communicate this concept to you as unequivocally as possible. Then all the claims and counterclaims you hear will fall into place.

Think of it this way:

A phonograph record doesn't know and doesn't care what kind of mechanism is spinning it,

as long as it's spinning properly. If your hand could turn it at exactly 33⅓ RPM, without the slightest fluctuations in speed, and keep it moving in the horizontal plane only, without the slightest jiggling or vibrations up-and-down or sideways, you could expect perfect reproduction.

Similarly, a phono cartridge has no idea what's holding it in the groove, as long as it's properly held. If your other hand were holding it, correctly aligned, with the right amount of downward force and without resisting its movement across the record, it would perform faultlessly.

That's really all there is to it.

The basic point is that the turntable and tonearm have exceedingly simple and purely mechanical functions, just like a chemist's analytical balance or a gyroscope. That's why turntable manufacturing is, above all, a matter of precision and integrity, with the emphasis on perfect operation rather than hi-fi pizzazz or features for features' sake.

Of course, theoretical perfection in an actual mechanical device is an unrealizable ideal. But even though 100% is impossible, there's a big difference between 99.9% and 98%.

It's in this most fundamental sense, we feel, that Garrard turntables are in a class by themselves.

For example, in the case of the Zero 100c changer and the Zero 100SB single-play automatic, tracking error has been reduced to a virtually unmeasurable quantity (in effect, zero) by the geometry of the tonearm design. Rumble, wow and flutter figures are also coming ever closer to theoretical perfection in these and other top Garrard models. (The Zero 100c and the Zero 100SB are both priced at $209.95.)

To a less spectacular degree, the lower-priced models, from $49.95 up, also come quite close to the theoretical ideal because of this emphasis on fundamentals.

Remember: all we want is to make your record revolve perfectly and to position your phono cartridge perfectly.

And we're almost there.

For your free copy of The Garrard Guide, a 16-page full-color reference booklet, write to Garrard, Dept. 10, 100 Commercial Street, Plainview, N.Y. 11803.

Garrard
Division of Plessey Consumer Products.

29

ARTIST / KÜNSTLER / ARTISTE:

23–28 Ernst Herzog
29 Don Ivan Punchatz
30 Herbert Leupin
31 Hanspeter Wyss
32 Janet Carr
33 Bahadur Merwan

DESIGNER / GESTALTER / MAQUETTISTE:

23–28 Ernst Herzog
29 Barbara Schubeck
30 Herbert Leupin
31 Hanspeter Wyss
32 Janet Carr
33 Bahadur Merwan

Advertisements / Inserate / Annonces

das Halbtaxabonnement halbiert Preise

30

23–28 From a campaign echoing the (originally Anglo-Chinese) toast "Chin-chin" and using colours familiar from the bottle label to promote *Cinzano* vermouth in Europe. (SWI)
29 Ad for *Garrard* record-player turntables. (USA)
30 For half-fare season tickets offered by Swiss Federal Railways. Magazine ad. (SWI)
31 "So well cared for and cosy." Magazine ad for Swiss Federal Railways. (SWI)
32 From a campaign in magazines, here for *Aqua Maid* pumps providing water under pressure for caravans and campers. Illustration in full colour. (AUL)
33 Black-and-white advertisement about tourism in India published by *Air-India.* (IND)

23–28 Kleinanzeigeserie für *Cinzano*, den weltbekannten Aperitif mit langjähriger Tradition. (SWI)
29 Inserat für den Plattenspieler *Garrard*. (USA)
30, 31 Zwei Zeitschriften-Inserate für die Schweizerischen Bundesbahnen. (SWI)
32 Zeitschriften-Inserat aus einer Kampagne, hier für *Aqua Maid*-Wasser-Druckpumpen, die hauptsächlich von Campers und Touristen benützt werden. Illustration mehrfarbig. (AUL)
33 Schwarzweisses Inserat über Tourismus in Indien, herausgegeben von der *Air-India*. (IND)

23–28 D'une campagne pour *Cinzano,* l'apéritif de longue tradition. Un message offrant la possibilité d'heureuses associations a été trouvé dans la syllabe Cin. Cin-Cin (à l'origine anglo-chinois) ne signifie rien que «A la tienne». Couleurs originales de l'étiquette. (SWI)
29 Annonce en faveur des plateaux tourne-disques de *Garrard*. (USA)
30 Annonce de revue pour les abonnements à demi-tarif qu'offrent les Chemins de fer fédéraux suisses. (SWI)
31 Annonce de magazine pour les Chemins de fer fédéraux suisses. (SWI)
32 D'une campagne publicitaire, ici pour les pompes foulantes *Aqua Maid,* utilisées pour l'alimentation en eau des caravanes de camping. (AUL)
33 Annonce noir-blanc pour la promotion touristique de l'Inde. Publicité d'*Air-India.* (IND)

ART DIRECTOR / DIRECTEUR ARTISTIQUE:

23–28 Ernst Herzog
29 Dick Calderhead
30, 31 Werner Belmont
32 George Conte/Janet Carr
33 Bahadur Merwan

AGENCY / AGENTUR / AGENCE – STUDIO:

23–28 Advico AG
29 Calderhead, Jackson, Inc.
30, 31 Schweizerische Bundesbahnen, Publizitätsdienst
32 E.G. Holt & Associates
33 Hindustan Thompson Associates Ltd.

THE PUMP AND THE CARAVAN

Mary's family had a maid,
A car and caravan too,
And everywhere the family went,
The maid was sure to go.
Aqua Maid is family's aid,
A pressure pump so true,
And everywhere the family went,
A shower was sure to flow.
Instant water from the tap,
A caravaner's dream come true,
And everywhere the family went,
Others followed too.

"Aqua Maid" automatic water pressure systems deliver a constant flow of water at a steady pressure for caravans, travel trailers, campers, and cabins with water storage tanks.

Standard battery operated models
12760 6V DC   12780 24V DC
12770 12V DC   12790 32V DC

Manufacturers and suppliers of domestic, industrial, commercial and agricultural pumps.

McPHERSON'S LIMITED
Pump Division,
Melbourne 62 0301, Sydney 51 0433,
Brisbane 5 0191, Adelaide 46 0271,
Perth 6 3211.

32

SBB
So wohl Behütet und Behaglich

31

70099

All that prevents tourists like me coming to India is you.

India, we keep telling ourselves, is a tourist paradise. And yet, though our tourist trade is growing, its growth rate is a mere one-third of the worldwide growth rate. So our share of the international tourist trade keeps declining every year.
Despite all that we have to offer, we attracted fewer than 3½ lakh tourists in 1972, while Spain, less than one-eighth our size, attracted 325 lakhs!
While the average tourist's spending increased worldwide by 10.8% in just five years, in India it actually fell by 4.2%.
Our earnings from tourism are today among the smallest in the world, and for every tourist who visits India, one just flies over without even stopping, while several thousand others ignore this country altogether.

Do we really want tourists?
Perhaps the full potential of what a tourist boom can do for India has not been fully understood by us.
According to official figures, tourists spent just Rs 67.5 crores in India during 1973. This, however, benefitted the economy to the tune of Rs 216 crores, and yielded a tax revenue of Rs 21.6 crores.
If tourism is considered—and it should be—as an export industry, it is easy to see how an increase in tourist traffic can benefit us. And yet, tourism receipts constitute only 1.5% of our total export earnings, as compared with 43.7% for Mexico and 33.5% for Spain.

What's wrong with the tourists?
Is it possible that tourists are more interested in bullfights than in temples? Is this why the tourist trade in Mexico and Spain is booming, while it is growing only sluggishly in India?

The fact is that India and everything Indian have never been as popular abroad as they are today. So if tourists are not coming to India in droves, it's not because they're not interested. They are.
Perhaps it would be closer to the truth to say that we have shown no interest in having them visit us.

What's wrong with us?
We do recognise how a booming tourist trade will help our small scale and cottage industries to grow, how it will help our National Income to grow, and how it will help our culture to flourish.
Or do we?
For, if we are honest with ourselves, we shall have to admit that we have so far only paid lip service to the tourist, our honoured guest.
If we had really wanted him to come, would we not have given the tourist trade the same status and incentives we give to our other export activities? Would we not have evolved a system of priorities, with clear-cut allocations of roles, resources, responsibility and authority? Would not the promotion of tourism have featured prominently in our five-year plans?
The bitter pill we all have to swallow is that we have not been up to the task. Each of us has a role to play if we want tourists to come to our country.
And till such time as we are prepared to play our roles in full, all our talk about India being a tourist paradise will be in vain.

HT-AI-8456

INDIAN MERCHANTS' CHAMBER

33

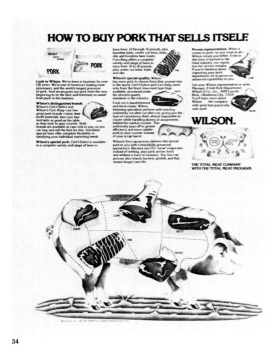

34

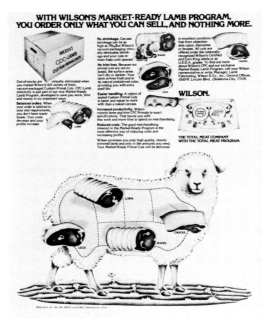

35

36

37

38

39

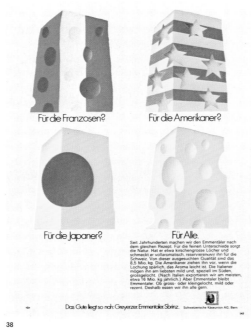

40

34–36 The *Wilson* "total" meat company advertises its pork, lamb and beef programmes to the trade. From a campaign. Illustrations in colour. (USA)

37, 38 "You may sometimes see black..."—"For the French..?" From a series of magazine advertisements for Emmental and other Swiss cheeses. (SWI)

39 Full-page magazine advertisement in the form of an entry in an encyclopaedia about *Old Red Fox* bourbon whiskey. (GER)

40 Advertisement (also used as a poster) for *Roth-Händle* (Red-Hand) cigarettes. (GER)

41–44 Colour magazine advertisements from a campaign for *Bonduelle* tinned vegetables. The green wheelbarrow is widely used in the company's publicity to suggest garden-fresh vegetables. Its human hands offer more scope for Tomi Ungerer's special brand of wit. (GER)

34–36 Une grande boucherie lance une campagne de publicité en faveur du grand choix qu'elle offre en viande de porc, d'agneau et de bœuf. Illustrations en couleurs. (USA)

37, 38 «De temps en temps vous verrez tout en noir...» «Pour les Français?» D'une série d'annonces de revue pour l'emmenthal et les autres fromages suisses. (SWI)

39 Annonce de revue pleine page sous forme d'un article tiré d'une encyclopédie pour une marque de whiskey. (GER)

40 Annonce (publiée aussi sous forme d'affiche) pour les cigarettes *Roth-Händle* (mains rouges). (GER)

41–44 Annonces de revue en couleurs figurant dans une campagne pour les conserves de légumes *Bonduelle*, société qui fait un usage intense du symbole de la brouette pour évoquer les légumes frais du jardin. Un trait d'humour féroce, mais brillant, typique de la manière d'Ungerer, incarné dans les couleurs délicates. (GER)

34–36 Aus einer Werbe-Kampagne einer Grossmetzgerei, die eine grosse Auswahl von Schweine-, Lamm- und Rindfleisch anbietet. Illustrationen mehrfarbig. (USA)

37, 38 Zwei Beispiele aus einer Serie von Zeitschriften-Inseraten für die Schweizerische Käseunion AG. (SWI)

39 Ganzseitiges Zeitschriften-Inserat für den Whiskey *Old Red Fox*. Das Inserat präsentiert sich wie eine Seite aus dem Brockhaus-Lexikon. (GER)

40 Inserat, auch als Plakat verwendet, für die Zigarettenmarke *Roth-Händle*. (GER)

41–44 Mehrfarbige Zeitschriften-Inserate aus einer Kampagne für *Bonduelle*-Konservengemüse. Der Stosskarren soll zeigen, dass das Gemüse dieser Firma immer frisch vom Garten ist. Die humoristischen Illustrationen von Tomi Ungerer sind in dezenten Farbtönen gehalten. (GER)

41

43

42

44

45, 46 Complete double-spread advertisement for *Levolor Riviera* blinds, with artwork (full colour). (USA)
47, 48 Artwork and complete magazine advertisement for food-warming trays by Salton Inc., which save women from being on their feet at mealtimes. (USA)
49 Ortho Pharmaceutical Corporation offers its family planning products in white print on black. (USA)
50 "We announce the end of the 'slap on the back'." Double-spread advertisement announcing a *Control* dossier about advertising agencies. (SPA)
51 "For us there are no big fish and little fish. We protect them all with the same care." Black-and-white ad for *Shell* marine lubricants. (ITA)

45, 46 Doppelseitiges Inserat für *Levolor Riviera*-Rolläden, und Detail. Mehrfarbig. (USA)
47, 48 Detail der Illustration und vollständiges, doppelseitiges Inserat für Tellerwärmer, die der Hausfrau das ständige Aufstehen während der Mahlzeiten ersparen. (USA)
49 «Fortpflanzung ist nicht der einzige Grund, sich zu lieben.» Schwarzweisses Inserat für Familienplanung. (USA)
50 «Wir verkünden, dass man sich nicht mehr auf die Schultern klopft.» Doppelseitiges Inserat, das für ein Dossier über Werbeagenturen wirbt. (SPA)
51 «Für uns existieren keine grossen oder kleinen Fische. Wir beschützen alle.» Schwarzweisses Inserat für *Shell* Schmiermittel. (ITA)

45, 46 Annonce complète sur page double pour une marque de jalousies, et détail de la composition (en couleurs). (USA)
47, 48 Détail de la composition et annonce de magazine complète sur double page pour des plateaux de repas autochauffants de Salton, Inc., qui économisent les pas de la ménagère. (USA)
49 Ortho Pharmaceutical Corporation offre ses divers produits destinés au planning familial. Texte blanc sur fond noir. (USA)
50 «Nous annonçons qu'on ne se tape plus sur l'épaule.» Annonce sur page double pour la promotion d'un dossier des agences publicitaires. (SPA)
51 «Pour nous il n'y existe pas de grands ou de petits poissons. Nous les protégeons tous.» Annonce noir-blanc *Shell* pour un lubrifiant marin. (ITA)

45

46

49

50

47

51

Per noi non ci sono
pesci grandi e pesci piccoli.
Li proteggiamo tutti
con la stessa cura.

SHELL ALEXIA OILS oli antiusura per cilindri dei grandi motori Diesel - SHELL MELINA OILS oli multifunzionali per motori Diesel - SHELL TURBO OILS per turbine principali e turboalternatori - SHELL RIMULA e GADINIA OILS per motori Diesel ausiliari - SHELL ARGINA OILS per motori Diesel a stantuffo tuffante funzionanti a olio combustibile - SHELL MACOMA OILS per ingranaggi - SHELL ALVANIA GREASES per cuscinetti a sfere, rulli e usi generali - SHELL ENSIS FLUIDS protettivi per parti di ricambio - SHELL TELLUS OILS per circuiti oleodinamici - E in più una serie di oli speciali per tutti i problemi particolari dei macchinari di bordo.

SHELL LUBRIFICANTI MARINA

ARTIST / KÜNSTLER / ARTISTE:

45–48 Roy Carruthers
50 Salvatore Adduci
51 Adelchi Galloni

DESIGNER / GESTALTER / MAQUETTISTE:

50 Carlos Rolando
51 Adelchi Galloni

ART DIRECTOR / DIRECTEUR ARTISTIQUE:

45, 46 Edward Rostock
47, 48 Alan Beaver
50 Carlos Rolando
51 Adelchi Galloni

AGENCY / AGENTUR / AGENCE – STUDIO:

45, 46 Muller, Jordan, Herrick, Inc.
47, 48 Leonard Sacks, Inc.
51 CPV Italiana S.p.A. Colman, Prentis & Varley

48

Advertisements / Inserate / Annonces

ARTIST / KÜNSTLER / ARTISTE:

52, 53 Jean Mulatier
54 Roy Carruthers
55 Cliff Andrea
56 Jack Davis

DESIGNER / GESTALTER / MAQUETTISTE:

52–55 Elmer Pizzi
56 Jerry Sullivan

ART DIRECTOR / DIRECTEUR ARTISTIQUE:

52–55 Elmer Pizzi
56 Jerry Sullivan

AGENCY / AGENTUR / AGENCE – STUDIO:

52–55 Gray & Rogers, Inc.
56 Cole Henderson Drake, Inc.

52

53

56

52–55 Complete advertisement, detail of artwork for "the hunchfrog of Notre Dame", and two further frogs ("Doctor Sigmund Frog" and "The Frog and the ad man") from a space promotion campaign for the weekly magazine *Grit,* which claims to be "a big frog in small towns". (USA)
56 Magazine advertisement addressed to pilots, placed in the trade press by Aviation Insurance Agency. Colour illustration. (USA)

52–55 Vollständiges Inserat, Detail mit dem Titel «Der Frosch von Notre Dame» und zwei weitere Beispiele («Doktor Sigmund Frosch» und «Der Frosch und die Werbeleute») aus einer Kampagne für die Wochenzeitschrift *Grit,* welche behauptet, «ein grosser Frosch in den kleinen Städten» zu sein. (USA)
56 Zeitschriften-Inserat einer Versicherungsgesellschaft, die sich hier an Piloten richtet. Mehrfarbige Illustration. (USA)

52–55 Annonce complète, détail de l'illustration de «la grenouille bossue de Notre Dame» et deux autres grenouilles (Docteur Sigmund Grenouille et La Grenouille et les publicitaires). Eléments figurant dans une série pour la promotion de l'hebdomadaire *Grit,* qui prétend être la grande grenouille dans les petites villes. (USA)
56 Annonce de magazine qui s'adresse aux pilotes. Elément publié dans la presse professionnelle par l'Aviation Insurance Agency. Illustration en couleur. (USA)

54

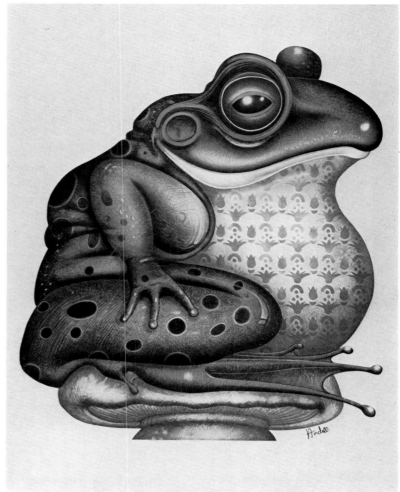

55

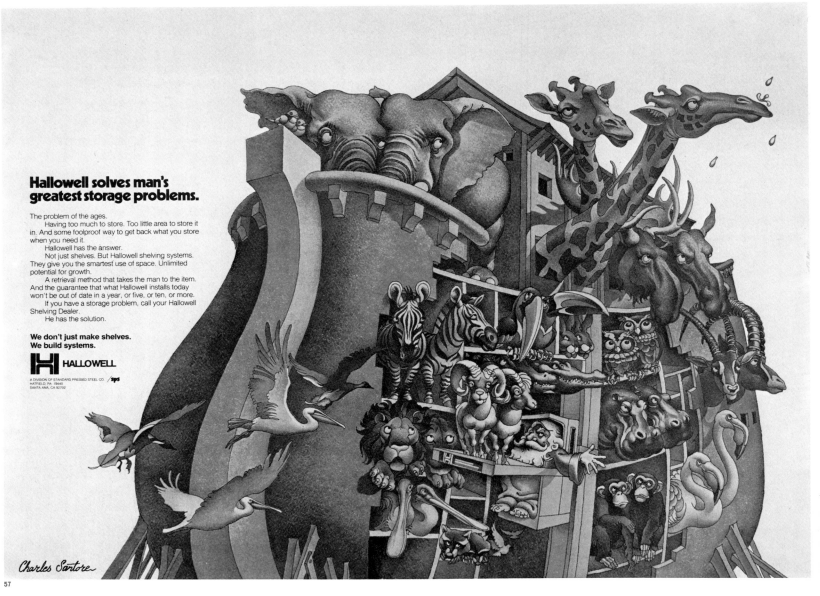

le CNRS est aussi un éditeur d'art

Editions du CNRS

57 The ark, depicted in shades of brown and pink, is used to advertise *Hallowell* storage systems. Double-spread trade magazine advertisement. (USA)
58 "CNRS is also an art publishing company." Black-and-white magazine advertisement for Editions du CNRS, better known as science publishers. (FRA)
59 Advertisement placed by *Oclae,* Havana. It promotes a magazine devoted to the influence of the USA in the universities of Latin America (the letters USA are falling out of the word for "university"). (CUB)
60, 61 "Folding boxes are stably stacked."—"Folding boxes are packed automatically." From a series of advertisements using a coloured arrow, placed in trade magazines by the association of West German folding-box manufacturers. (GER)

57 Die Arche, in Braun- und Rosatönen, wirbt hier für *Hallowell*-Lagerungssysteme. Doppelseitiges Zeitschriften-Inserat. (USA)
58 «Der CNRS ist auch ein Kunst-Verlag.» Schwarzweisses Zeitschriften-Inserat für Editions du CNRS, ein Verlag, der vor allem wissenschaftliche Publikationen herausgibt. (FRA)
59 Inserat, herausgegeben von *Oclae,* Havana. Man wirbt hier für eine Zeitschrift, die über die Einmischung der USA in die lateinamerikanischen Universitäten berichtet. (Die Buchstaben USA haben sich vom Wort «Universität» gelöst.) (CUB)
60, 61 Vollständiges Inserat und Illustration aus einer Serie von Zeitschriften-Inseraten für die besonders praktischen Faltschachteln. Herausgegeben vom Fachverband Faltschachtel-Industrie e.V., Offenbach a.M. (GER)

57 L'arche, représentée en divers tons bruns et roses, sert ici en tant qu'élément de publicité pour un système d'entreposage. Annonce sur page double. (USA)
58 Annonce de revue en noir et blanc pour les livres sur l'art publiés par le CNRS, mieux connu pour ses publications scientifiques. (FRA)
59 Annonce publiée par *Oclae,* La Havane. Elle lance une revue consacrée à l'influence néfaste qu'exercent les Etats-Unis dans les universités de l'Amérique Latine (les trois lettres U-S-A se sont détachées du mot «université»). (CUB)
60, 61 «On empile facilement les boîtes pliantes.» – «Les boîtes pliantes s'emballent automatiquement.» Série d'annonces, toutes avec une flèche en couleurs, publiée par une association des fabricants de boîtes pliantes de l'Allemagne fédérale. (GER)

58

60

59

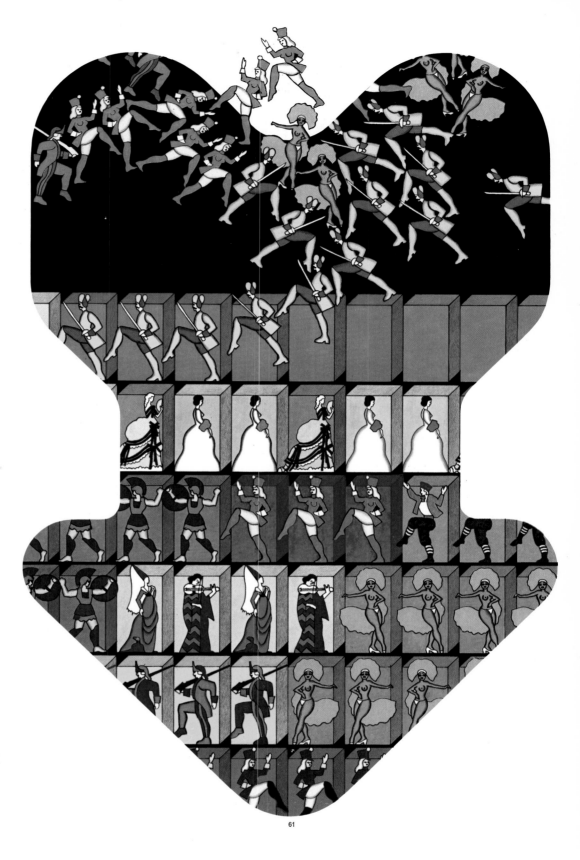

61

63

ARTIST / KÜNSTLER / ARTISTE:

62–64 Richard Hess
65 Haruo Miyauchi

DESIGNER / GESTALTER / MAQUETTISTE:

65 Gerry Severson

ART DIRECTOR / DIRECTEUR ARTISTIQUE:

62–64 Robert Pütz
65 Gerry Severson

AGENCY / AGENTUR / AGENCE – STUDIO:

62–64 Robert Pütz GmbH & Co.
65 Richard K. Manoff, Inc.

Advertisements / Inserate / Annonces

64

65

66

67

68

69

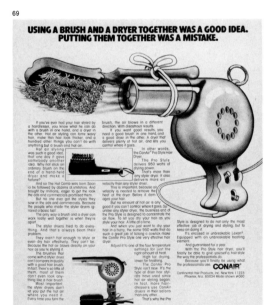

70

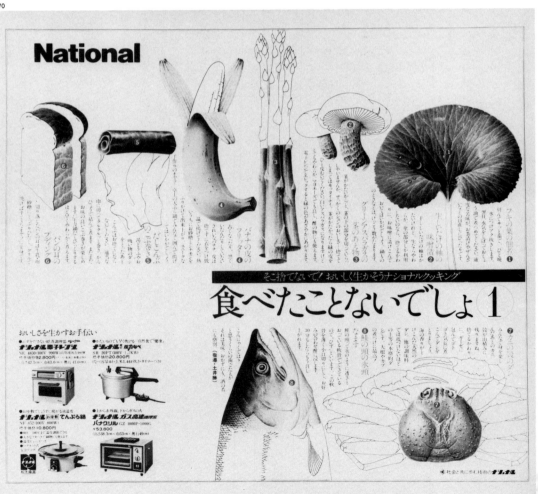

71

72

73

66—68 "The inner life begins with comfort." From a series of full-colour magazine advertisements for *Chaffoteaux et Maury* gas-fired water heaters. (FRA)
69 The *Conair* hair dryer comes without a brush. Capital is made out of this fact in this magazine advertisement. (USA)
70 Advertisement with colour illustrations for *National* kitchen appliances. (JPN)
71—73 Three full-page magazine advertisements in full colour using fairy tales (here Jack the Giant-Killer, Goldilocks and the Three Little Pigs) to promote *Fender* electric instruments. Posters of the various motifs are also available. (USA)

66—68 «Das Innenleben beginnt mit Komfort.» Drei Beispiele aus einer Serie von mehrfarbigen Zeitschriften-Inseraten für Durchlauferhitzer. (FRA)
69 Inserat für den Haartrockner *Conair*, der auf eine Bürste verzichtet. (USA)
70 Inserat mit farbigen Illustrationen für *National*-Küchengeräte. (JPN)
71—73 Drei ganzseitige Zeitschriften-Inserate für elektrische Musikinstrumente von *Fender*. Die mehrfarbigen Illustrationen beziehen sich auf drei Märchen. (USA)

66—68 Exemples d'une série d'annonces de revue en couleurs pour les chauffe-eau à gaz fabriqués par *Chaffoteaux et Maury*. (FRA)
69 Le sèche-cheveux de *Conair* est sans brosse. Dans cette annonce de revue l'entreprise en question exploite ce fait à son avantage. (USA)
70 Annonce avec illustration en couleurs pour les ustensiles de cuisine de *National*. (JAP)
71—73 Trois annonces pleines pages (en couleurs) pour la promotion d'instruments électriques. Les motifs de cette série ont été empruntés à divers contes (Jack, le tueur de géants, La fille aux boucles dorées et Les trois petits cochons). Les différentes illustrations peuvent être obtenues aussi sous forme d'affiches décoratives. (USA)

74

75

ARTIST / KÜNSTLER / ARTISTE:

74–77 Richard Brown
78–80 Sam Cooperstein
81 Philip Oldfield
82, 83 Jean Michel Folon

DESIGNER / GESTALTER:

74–77 Richard Brown/Joe Rizzuto
81 Philip Oldfield
82, 83 Jack Gregory

ART DIRECTOR:

74–77 Joe Rizzuto
78–80 Sam Cooperstein
81 Cariou
82, 83 Alan J. Klawans

AGENCY / AGENTUR / AGENCE:

78–80 Benton & Bowles, Inc.
81 Orange
82, 83 Smith, Kline & French Labs.,
Advertising Dept.

76

77

Advertisements

Inserate

Annonces

46

à l'heure de la ménopause
ondogyne

ROUSSEL

81

74–77 Complete trade advertisement and examples of the artwork (red, green and orange shades respectively) from a series about a *Rohm and Haas* surfactant. (USA)
78–80 From a campaign for *Vicks NyQuil*, which claims to relieve five major cold symptoms. (USA)
81 Magazine advertisement for a *Roussel* pharmaceutical recommended for women during the menopause. (FRA)
82, 83 Artwork and complete double-spread trade magazine advertisement for a *Smith, Kline & French* low-cost anti-depressant drug. (USA)

74–77 Vollständiges Inserat und drei Illustrationen aus einer Serie über ein oberflächenaktives Produkt. (USA)
78–80 Drei Beispiele aus einer Kampagne für ein Medikament gegen Erkältungen. (USA)
81 Zeitschriften-Inserat für ein *Roussel*-Medikament, welches man Frauen zur Einnahme während der Menopause empfiehlt. Mehrfarbig. (FRAU)
82, 83 Illustration und vollständige Doppelseite eines Fachzeitschriften-Inserates für ein *Smith, Kline & French*-Medikament gegen Depressionen. (USA)

74–77 Annonce de presse et exemples des illustrations (en tons rouges, verts et orange respectivement) figurant dans une série pour une marque de surfactant. (USA)
78–80 D'une campagne publicitaire pour un produit allégeant cinq symptômes des refroidissements. (USA)
81 Annonce de magazine pour un produit pharmaceutique *Roussel* qu'on recommande aux femmes pendant la ménopause. (FRA)
82, 83 Illustration et annonce (sur page double) pour un antidépresseur bon marché. (USA)

83

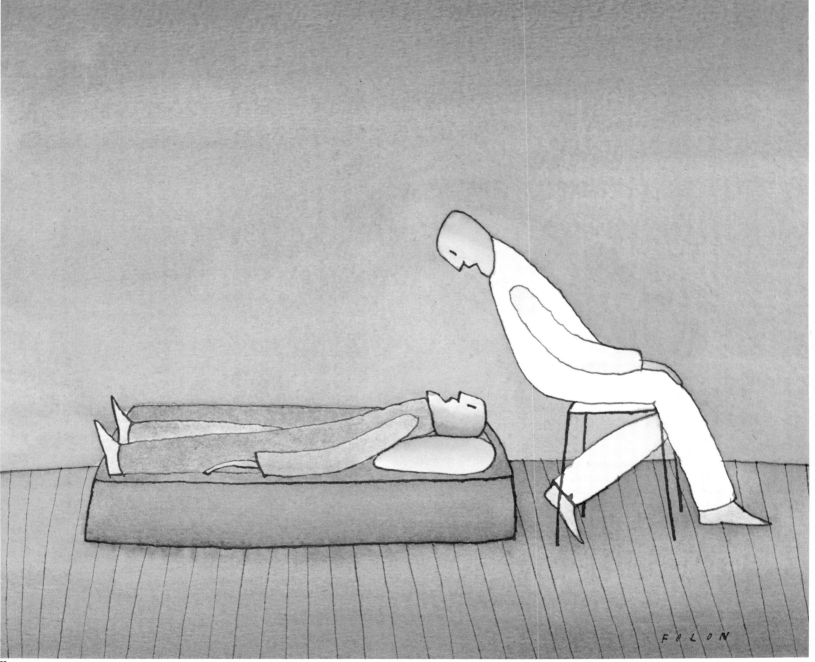

82

84

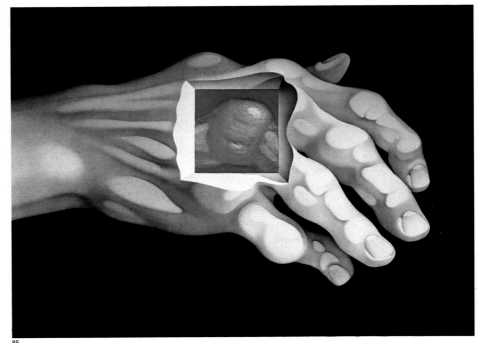

85

Advertisements / Inserate / Annonces

89

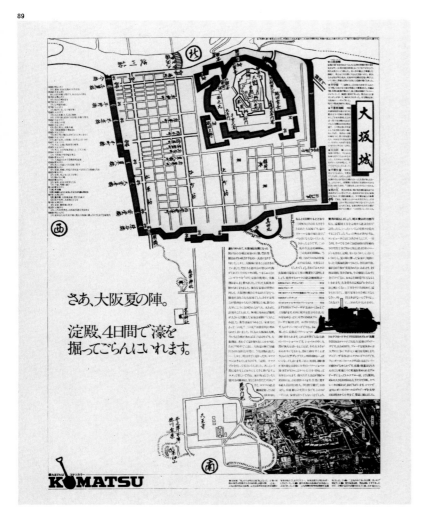

90

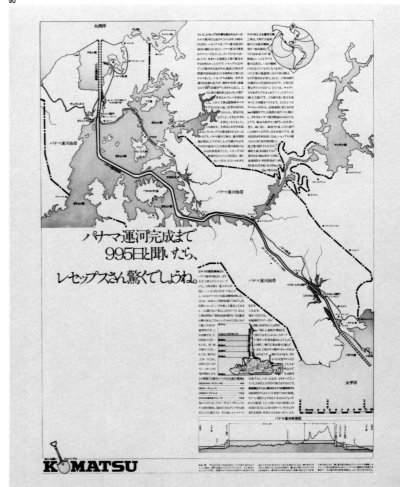

86

87

88

91

ARTIST / KÜNSTLER / ARTISTE:

84, 85 Lou Bory
86–88 Tomi Ungerer
89–91 Kazuo Aoki (Photo)

DESIGNER / GESTALTER / MAQUETTISTE:

84, 85 Ken Jordan/Joseph J. Fazio
89–91 Tadashi Ishiura/Yasunobu Aso

ART DIRECTOR / DIRECTEUR ARTISTIQUE:

84, 85 John de Cesare
86–88 Robert Pütz
89–91 Hiroaki Koga/Tadashi Ishiura

AGENCY / AGENTUR / AGENCE – STUDIO:

84, 85 Geigy Promotion Department
86–88 Robert Pütz GmbH & Co.
89–91 Hakuhodo, Inc.

84, 85 Advertisement from the trade press, with illustration in roughly actual size, for *Tandearil*, a drug for the treatment of painful inflammatory processes. (USA)
86–88 Artwork and one example of a complete advertisement for *Hafties*, small stickers made by *Henkel*. Black and white, with magenta *Hafties*. (GER)
89–91 From a series of black-and-white magazine advertisements for earth-moving equipment made by *Komatsu*. (JPN)

84, 85 Inserat aus einer Fachzeitschrift, und Illustration in ungefährer Originalgrösse, für das Medikament *Tandearil* zur Behandlung von entzündlichen Prozessen. (USA)
86–88 Zwei Illustrationen und vollständiges Inserat für *Hafties*-Kleber, hergestellt von *Henkel*. Schwarzweiss mit magentafarbenen *Hafties*. (GER)
89–91 Aus einer Serie von schwarzweissen Zeitschriften-Inseraten für Baumaschinen von der japanischen Firma *Komatsu*. (JPN)

84, 85 Annonce publiée dans des périodiques médicaux et illustration (approx. en grandeur nature) pour *Tandearil*, un produit pharmaceutique pour le traitement d'inflammations douloureuses et d'affections cutanées. (USA)
86–88 Compositions et l'une des annonces complètes pour les *Hafties*, une marque de petites étiquettes gommées. Noir et blanc, *Hafties* en magenta. (GER)
89–91 Exemples d'une série d'annonces en noir et blanc publiée par un fabricant d'excavatrices et d'autres machines de construction. (JPN)

Regenbogen-Farben zaubern die schönsten Druckergebnisse auf's Papier.

Hut ab vor den Druckergebnis-
sen mit Siegwerk-Regenbogenfarben.
Hut ab vor dem Service, der mit
Regenbogenfarben zaubern hilft.
Der Regenbogen-Service ist
immer für Sie da, denn er ist hilf-

reich gut: der Service durch ein um-
fangreiches, aufeinander abgestimm-
tes Programm von Druckhilfsmitteln,
der Service durch die praktischen.
Hilfen für die problemfreie Praxis des
Qualitätsdrucks.

Und wenn es trotz allem zu
Problemen kommt: mit dem
Know-how vom Ende des Regenbogens
kann man immer was anfangen.

SIEGWERK-FARBENFABRIK
52 Siegburg

92

92, 93 "Rainbow colours conjure the finest printing results on to the paper."—"All good things come from the rainbow." From a continuing series of magazine advertisements for *Siegwerk* "rainbow" printing inks. Full colour. (GER)
94 Black-and-white advertisement for a play starring Henry Fonda on NBC television. (USA)
95, 96 Artwork and complete full-page newspaper ad to promote *The New York Times,* which claims to be "plum full of surprises" (hence the portrait of Little Jack Horner). (USA)

92, 93 Aus einer grossen Serie von Zeitschriften-Inseraten für die *Siegwerk*-Farbenfabrik. Alle Mehrfarbig. (GER)
94 Schwarzweisses Inserat für ein Stück mit Henry Fonda in der Hauptrolle, das im NBC-Fern-sehen ausgestrahlt wurde. (USA)
95, 96 Illustration und vollständiges, ganzseitiges Zeitungsinserat für die *New York Times,* die behauptet, immer voller Überraschungen zu sein. (USA)

92, 93 «Les couleurs de l'arc-en-ciel donnent de merveilleux résultats.» – «Les bonnes choses viennent de l'arc-en-ciel.» Exemples d'une longue série d'annonces de revue pour les encres d'imprimerie «arc-en-ciel» de *Siegwerk*. En polychromie. (GER)
94 Annonce en noir et blanc pour une pièce télévisée avec Henry Fonda en vedette. (USA)
95, 96 Composition et annonce de presse où elle figure. Elément pour la promotion du *New York Times* qui prétend être plein de surprises. (L'illustration fait allusion à Little Jack Horner qui dans un conte d'enfants anglais avait une tarte aux prunes.) (USA)

Alles Gute kommt vom Bogen.

Wenn es um den Qualitätsdruck
geht, um das problemfreie, schnelle
Drucken, um die Sicherheit beim
Druck und die Zufriedenheit mit dem
Druckergebnis:

am Regenbogen führt kein Weg vorbei.
Denn Siegwerk hat zu den
Regenbogenfarben den Regenbogen-
Service: das umfangreiche, aufein-
ander abgestimmte Programm von

Druckhilfsmitteln, das für bessere
Druckergebnisse gut ist.
Alles Gute. Ihr Regenbogen.

SIEGWERK-FARBENFABRIK
52 Siegburg

93

Henry Fonda
in CLARENCE DARROW
O:OOPM
On NBC OO

94

ARTIST / KÜNSTLER / ARTISTE:

92, 93 Tomi Ungerer
94 Robert Heindel
95, 96 Joyce MacDonald

DESIGNER / GESTALTER / MAQUETTISTE:

92, 93 Robert Pütz
94 Dolores Gudzin
95, 96 Emil T. Micha

ART DIRECTOR / DIRECTEUR ARTISTIQUE:

92, 93 Alfred Limbach
94 Dolores Gudzin
95, 96 Emil T. Micha

AGENCY / AGENTUR / AGENCE – STUDIO:

92, 93 Robert Pütz GmbH & Co.
94 National Broadcasting Co., Advertising Dept.

Must you miss the latest talk about a play?
Unthinkable!
Must you only hear what others say about it?
Impossible!

CALL TOLL FREE   800-325-6400
The New York Times
FOR HOME DELIVERY

97 a

Can you bear not knowing what the market's doing?
Can you bear not knowing what the pundits say?
Can you stand it if The Times is quoted at you?
Instead of just the other way?

CALL TOLL FREE   800-325-6400
The New York Times
FOR HOME DELIVERY

b

Good Heavens, Sir or Madam, call today! 800-325-6400. That's the splendid toll-free number that you phone. And say, "By George, I want The New York Times at home!"

CALL TOLL FREE   800-325-6400
The New York Times
FOR HOME DELIVERY

c

Did you know that you could have The Times for breakfast... That you could scan the world while sipping your cafe au lait?

CALL TOLL FREE   800-325-6400
The New York Times
FOR HOME DELIVERY

d

Did you know that you could get The New York Times at home?
Did you know that you don't have to miss it, ever?

CALL TOLL FREE   800-325-6400
The New York Times
FOR HOME DELIVERY

e

Must you sit around regretfully without it?
Unthinkable!

CALL TOLL FREE   800-325-6400
The New York Times
FOR HOME DELIVERY

f

97 a–f Black-and-white newspaper advertisements to promote home delivery of *The New York Times*. (USA)
98, 99 Artwork and complete full-page newspaper advertisement for *autofon* self-copying paper as a means of overcoming "lentocracy" (the rule of the slow). (ITA)

97 a–f Schwarzweisse Zeitungs-Inserate, die für die Hauslieferung der *New York Times* werben. (USA)
98, 99 Illustration und vollständiges Zeitungs-Inserat für ein schnelleres Photokopier-System zur Bekämpfung der «Lentocratie» (Herrschaft der Langsamen). (ITA)

97 a–f Annonces de presse en noir et blanc pour la promotion du service de distribution du *New York Times*. (USA)
98, 99 Illustration et annonce de presse pleine page vantant les papiers autocopiants en tant que moyen pour vaincre la «lentocratie». (ITA)

ARTIST / KÜNSTLER / ARTISTE:

97 Isadore Seltzer
98, 99 Adelchi Galloni

DESIGNER / GESTALTER / MAQUETTISTE:

97 Andrew Kner

ART DIRECTOR / DIRECTEUR ARTISTIQUE:

97 Andrew Kner
98, 99 Roberto Borioli

Advertisements / Inserate / Annonces

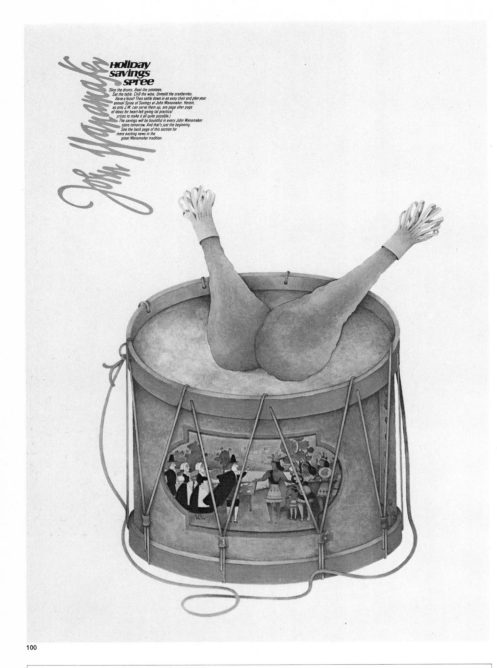

100

102

100, 102–107 Full-page newspaper advertisements, all in full colour, for the *John Wanamaker* department stores. Figs. 100 and 107 are institutional ads for Christmas, Figs. 103 and 106 are institutional ads for Valentine's Day and the Fourth of July, and Figs. 102, 104 and 105 are ads for boys' back-to-school jeans and jackets. (USA)
101 Newspaper advertisement for shoes and pantyhose sold by the *Neiman-Marcus* department stores. Shoes and hose in full colour. (USA)
108, 109 "Let him speak even if he's wrong."—"You've had your mouth open too long—your ears have closed." Black-and-white public service ads placed by an advertising confederation to promote respect for others. (ITA)

100, 102–107 Ganzseitige Zeitungs-Inserate, alle mehrfarbig, für das Warenhaus *John Wanamaker*. Abb. 100 und 107 sind Weihnachtsinserate, Abb. 103 und 106 sind für den Valentinstag und den 14. Juli, und Abb. 102, 104 und 105 sind für Knaben-Jeans und Jacken. (USA)
101 Zeitungs-Inserat für Schuhe und Strumpfhosen vom Warenhaus *Neiman-Marcus*. Mehrfarbig. (USA)
108, 109 «Lassen Sie ihn sprechen, auch wenn er unrecht hat.» — «Sie hatten Ihren Mund zu lange offen – Ihre Ohren sind nun verstopft.» Schwarzweisse Inserate einer Werbe-Gesellschaft, die für mehr Respekt gegenüber den Mitmenschen appelliert. (ITA)

Total Leg Color . . . *the well put-together continuing flow of coordinating color, leg to shoe. The whole point of it . . . nothing to break the line of a pretty leg, a neat ankle. Very new footnote, the calf-with-suede wedge ghillie, grey, rust, green or Burgundy 36.00, Galleria Shoes Downtown; Shoe Salon at NorthPark and Fort Worth. Our color-cued Neiman-Marcus sheer leg pantyhose, 3 pairs 9.00. Hosiery* Neiman-Marcus

101

103

108

104

106

109

105

107

ARTIST / KÜNSTLER / ARTISTE:

100, 102–105, 107 Linda + John Gist
101 Dorothy Michaelson
106 Jacqueline Miles
108, 109 Adelchi Galloni

DESIGNER / GESTALTER / MAQUETTISTE:

100, 103, 107 Louise Regues
101 Walter Lamb
102, 104–106 Jacqueline Miles
108, 109 Adelchi Galloni

ART DIRECTOR / DIRECTEUR ARTISTIQUE:

100, 102–107 Albin Smagala
101 Richard Nelson
108, 109 Angelo Traversa

AGENCY / AGENTUR / AGENCE – STUDIO:

101 Neiman-Marcus
108, 109 O.D.G.

Advertisements / Inserate / Annonces

2

Booklets

Folders

Catalogues

Invitations

Programmes

Broschüren

Faltprospekte

Kataloge

Einladungen

Programme

Brochures

Dépliants

Catalogues

Invitations

Programmes

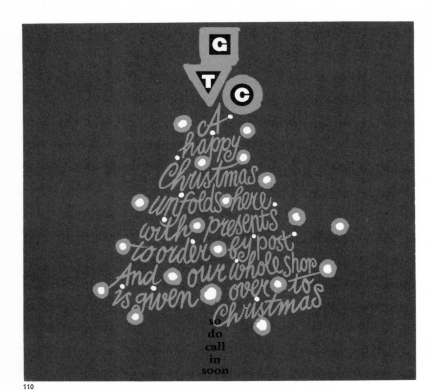

110

113

ARTIST / KÜNSTLER / ARTISTE:

110 Klaus Friedeberger
111 Bob Byro
112 Burton Kramer/Jeffry Dawson
113, 114 Nicolas Sidjakov

DESIGNER / GESTALTER / MAQUETTISTE:

111 Rodeni Lubbens
113, 114 Jerry Berman/Gene Icardi

ART DIRECTOR / DIRECTEUR ARTISTIQUE:

111 Eric Hall
112 Burton Kramer
113, 114 Jerry Berman

AGENCY / AGENTUR / AGENCE – STUDIO:

110 National Advertising Corp.
111 Lewis & Gilman, Inc.
112 Burton Kramer Associates Ltd.
113, 114 Jerry Berman & Associates, Inc.

111

112

110 Two panels of a Christmas folder sent out by The General Trading Company Ltd. Yellow letter-ing on green ground. (GBR)
111 Folder about a mastic for spraying tanks, etc., made by Anchem Products, Inc. (USA)
112 Folder-poster listing performances at the Shaw Festival in Niagara-on-the-Lake, Ontario. White print on blue, red and purple. (CAN)
113, 114 Full-page illustration from a newspaper-size mailer sent to newspapers by the paper-makers *Crown Zellerbach* to promote fashion advertising in the daily press. (USA)

110 Ausschnitte aus einem Weihnachtsprospekt für ein Londoner Kaufhaus. Gelbe Schrift auf grünem Grund. (GBR)
111 Faltprospekt für ein Farb-Spray für Tanks usw. von *Anchem*. (USA)
112 Prospekt und Plakat für das Shaw-Festival, das in Kanada stattfindet. Weisse Schrift auf Blau, Rot und Violett. (CAN)
113, 114 Ganzseitige Illustration aus einem Prospekt der Papierfabrik *Crown Zellerbach*, welcher an Zeitungen verschickt wird, um Modewerbung in der Tagespresse zu fördern. (USA)

110 Deux panneaux d'un dépliant de Noël distribué par la General Trading Company Ltd. Typo-graphie en jaune sur fond vert. (GBR)
111 Dépliant en faveur d'un mastic pour des citernes etc. fabriqué par *Anchem*. (USA)
112 Dépliant au format d'affiche contenant le programme des manifestations du Shaw Festival à Niagara-on-the-Lake, Ontario. Typo blanc sur fond bleu, rouge et violet. (CAN)
113, 114 Illustration pleine page d'une brochure au format de journal qu'une papeterie a distribuée aux journaux afin de promouvoir la publicité d'articles de modes dans la presse. (USA)

114

115–122 Vignettes from a large mailer about a thirteen-part *Xerox* television series on the making of America. Each vignette represents a phase of history. (USA)
123 Cover of a folder about an open house in the IBM plant at Boulder, Colorado. (USA)
124–127 Cover, page and two double spreads from an eight-page promotional mailer sent to past and prospective clients by Hinrichs Design Associates. It lists all sorts of famous and less-known "firsts" in history and is printed in brown and blue on brown "packing-paper" stock. The tiger-into-man drawing refers to the first circus show with a mixed group of animals, staged by the American Van Amburgh in London in 1838. (USA)

115–122

123

Family Open House
IBM
Boulder, Colorado
August 16, 1975

ARTIST / KÜNSTLER / ARTISTE:

115–122 Richard Hess
123 Tom Bluhm
124–127 Skip Andrews/Christoph Blumrich/
Ken Korsh/Carveth Kramer/Tim Lewis/
George Masi/Marvin Mattelson/
Nancy Stahl/Philip Weisbecker

DESIGNER / GESTALTER / MAQUETTISTE:

126, 127 Paul Hardy/Kit + Linda Hinrichs

ART DIRECTOR / DIRECTEUR ARTISTIQUE:

115–122 Ted Heidipream
123 Ken White
124, 125 Robert Pütz

AGENCY / AGENTUR / AGENCE – STUDIO:

115–122 Richard Hess, Inc.
123 IBM Boulder, Design Center
124, 125 Robert Pütz GmbH & Co.
126, 127 Hinrichs Design Associates

124

125

115–122 Vignetten aus einem Prospekt der *Xerox* über eine dreizehnteilige Fernsehserie über die Entstehung Amerikas. Jede Vignette stellt einen Ausschnitt aus der Geschichte dar. (USA)
123 Umschlag einer Einladung zum Besuch der IBM in Boulder, Colorado. (USA)
124–127 Umschlag, Seite und zwei Doppelseiten aus einer 8seitigen Propaganda-Broschüre, die von Hinrichs Design Associates an alle alten und zukünftigen Kunden verschickt wird. Sie zeigt verschiedene berühmte und weniger bekannte Persönlichkeiten der Geschichte. Braun und blau auf braunem Packungspapier. Abb. 127 bezieht sich auf die erste Zirkusaufführung mit gemischten Tieren in London 1838. (USA)

115–122 Vignettes figurant dans un dépliant grand format consacré à une série TV en 13 suites sur la fondation de l'Amérique. Chaque vignette représente un épisode historique. (USA)
123 Couverture de l'invitation pour une visite de la fabrique IBM à Boulder. (USA)
124–127 Couverture, page et pages doubles figurant dans un prospectus de huit pages. Elément de publicité adressé aux anciens clients et aux clients prospectifs par Hinrichs Design Assoc. Il présente des figures historiques bien connues et moins connues. Impression en brun et bleu sur papier d'emballage. Le dessin d'un tigre se déguisant en homme se réfère à la première présentation d'un groupe de divers animaux par l'Américain Van Amburgh à Londres en 1838. (USA)

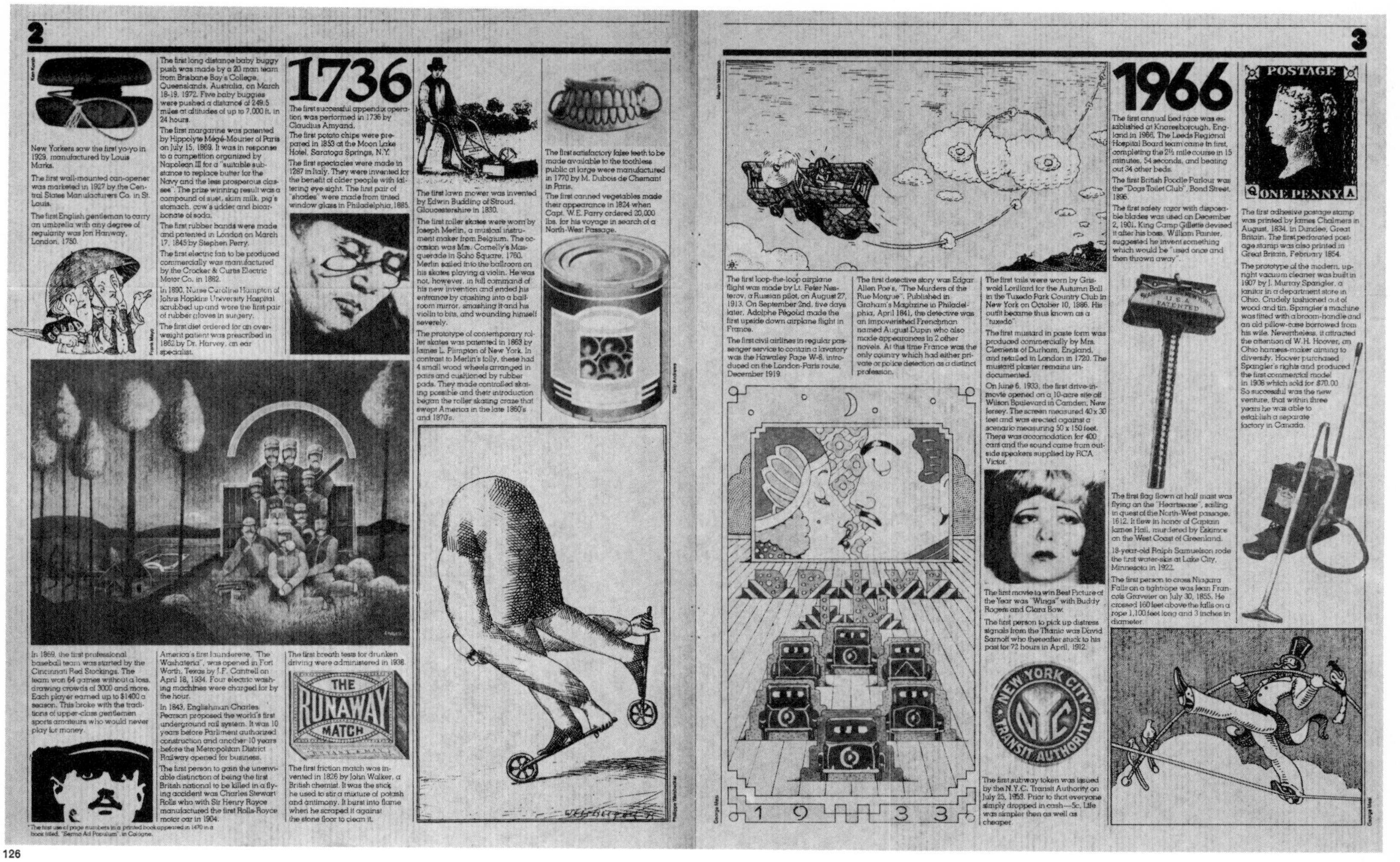

2

New Yorkers saw the first yo-yo in 1929, manufactured by Louis Marks.

The first wall-mounted can-opener was marketed in 1927 by the Central States Manufacturers Co. in St. Louis.

The first English gentleman to carry an umbrella with any degree of regularity was Jon Hanway, London, 1750.

The first long distance baby buggy push was made by a 20 man team from Brisbane Boy's College, Queenslands, Australia, on March 18-19, 1972. Five baby buggies were pushed a distance of 249.5 miles at altitudes of up to 7,000 ft. in 24 hours.

The first margarine was patented by Hippolyte Mégé-Mourier of Paris on July 15, 1869. It was in response to a competition organized by Napolean III for a "suitable substance to replace butter for the Navy and the less prosperous classes". The prize winning result was a compound of suet, skim milk, pig's stomach, cow's udder and bicarbonate of soda.

The first rubber bands were made and patented in London on March 17, 1845 by Stephen Perry.

The first electric fan to be produced commercially was manufactured by the Crocker & Curtis Electric Motor Co. in 1882.

In 1890, Nurse Caroline Hampton of Johns Hopkins University Hospital scrubbed up and wore the first pair of rubber gloves in surgery.

The first diet ordered for an overweight patient was prescribed in 1862 by Dr. Harvey, an ear specialist.

1736

The first successful appendix operation was performed in 1736 by Claudius Amyand.

The first potato chips were prepared in 1853 at the Moon Lake Hotel, Saratoga Springs, N.Y.

The first spectacles were made in 1287 in Italy. They were invented for the benefit of older people with faltering eye sight. The first pair of "shades" were made from tinted window glass in Philadelphia, 1885.

The first lawn mower was invented by Edwin Budding of Stroud, Gloucestershire in 1830.

The first roller skates were worn by Joseph Merlin, a musical instrument maker from Belgium. The occasion was Mrs. Cornelly's Masquerade in Soho Square, 1760. Merlin sailed into the ballroom on his skates playing a violin. He was not, however, in full command of his new invention and ended his entrance by crashing into a ballroom mirror, smashing it and his violin to bits, and wounding himself severely.

The prototype of contemporary roller skates was patented in 1863 by James L. Plimpton of New York. In contrast to Merlin's folly, these had 4 small wood wheels arranged in pairs and cushioned by rubber pads. They made controlled skating possible and their introduction began the roller skating craze that swept America in the late 1860's and 1870's.

The first satisfactory false teeth to be made available to the toothless public at large were manufactured in 1770 by M. Dubois de Chemant in Paris.

The first canned vegetables made their appearance in 1824 when Capt. W.E. Parry ordered 20,000 lbs. for his voyage in search of a North-West Passage.

In 1869, the first professional baseball team was started by the Cincinnati Red Stockings. The team won 64 games without a loss, drawing crowds of 3000 and more. Each player earned up to $1400 a season. This broke with the traditions of upper-class gentlemen sports amateurs who would never play for money.

America's first launderette, "The Washateria", was opened in Fort Worth, Texas by J.F. Cantrell on April 18, 1934. Four electric washing machines were charged for by the hour.

In 1843, Englishman Charles Pearson proposed the world's first underground rail system. It was 10 years before Parliment authorized construction and another 10 years before the Metropolitan District Railway opened for business.

The first person to gain the unenviable distinction of being the first British national to be killed in a flying accident was Charles Stewart Rolls who with Sir Henry Royce manufactured the first Rolls-Royce motor car in 1904.

The first breath tests for drunken driving were administered in 1938.

THE RUNAWAY MATCH

The first friction match was invented in 1826 by John Walker, a British chemist. It was the stick he used to stir a mixture of potash and antimony. It burst into flame when he scraped it against the stone floor to clean it.

*The first use of page numbers in a printed book appeared in 1470 in a book titled, "Sermo Ad Populum", in Cologne.

3

The first loop-the-loop airplane flight was made by Lt. Peter Nesterov, a Russian pilot, on August 27, 1913. On September 2nd, five days later, Adolphe Pégoud made the first upside down airplane flight in France.

The first civil airlines in regular passenger service to contain a lavatory was the Hawaley Page W-8, introduced on the London-Paris route, December 1919.

The first detective story was Edgar Allen Poe's, "The Murders of the Rue Morgue". Published in Graham's Magazine in Philadelphia, April 1841, the detective was an impoverished Frenchman named August Dupin who also made appearances in 2 other novels. At this time France was the only country which had either private or police detection as a distinct profession.

The first tails were worn by Griswold Lorillard for the Autumn Ball in the Tuxedo Park Country Club in New York on October 10, 1886. His outfit became thus known as a "tuxedo".

The first mustard in paste form was produced commercially by Mrs. Clements of Durham, England, and retailed in London in 1720. The mustard plaster remains undocumented.

On June 6, 1933, the first drive-in-movie opened on a 10-acre site off Wilson Boulevard in Camden, New Jersey. The screen measured 40 x 30 feet and was erected against a scenario measuring 50 x 150 feet. There was accomodation for 400 cars and the sound came from outside speakers supplied by RCA Victor.

1 9 3 3

The first movie to win Best Picture of the Year was "Wings" with Buddy Rogers and Clara Bow.

The first person to pick up distress signals from the Titanic was David Sarnoff who thereafter stuck to his post for 72 hours in April, 1912.

NEW YORK CITY TRANSIT AUTHORITY

The first subway token was issued by the N.Y.C. Transit Authority on July 25, 1953. Prior to that everyone simply dropped in cash—5c. Life was simpler then as well as cheaper.

1966

The first annual bed race was established at Knaresborough, England in 1966. The Leeds Regional Hospital Board team came in first, completing the 2½ mile course in 15 minutes, 54 seconds, and beating out 34 other beds.

The first British Poodle Parlour was the "Dogs Toilet Club", Bond Street, 1896.

The first safety razor with disposable blades was used on December 2, 1901. King Camp Gillette devised it after his boss, William Painter, suggested he invent something which would be "used once and then thrown away".

The first flag flown at half mast was flying on the "Heartsease", sailing in quest of the North-West passage, 1612. It flew in honor of Captain James Hall, murdered by Eskimos on the West Coast of Greenland.

18-year-old Ralph Samuelson rode the first water-skis at Lake City, Minnesota in 1922.

The first person to cross Niagara Falls on a tightrope was Jean Francois Graveler on July 30, 1855. He crossed 160 feet above the falls on a rope 1,100 feet long and 3 inches in diameter.

POSTAGE ONE PENNY

The first adhesive postage stamp was printed by James Chalmers in August, 1834, in Dundee, Great Britain. The first perforated postage stamp was also printed in Great Britain, February 1854.

The prototype of the modern, upright vacuum cleaner was built in 1907 by J. Murray Spangler, a janitor in a department store in Ohio. Crudely fashioned out of wood and tin, Spangler's machine was fitted with a broom-handle and an old pillow-case borrowed from his wife. Nevertheless, it attracted the attention of W.H. Hoover, an Ohio harness-maker aiming to diversify. Hoover purchased Spangler's rights and produced the first commercial model in 1908 which sold for $70.00. So successful was the new venture, that within three years he was able to establish a separate factory in Canada.

126

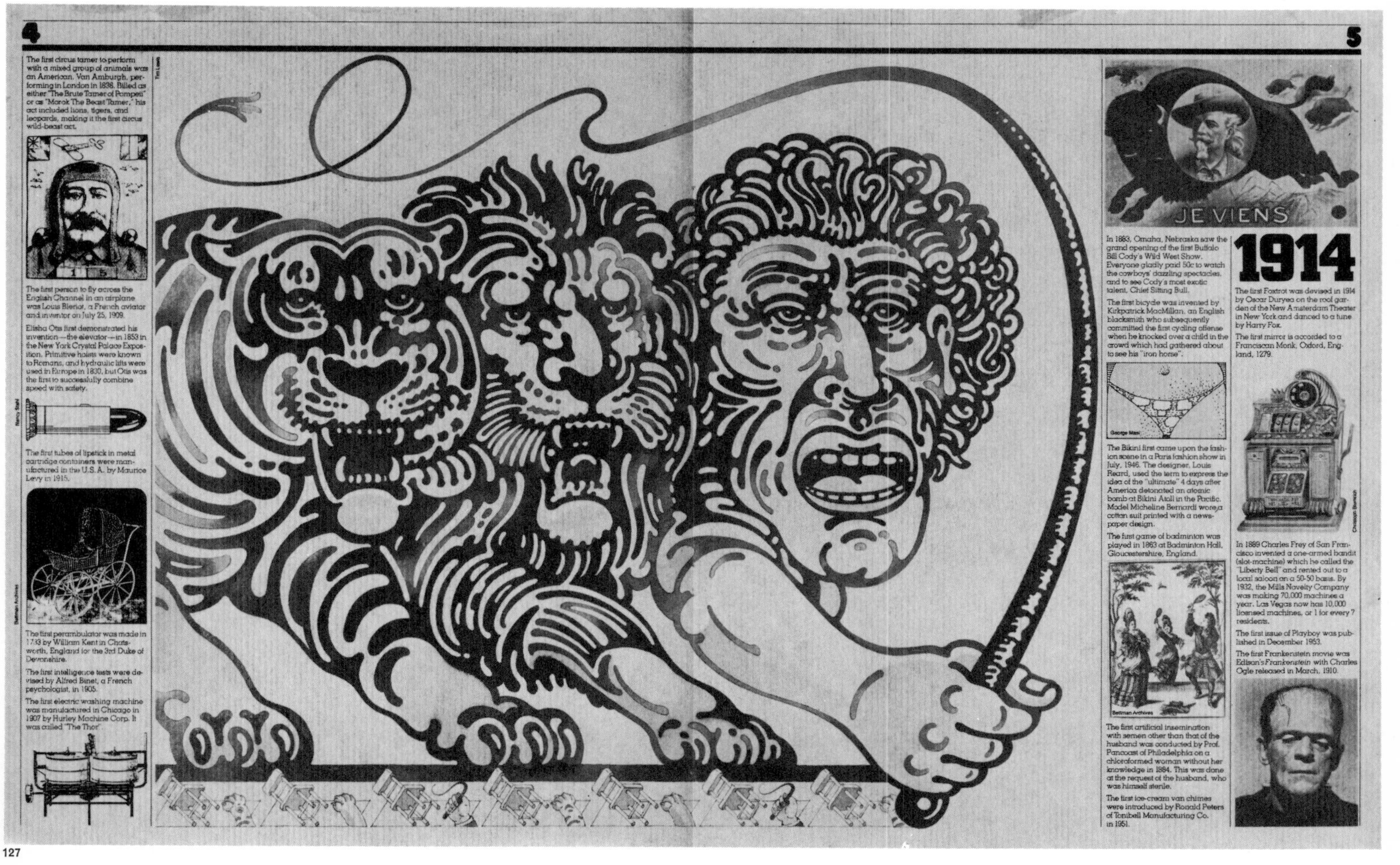

4

The first circus tamer to perform with a mixed group of animals was an American, Van Amburgh, performing in London in 1838. Billed as either "The Brute Tamer of Pompeii" or as "Morok The Beast Tamer," his act included lions, tigers, and leopards, making it the first circus wild-beast act.

The first person to fly across the English Channel in an airplane was Louis Bleriot, a French aviator and inventor on July 25, 1909.

Elisha Otis first demonstrated his invention—the elevator—in 1853 in the New York Crystal Palace Exposition. Primitive hoists were known to Romans, and hydraulic lifts were used in Europe in 1830, but Otis was the first to successfully combine speed with safety.

The first tubes of lipstick in metal cartridge containers were manufactured in the U.S.A. by Maurice Levy in 1915.

The first perambulator was made in 1733 by William Kent in Chatsworth, England for the 3rd Duke of Devonshire.

The first intelligence tests were devised by Alfred Binet, a French psychologist, in 1905.

The first electric washing machine was manufactured in Chicago in 1907 by Hurley Machine Corp. It was called "The Thor".

5

JE VIENS

In 1883, Omaha, Nebraska saw the grand opening of the first Buffalo Bill Cody's Wild West Show. Everyone gladly paid 50c to watch the cowboys' dazzling spectacles, and to see Cody's most exotic talent, Chief Sitting Bull.

The first bicycle was invented by Kirkpatrick MacMillan, an English blacksmith who subsequently committed the first cycling offense when he knocked over a child in the crowd which had gathered about to see his "iron horse".

The Bikini first came upon the fashion scene in a Paris fashion show in July, 1946. The designer, Louis Reard, used the term to express the idea of the "ultimate" 4 days after America detonated an atomic bomb at Bikini Atoll in the Pacific. Model Micheline Bernardi wore a cotton suit printed with a newspaper design.

The first game of badminton was played in 1863 at Badminton Hall, Gloucestershire, England.

The first artificial insemination with semen other than that of the husband was conducted by Prof. Pancoast of Philadelphia on a chloroformed woman without her knowledge in 1884. This was done at the request of the husband, who was himself sterile.

The first ice-cream van chimes were introduced by Ronald Peters of Tonibell Manufacturing Co. in 1951.

1914

The first Foxtrot was devised in 1914 by Oscar Duryea on the roof garden of the New Amsterdam Theater in New York and danced to a tune by Harry Fox.

The first mirror is accorded to a Franciscan Monk, Oxford, England, 1279.

In 1889 Charles Frey of San Francisco invented a one-armed bandit (slot-machine) which he called the "Liberty Bell" and rented out to a local saloon on a 50-50 basis. By 1932, the Mills Novelty Company was making 70,000 machines a year. Las Vegas now has 10,000 licensed machines, or 1 for every 7 residents.

The first issue of Playboy was published in December 1953.

The first Frankenstein movie was Edison's *Frankenstein* with Charles Ogle released in March, 1910.

127

128

129

128 Double spread in colour on brown stock from a sales promotion booklet with sidelights on food history issued by N. Merberg & Son., Inc. (USA)
129 Double spread from a brochure on the *Hermes* instrument landing system. Blue shades and white. (NOR)
130 One side of a large call for entries for the AIGA packaging contest, 1976. Design in red and blue. (USA)
131 One side of a large folder announcing a programme of visits to plants in the graphic trades organized by the AIGA. Green figure, red and green type. (USA)
132, 133 Opening illustration (full colour) and complete double spread from a brochure about *Sony* radios. (USA)
134 Cover of a spirally bound booklet about R.S. Platou A/S, shipbrokers. (NOR)
135 Invitation to the *Olivetti* stand at an office equipment exhibition. Yellow spheres on blue ground, lettering in blue, red and green. (SWI)
136 Page showing a block diagram in brown, yellow, blue and red on olive from a brochure on microprocessing issued by National Semiconductor Corp. (USA)

128 Mehrfarbige Doppelseite (auf braunem Papier) aus einer Promotion-Broschüre, hier mit einer kleinen Erläuterung über die Entstehung verschiedener Lebensmittel. (USA)
129 Doppelseite aus einer Broschüre über ein Landesystem mit *Hermes*-Instrumenten. Blautöne auf Weiss. (NOR)
130 Eine Seite aus einer grossformatigen Einladung der AIGA zum Packungs-Wettbewerb 1976. Design in Rot und Blau. (USA)
131 Eine Seite aus einem grossen Faltprospekt der AIGA, die zu Besuchen in verschiedenen Graphischen Betrieben einlädt. Grün und rot. (USA)
132, 133 Mehrfarbige Illustration und vollständige Doppelseite aus einer Broschüre über *Sony*-Radios. (USA)
134 Farbiger Umschlag einer Broschüre über eine Schiffsgesellschaft. (NOR)
135 Einladung der *Olivetti* zum Besuch ihres Standes an der Büfa 1975 (Bürofachmesse). Gelbe Kugeln auf blauem Grund, Schrift blau, rot und grün. (SWI)
136 Seite aus einer Broschüre über Datenverarbeitungs-Systeme. Diagramm in Braun, Gelb, Blau und Rot auf olivem Grund. (USA)

128 Page double en couleur (imprimée sur papier brun) figurant dans une brochure promotionnelle, avec un aperçu sur l'histoire de l'art culinaire. (USA)
129 Page double tirée d'une brochure pour un système d'atterrissage aux instruments. Tons bleus et blancs. (NOR)
130 Recto d'une invitation grand format pour la soumission de travaux pour le concours AIGA de création d'emballages. Design en rouge et bleu. (USA)
131 Panneau d'un dépliant grand format annonçant une série de visites dans diverses entreprises graphiques, organisées par l'AIGA. Vert et rouge. (USA)
132, 133 Illustration (en couleurs) et première page double où elle figure. Eléments d'une brochure en faveur des radios *Sony*. (USA)
134 Couverture d'une brochure à reliure spirale d'un courtier maritime. (NOR)
135 Invitation pour une visite du stand *Olivetti* à une exposition d'articles de bureaux. Jaune sur fond bleu, typo bleu, rouge et vert. (SWI)
136 Page présentant un diagramme en brun, jaune, bleu et rouge sur fond olive. Elément figurant dans une brochure sur le traitement de l'information. (USA)

ARTIST / KÜNSTLER / ARTISTE:

128 W. Chris Gorman
129 Rainer Jucker/Bruno Oldani
130, 131 David L. Romanoff
132, 133 Stanislaw Zagorski
134 Leif F. Anisdahl
135 Giovanni Ferioli
136 Jean-Claude Muller

DESIGNER / GESTALTER / MAQUETTISTE:

128 W. Chris Gorman
129 Rainer Jucker/Bruno Oldani
130, 131 David L. Romanoff
132, 133 John Channell
134 Leif F. Anisdahl
135 Enzo Ragazzini
136 Jean-Claude Muller

ART DIRECTOR / DIRECTEUR ARTISTIQUE:

128 W. Chris Gorman
129 Bruno Oldani/Rainer Jucker
130, 131 David L. Romanoff
132, 133 John Channell
134 Leif F. Anisdahl
135 Giovanni Ferioli
136 Ken Parkhurst

AGENCY / AGENTUR / AGENCE – STUDIO:

128 Martin E. Janis & Co., Inc.
129 Designstudio Bruno Oldani
130, 131 Romanoff Design
132, 133 Group One Inc.
134 Anisdahl/Christensen A/S
135 Ufficio Pubblicità Olivetti
136 Ken Parkhurst & Associates, Inc.

Booklets / Prospekte / Brochures

130

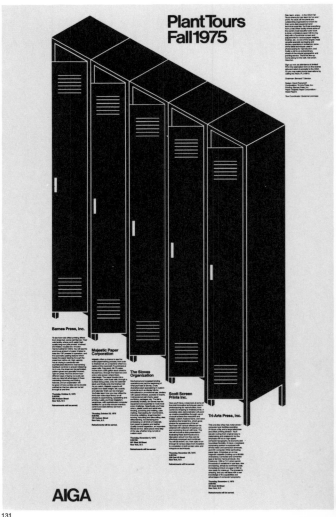

131

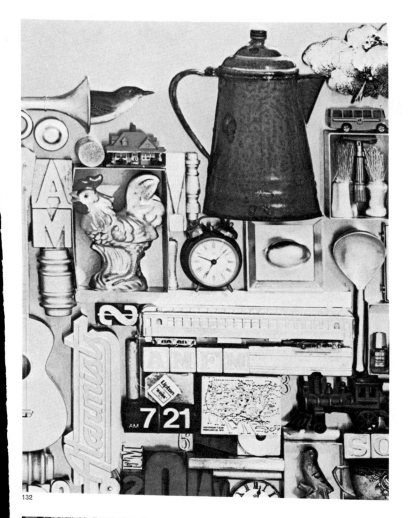

132

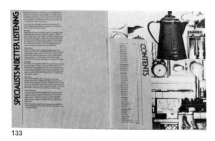

SPECIALISTS IN BETTER LISTENING

133

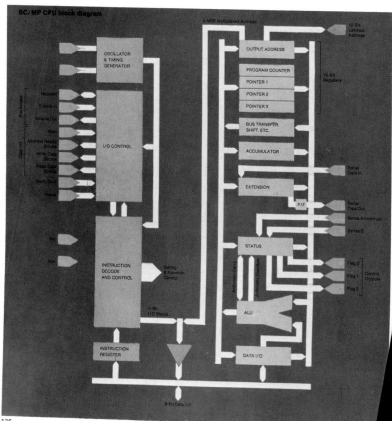

134

35

SC/MP CPU block diagram

136

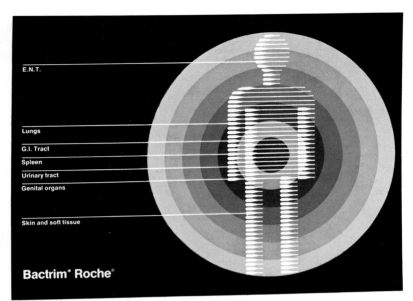

137

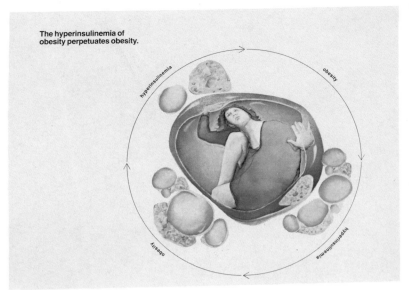

138

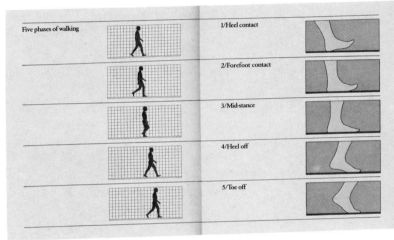

139

ARTIST / KÜNSTLER / ARTISTE:

137 Andy Graetz/Rolf Harder
138 Paul Giovanopoulos
139 Dawn Tennant/Heather Cooper
140 Ewald Becker
141, 142 Alain Gauthier

DESIGNER / GESTALTER / MAQUETTISTE:

137 Rolf Harder
138 Ron Vareltzis
139 Robert Burns/Richard Male
140 Ewald Becker/Grit von Fransecky

ART DIRECTOR / DIRECTEUR ARTISTIQUE:

137 Monique Simond/Doug Mahoney
138 Ron Vareltzis
139 Robert Burns
141, 142 Jean-François Feige

AGENCY / AGENTUR / AGENCE – STUDIO:

137 Design Collaborative
138 Geigy Pharmaceuticals
139 Burns & Cooper
141, 142 Industrie Service

141

137 Cover of a folder about a *Roche* broad-spectrum bactericide. White figure on coloured concentric circles, black background. (CAN)
138 Cover of a booklet about a *Geigy* product against obesity. The illustration, in delicate colours, appeared through a die-cut circle in the envelope used for dispatch. (USA)
139 Double spread from a promotional booklet about *Roots* footwear. Illustrations brown, grey and pink on yellow stock. (CAN)
140 "The cook's ladle is more important than her grammar." Colour illustration on the front of a folder about *Pankreon forte* for regulating the digestion. (GER)
141, 142 Double spread and detail in roughly actual size from a booklet issued by a tube company. It tells the story of two children whose interest in tubes begins when they realize that flower stalks are tubes, then passes via the tubes of the circulatory system to end up with technical tubes made in the factory. (FRA)

63

142

137 Umschlag eines Faltprospektes über das *Roche*-Produkt *Bactrim.* Weisse Figur auf mehr-farbigen Kreisen, schwarzer Grund. (CAN)
138 Umschlag einer Broschüre über ein *Geigy*-Produkt gegen Fettleibigkeit. Illustration in sanften Farben. (USA)
139 Doppelseite aus einer Werbe-Broschüre über *Roots*-Schuhe. Illustration in Braun, Grau und Rosa auf gelbem Papier. (CAN)
140 Mehrfarbiger Umschlag eines Prospekts über *Pankreon forte,* ein Medikament gegen Ver-dauungsstörungen. (GER)
141, 142 Doppelseite und Detail aus einer Broschüre der Röhrenfabrik Compagnie des Tubes de Normandie. Das Märchen erzählt von zwei Kindern, die bemerken, dass Blumenstiele eigentlich Röhren sind, und so steigert sich ihr Interesse bis zu den technischen Röhren der Fabrik. Sie sind von der vielseitigen Verwendbarkeit dieser Röhren begeistert. (FRA)

137 Couverture d'un dépliant *Roche* pour un bactéricide à large spectre d'activité. Figure blanche, cercles concentriques en couleurs sur fond noir. (CAN)
138 Couverture d'une brochure *Geigy* pour un produit pharmaceutique contre l'obésité. L'illus-tration en couleurs atténuées se fait voir à travers la découpe de l'enveloppe. (USA)
139 Page double d'une brochure promotionnelle pour les chaussures *Roots.* Illustrations en brun, gris et rose sur papier vergé jaune. (CAN)
140 «La louche de la cuisinière est beaucoup plus importante que sa grammaire.» Illustration couleur figurant sur le recto d'un dépliant pour un produit digestif. (GER)
141, 142 Page double et détail (approx. grandeur nature) figurant dans une brochure de la Com-pagnie des Tubes de Normandie. Elle raconte l'histoire de deux enfants qui découvrent successive-ment les différents genres de tubes: les minces tubes dont consistent les tiges, les tuyaux condui-sant le sang, les tubes servant à toutes sorte de choses techniques. (FRA)

143

144

ARTIST / KÜNSTLER / ARTISTE:

143, 144 Nobuhiko Nobuki
147 B Communications
148 Victor Jennings
149 Gavin Healey

DESIGNER / GESTALTER / MAQUETTISTE:

143, 144 Osamu Asao
145, 146 Tom Bluhm
147 B Communications
148 Victor Jennings
149 Gavin Healey

ART DIRECTOR / DIRECTEUR ARTISTIQUE:

143, 144 Mitsumasa Nagata
145, 146 Ken White
148 Victor Jennings
149 Gavin Healey

AGENCY / AGENTUR / AGENCE – STUDIO:

145, 146 IBM Boulder, Design Center
147 B Communications
148 Chrysler Graphic Art Services
149 Gavin Healey Design

**Booklets
Prospekte
Brochures**

145

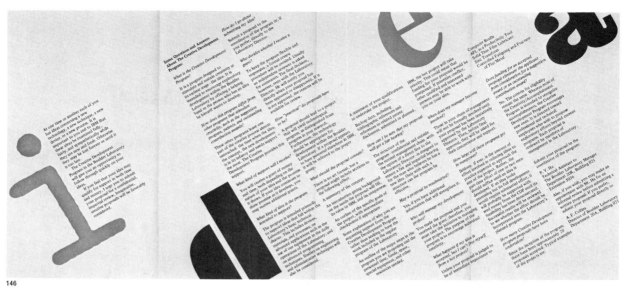

146

147

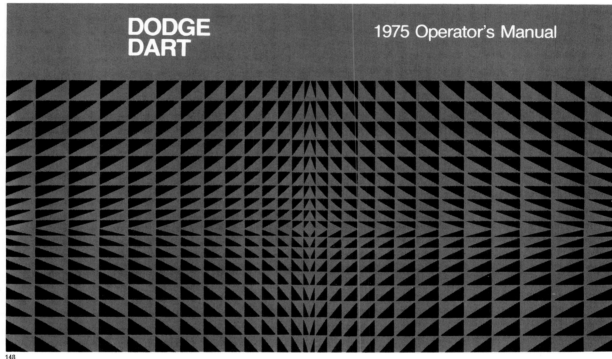

148

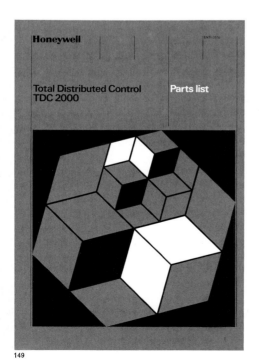

149

143, 144 Illustration in actual size and complete cover of a folder about *National* air conditioning units. (JPN)
145, 146 Cover and inside spread of a folder about the utilization of creative ideas in an IBM plant. Letters in yellow and brownish grey, black type matter. (USA)
147 Brochure about a range of cosmetics for men called *Blue Max*. Blue and white seal, cigar in natural colours. (ITA)
148 Cover of an owner's manual about the operation of a *Dodge* car. Design blue and red with white lettering. (USA)
149 Cover of a parts list for a *Honeywell* computer system. Design in green, blue and white on a green ground. (USA)

143, 144 Illustration in Originalgrösse und vollständiger Umschlag eines Katalogs über verschiedene Klima-Anlagen der Marke *National*. (JPN)
145, 146 Umschlag und Innenseite einer Broschüre, herausgegeben von der IBM, mit der Aufforderung an Angestellte, kreativ zu sein, neue Ideen und Erfindungen anzubringen. Buchstaben in Gelb und Braun-Grau, Schrift schwarz. (USA)
147 Umschlag einer Broschüre über die Herrenkosmetik-Marke *Blue Max*. Weisse Schrift auf blauem Grund, Cigarre naturfarben. (ITA)
148 Umschlag einer Betriebsanleitung für die Automarke *Dodge*. Design in Rot und Blau, weisse Schrift. (USA)
149 Titelblatt einer Broschüre über Zubehörteile eines *Honeywell*-Computers. Design in Grün, Blau und Weiss auf grünem Grund. (USA)

143, 144 Illustration (en grandeur nature) et couverture du dépliant où elle figure. Elément de publicité pour les climatiseurs *National*. (JPN)
145, 146 Couverture et double page intérieure d'un dépliant consacré à la mise en œuvre d'idées créatives chez IBM. Caractères jaunes et grisâtres, typo noir. (USA)
147 Brochure pour la gamme de produits cosmétiques *Blue Max* pour hommes. Bande bleue et blanche, cigare en couleur naturelle. (ITA)
148 Couverture d'un manuel sur le fonctionnement des voitures *Dodge*. Design en bleu et rouge, texte en blanc. (USA)
149 Couverture de la liste des pièces détachées et des accessoires pour les systèmes d'ordinateur *Honeywell*. Design en vert, bleu et blanc sur fond vert. (USA)

ARTIST / KÜNSTLER / ARTISTE:

150, 151 J. P. Desclozeaux
152, 154 May Néama
153 Edward Sorel
155 Rebecca Anderson
156 Alex Gniedziejko

150, 151 Illustration pages in colour from a booklet of rules for coronary patients—here as car drivers and hunters—and their treatment with the pharmaceutical *Lénitral*. (FRA)
152 Cover of a brochure about a *Roche* tranquillizer. (BEL)
153 Cover in pale hues of a folder about a menopausal treatment, issued by *Abbott Laboratories*. (USA)
154 "When anxiety affects morale." Folder about the tranquillizer *Librium*, shown closed and open. (BEL)
155 Full-page illustration from a report on an AT&T management conference in Santa Cruz. (USA)
156 Page from a booklet on *Aldactone* as an antidote for hypertension. (USA)

150, 151 Farbige Illustrationen aus einer Broschüre mit Ratschlägen für herzkranke Patienten – hier als Autofahrer und als Jäger – und ihre Behandlung mit dem Medikament *Lénitral*. (FRA)
152 Umschlag einer Broschüre über das Beruhigungsmittel *Nobrium*, ein *Roche*-Medikament. (BEL)
153 Titelblatt in sanften Farben eines Faltprospektes über ein Medikament gegen Beschwerden in der Menopause. (USA)
154 «Wenn Angst die Moral beeinträchtigt.» Faltprospekt über das *Roche*-Beruhigungsmittel *Librium*. (BEL)
155 Ganzseitige Illustration aus einem Bericht über eine Konferenz in Santa Cruz über Management. (USA)
156 Seite aus einem Prospekt über ein Medikament gegen hohen Blutdruck. (USA)

150, 151 Pages illustratives (en couleurs) d'une brochure contenant des règles pour le coronarien – le coronarien et la conduite automobile et le coronarien et la chasse – et le traitement des affections des vaisseaux coronaires avec *Lénitral*. (FRA)
152 Couverture d'une brochure sur un tranquilisant *Roche*. (BEL)
153 Couverture (en couleurs atténuées) d'un dépliant consacré à un produit recommandé pendant la ménopause. (USA)
154 Dépliant (montré ouvert et fermé) pour le tranquilisant *Librium.* (BEL)
155 Illustration pleine page consacrée à une conférence organisée par AT&T à Santa Cruz sur la direction et la gestion. (USA)
156 Page d'une brochure sur l'hypertenseur *Aldactone*. (USA)

150

151

DESIGNER / GESTALTER / MAQUETTISTE:

150, 151 B. Duparc
152, 154 May Néama
153 William R. Sample
156 Leslie Sisman

ART DIRECTOR / DIRECTEUR ARTISTIQUE:

150, 151 A. Bernardo
153 William R. Sample
156 Leslie Sisman

AGENCY / AGENTUR / AGENCE – STUDIO:

153 Bert Ray Studio
155 Reis and Manwaring
156 VIS-U-Com., Inc.

154

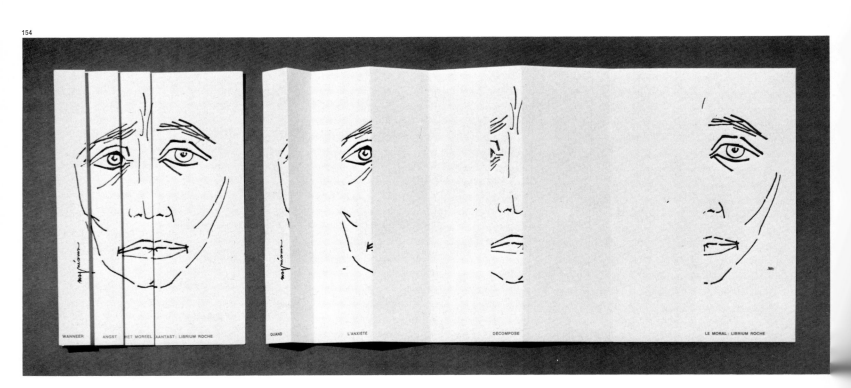

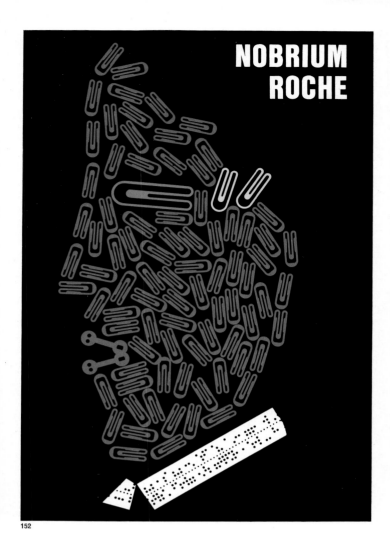

NOBRIUM
ROCHE

152

MIDDLE
AGE
is when
bifocals
are no longer
a funny
subject.

153

Booklets / Prospekte / Brochures

155

156

To keep excess urates out of circulation

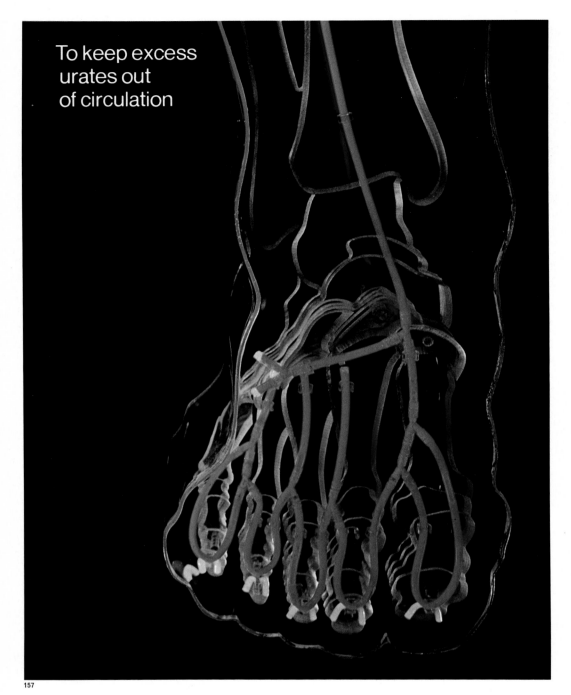

157

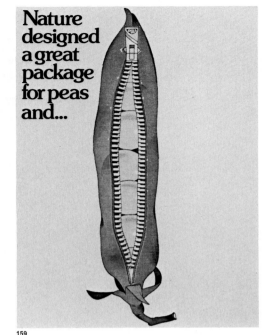

Nature designed a great package for peas and...

159

Nature designed a great package for corn and...

160

Nature designed a great package for bananas and...

161

ARTIST / KÜNSTLER / ARTISTE:

157 John Wilson/Mel Small (Photo)
158 Hans Falk
159–161 Ron Becker
162 John de Cesare
163, 164 Tomi Ungerer
165, 166 Anita Siegal

DESIGNER / GESTALTER / MAQUETTISTE:

157 Ron Vareltzis
159–161 Al Zalon
162 John de Cesare
163, 164 John de Cesare/Karen Kutner
165, 166 Ken Jordan

ART DIRECTOR / DIRECTEUR ARTISTIQUE:

157 Ron Vareltzis
159–161 Al Zalon
162–164 John de Cesare
165, 166 Ken Jordan

AGENCY / AGENTUR / AGENCE – STUDIO:

157, 162–166 Geigy Pharmaceuticals
159–161 Kallir, Philips, Ross, Inc.

Booklets / Prospekte Brochures

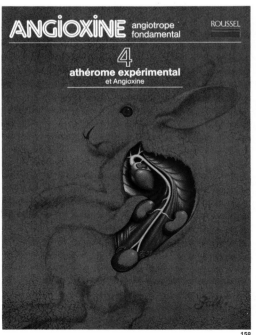

ANGIOXINE angiotrope fondamental ROUSSEL

4

athérome expérimental
et Angioxine

158

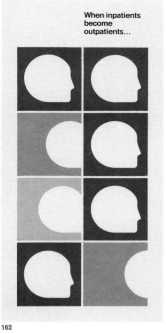

162

When inpatients become outpatients...

157 Cover of a *Geigy* brochure for a pharmaceutical against gout. (USA)
158 Cover of a *Roussel* brochure about a drug against atherosclerosis and the results obtained in experiments. (FRA)
159–161 Series of folders about new 21-day and 28-day dispensers for the oral contraceptive *Ortho-Novum*. The "zippers" of the coloured drawings can be pulled open. (USA)
162 Cover of a mailer about a one-capsule-a-day treatment now possible with a *Geigy* antidepressant. Red, orange and yellow squares. (USA)
163–166 Pages from two *Geigy* booklets from a series on creative psychiatry. Figs. 165 and 166 refer specially to the contribution of Jung. (USA)

157 Titelblatt einer *Geigy*-Broschüre für ein Medikament gegen Gicht. (USA)
158 Titelblatt einer *Roussel*-Broschüre über ein Medikament gegen Arteriosklerose und dessen Erprobung. (FRA)
159–161 «Die Natur entwarf eine grossartige Verpackung für Bananen und...» Aus einer Serie von Faltprospekten über die neue Verpackung der empfängnisverhütenden Pille *Ortho-Novum*. Der Reissverschluss in den Illustrationen kann geöffnet werden. (USA)
162 Umschlag eines Versand-Prospekts über eine «Einmal täglich eine Tablette»-Behandlung mit einem *Geigy*-Medikament gegen Depressionen. (USA)
163–166 Seiten aus zwei *Geigy*-Broschüren über kreative Psychiatrie. Abb. 165 und 166 beziehen sich speziell auf die Arbeit von C.G. Jung. (USA)

157 Couverture d'une brochure *Geigy* pour un produit contre la goutte. (USA)
158 Couverture d'une brochure *Roussel* en faveur d'un produit pour le traitement de l'artériosclérose, avec des résultats d'expérimentations. (FRA)
159–161 D'une série de dépliants pour un nouveau distributeur de pillules contraceptives (21 et 28 jours). Les «fermetures éclair» des dessins couleurs peuvent être tirées en bas. (USA)
162 Couverture d'un prospectus annonçant un traitement rendu possible grâce à un antidépresseur *Geigy* dont il ne faut plus qu'une seule capsule par jour. Carrés en rouge, orange et jaune. (USA)
163–166 D'une brochure *Geigy* figurant dans une série sur la psychiatrie créative. Les figs. 165 et 166 se réfèrent à la contribution de C.G. Jung. (USA)

individual might take, the attitude he could assume and the conditions he might seek out in order to be ready to engage in the creative experience. These various things that an individual might do we call "preparers."

There are two basic sets of preparers. One concerns itself with the *input* of information, the other with its *output*.

Information Input

To arrive at creative combinations of things and ideas requires having a storehouse of information and knowledge from which the necessary building blocks can be withdrawn. If there is no information or a limited amount of information, or if that which is available is large quantitatively but very similar qual-

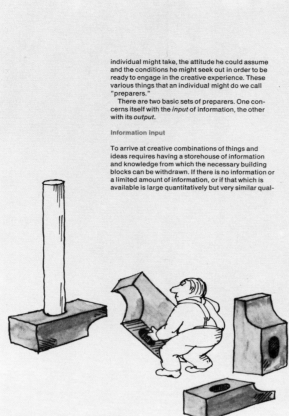

12

163

(1) *Personal analogy.*
In using personal analogy, an individual tries to feel what it is to be like the object he is working with. Thus he *becomes* the spring in the apparatus and *feels* its tension. He *becomes* the pane of glass and sees what it *feels* like to be looked through.

Four levels of personal analogy have been specified (Synectics, Inc. 1968).

(a) *First-person description of facts.*
A person imagines he is something else and simply describes the facts. An example we shall follow through in all four levels of analogy is that of the fiddler crab, which comes from the Synectics' *Teacher's Manual*. At this level, when a person feels he is like the fiddler crab, he might say that he has a hard outside and a soft inside.

(b) *Empathic identification with a living thing.*
This level involves both emotional and kinesthetic involvement with the object with which one empathizes. In the case of the fiddler crab, a person might say that his big claw is rather burdensome and useless. It is quite heavy and even though he waves it around nobody is frightened.

Becoming the object one is working with.

27

164

between the approach Freud took and that of Jung
in the following remarks:
Deeply as Freud's genius probed beneath the surface of his age, he was still so much influenced by its rationalistic trends that he could understand instinct only as a biological phenomenon that left no room for such "unscientific" questions as the question of meaning. This is where Jung's analytical psychology comes in: even though it is directed toward the sickness of the individual, it goes beyond the bounds of pure therapy of the neuroses and expands into a cultural psychology, in which "sickness" is a symbol and starting point for wider insights. In such a context the question of meaning assumes a special importance.

Freud saw instinct only as a biological phenomenon.

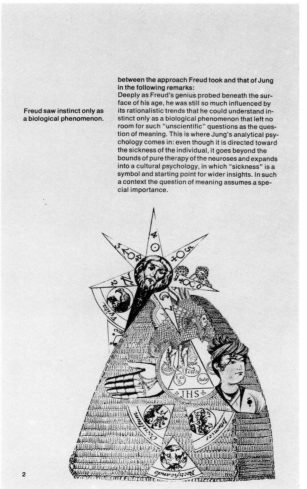

2

165

by presenting it in the familiar context of Rorschach's work. One chapter in particular, "The Archaeology of Archetypes," strives to remove the cloak of mysticism surrounding the concept of archetypes. Instead of focusing on the Rorschach as a diagnostic method of a means to discern personality dynamics, I tried to show how the Rorschach may contribute to an expansion of theory about psychic structure itself. I suggested that this

12

166

71

167

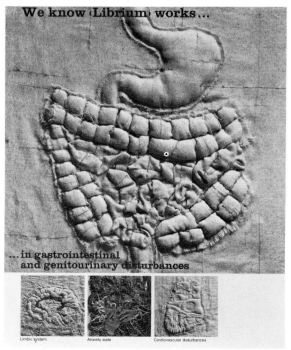

We know ‹Librium› works…

…in gastrointestinal
and genitourinary disturbances

Limbic system   Anxiety state   Cardiovascular disturbances

168

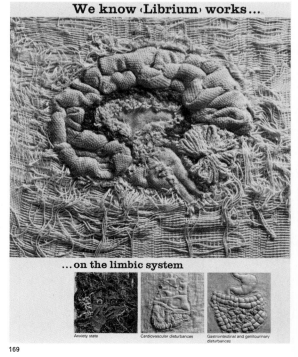

We know ‹Librium› works…

…on the limbic system

Anxiety state   Cardiovascular disturbances   Gastrointestinal and genitourinary disturbances

169

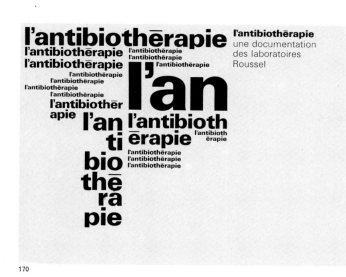

170

167–169 Illustration in actual size and two complete covers from a series of folders on the action of the tranquillizer *Librium,* here for instance on anxiety states, on the gastro-intestinal tract and on the limbic system. Illustrations in shades of grey-brown. (SWI)
170 Typographic cover of a *Roussel* booklet on antibiotic therapy. Black and red. (FRA)
171–173 Two illustrations (full colour) and one of the complete brochures from a series about the drug *Triavil* for the treatment of depression and anxiety. Each brochure quotes a work of fiction to illustrate the predicament of a woman—here Helen Alving from Ibsen's *Ghosts,* Birdie Hubbard from Lillian Hellman's *The Little Foxes* and Toby Landau from Neil Simon's *The Gingerbread Lady.* (USA)

167–169 Illustration in Originalgrösse und zwei vollständige Umschläge aus einer Serie von Faltprospekten über das Beruhigungsmittel *Librium* von *Roche,* das zur Behandlung von Angstzuständen mit funktionellen oder organischen Störungen dient. Illustration in grau-braunen Tönen. (SWI)
170 Typographischer Umschlag einer *Roussel*-Broschüre über die Antibiotika-Therapie. Schwarz und rot. (FRA)
171–173 Zwei mehrfarbige Illustrationen und ein vollständiger Umschlag aus einer Serie von Broschüren über ein Medikament zur Behandlung von Depressionen und Angstzuständen. Jede Illustration steht im Zusammenhang mit einem Werk aus der Literaturgeschichte, welches die missliche Lage einer Frau schildert. (USA)

167–169 Illustration (grandeur nature) et deux couvertures figurant dans une série de dépliants pour *Librium.* Ils illustrent le spectre d'activité de ce tranquilisant pour le traitement d'anxiété et d'affections gastro-intestinales et ses effets sur le système moteur. Illustrations en tons gris brunâtres. (SWI)
170 Couverture typographique d'une documentation *Roussel* pour une antibiothérapie. Noir et rouge. (FRA)
171–173 Illustrations couleurs et brochure d'une série pour *Triavil* pour le traitement d'anxiété et de dépressions. Chaque brochure est consacrée au principal personnage féminin d'un roman: Helen Alving (*Les Revenants* d'Ibsen), Birdie Hubbard (*The Little Foxes* de L. Hellman) et Toby Landau (*The Gingerbread Lady* de N. Simon). (USA)

171

173

ARTIST / KÜNSTLER / ARTISTE:

167–169 Erika Franke
171–173 Peter Schauman

DESIGNER / GESTALTER / MAQUETTISTE:

170 Theo Ballmer
173 Matthew Bennett

ART DIRECTOR / DIRECTEUR ARTISTIQUE:

167–169 Jacques Hauser
170 Theo Ballmer
171–173 Matthew Bennett

AGENCY / AGENTUR / AGENCE – STUDIO:

170 Studio Ballmer

172

Booklets / Prospekte / Brochures

ARTIST / KÜNSTLER / ARTISTE:

174, 175 Joseph J. Fazio
176 Nicholas Gaetano
177 Rick McCollum
178, 179 José Reyes
180 Norm Walker

DESIGNER / GESTALTER:

174, 175 Joseph J. Fazio
177–180 Ron Vareltzis

ART DIRECTOR:

174, 175 Joseph J. Fazio
176 Ken Jordan
177–180 Ron Vareltzis

AGENCY / AGENTUR:

174–180 Geigy
　　　　 Pharmaceuticals

CLINICAL FORUM ON ARTHRITIS — Geigy

Forty tons of joint pain.

174

Geigy — CLINICAL FORUM ON ARTHRITIS

Another tale from the Persian Nights

176

175

Documenta Geigy

Arteriosclerosis
the prospects for prevention

Introduction

177

174, 175 Cover and double spread from a newspaper-like *Geigy* mailer in the "Clinical Forum" series, here on arthritis. Illustrations in colour. (USA)
176 Cover of another mailer from the *Geigy* "Clinical Forum" series. The drawing illustrates an old Persian cure for rheumatoid arthritis. (USA)
177–180 Cover for a newspaper-like mailer from the "Documenta *Geigy*" series, with two double spreads and one illustration in actual size. The articles deal with various aspects of arteriosclerosis. (USA)

174, 175 Umschlag und Doppelseite aus einer zeitungsähnlichen Versand-Broschüre der *Geigy*, hier über Arthritis. Mehrfarbig. (USA)
176 Titelblatt aus der gleichen Serie von Broschüren der *Geigy*. Die Zeichnung zeigt eine alte persische Kur gegen rheumatische Arthritis. (USA)
177–180 Umschlag, Illustration und zwei vollständige Doppelseiten aus der Versand-Serie «Documenta *Geigy*». Es handelt sich hier um eine Nummer über Arteriosklerose. (USA)

174, 175 Couverture et page double d'une brochure *Geigy* (format de journal) sur l'arthrite. Publication de la série «Clinical Forum». Polychromie. (USA)
176 Couverture d'une autre brochure de la série «Clinical Forum» de *Geigy*. Le dessin se réfère à un ancien remède persan contre la polyarthrite. (USA)
177–180 Couverture d'une brochure en format de journal, deux pages doubles et une illustration (grandeur nature). Publication de la série «Documenta *Geigy*». Les articles se réfèrent aux divers aspects de l'artériosclérose. (USA)

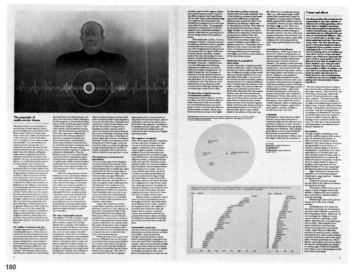

179

180

178

Booklets / Prospekte / Brochures

ARTIST / KÜNSTLER / ARTISTE:

181, 181a Ulrich Lehmann/Garry Emery
183 P. Kilmer/A. Sardina/G. Perraud
184, 185 Walter Pepperle
186, 187 Gervasio Gallardo
188 Joseph J. Fazio

DESIGNER / GESTALTER / MAQUETTISTE:

181, 181a Garry Emery
184, 185 Olaf Leu/Fritz Hofrichter
188 Joseph J. Fazio

181

183

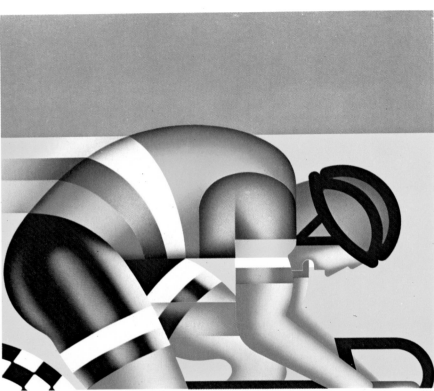

181a

184

182

185

181, 181a Complete cover of a notebook sent to doctors by Alan & Hanburys, and detail of the cover design. The product advertised is the bronchodilator *Ventolin,* said to have "a track record to depend on". (AUL)
182 Mailer sent to garment manufacturers by the Soabar Company offering them (on folder in pocket) *Permagraphic* labels. (USA)
183 Cover of a booklet about the metric system issued by Nekoosa Edwards Paper Co. (USA)
184, 185 Cover and inside of a folder on and about *Chromolux* glossy paper board. The tiger's hide appears through the die-cut contours of the pin-up girl's swimsuit. (GER)
186–188 Covers of *Geigy* folders in the *Pharmascan* series mailed to doctors. Each contains reprints of reports on medical and allied subjects. The covers refer to eight ecological surprises (fig. 186), hazards in the home (fig. 187) and sunburn complications (fig. 188). (USA)

181, 181a Vollständiger Umschlag und Detail eines Notizblocks für Ärzte. Die Firma Allen & Hanburys wirbt hier mit einem Medikament gegen Atembeschwerden. (AUL)
182 Versandprospekt für Etiketten der Soabar Company. Mehrfarbig. (USA)
183 Umschlag einer Broschüre über die Einführung des metrischen Systems in Amerika, herausgegeben von einer Papierfabrik. (USA)
184, 185 Umschlag und Innenseite eines Prospekts der Zanders Feinpapiere GmbH für das Kunstdruckpapier *Chromolux*. (GER)
186–188 Umschläge für die *Geigy*-Prospekte in der *Pharmascan*-Serie, die an Ärzte verschickt wird. Jeder Prospekt enthält Artikel über medizinische und damit verbundene Probleme. Die Umschläge beziehen sich auf acht ökologische Überraschungen (Abb. 186), Gefahren zu Hause (Abb. 187) und Sonnenbrände (Abb. 188). (USA)

181, 181a Couverture d'un bloc notes adressé aux médecins et détail de l'illustration. Elément de publicité en faveur d'un produit pour la dilatation des bronches. (AUL)
182 Publicité adressée aux fabricants de vêtements. On leur offre (dans le dépliant-accordéon) des étiquettes *Permagraphic*. (USA)
183 Couverture de la brochure d'une papeterie discutant le système métrique. (USA)
184, 185 Eléments d'un dépliant pour le carton brillant *Chromolux*. La peau du tigre se fait voir à travers la découpe du costume de bain d'un pin-up. (GER)
186–188 Couvertures de dépliants *Geigy* parus dans la série *Pharmascan*. Chacun comprend des rapports médicaux sur divers sujets. Les couvertures se réfèrent à huit surprises écologiques (fig. 186), aux risques qu'on court à la maison (fig. 187) et aux complications provoquées par les coups de soleil (fig. 188). (USA)

ART DIRECTOR / DIRECTEUR ARTISTIQUE:

181, 181a Garry Emery
183 Angelo G. Sardina
184, 185 Olaf Leu/Fritz Hofrichter
186–188 Joseph J. Fazio

AGENCY / AGENTUR / AGENCE – STUDIO:

181, 181a Interact Communications
183 Grant-Jacoby
184, 185 Olaf Leu Design
186–188 Geigy Pharmaceuticals

186

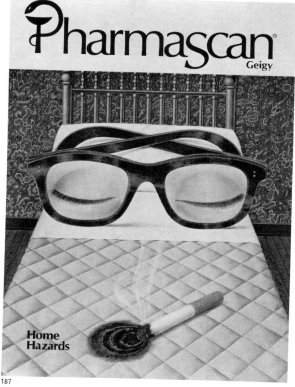

187

188

189

ARTIST / KÜNSTLER / ARTISTE:

189–193 André François
194 Bob Conrad
195 Jerry Pinkney

DESIGNER / GESTALTER / MAQUETTISTE:

189–193 Alain Pontecorvo
194 Bob Salpeter

190

191

192

193

194

189–193 Complete double spread and four of the large illustration pages (in colour) from a brochure sent to clients by *Artra*, printers and consultants. The illustrations allude to quality (Fig. 190), deadlines (Fig. 191), contacts (Fig. 192) and creativity (Fig. 193). (FRA)
194 Double spread from a brochure issued by the Gold Bronze Powder Council to illustrate the use of gold bronze pigments. The ''record'' emerging from the sleeve is gold. (USA)
195 Page from a mailer on the subject of childhood for *Warren* papers, here giving an illustrator's idea of childhood. (USA)

189–193 Vollständige Doppelseite und vier mehrfarbige Illustrationen aus einer grossformatigen Broschüre, die an Kunden der *Artra*, Druckerei und Beratungsfirma, verschickt wird. Die Illustrationen beziehen sich auf Qualität (Abb. 190), Termine (Abb. 191), Kontakte (Abb. 192) und Kreativität (Abb. 193). (FRA)
194 Doppelseite aus einer Broschüre, die über die Verwendung von Goldfarben für Illustrationen informiert. Die «Schallplatte» ist in Gold. (USA)
195 Seite aus einem Versandprospekt mit dem Thema «Kindheit», herausgegeben von der Papierfabrik *Warren*. (USA)

189–193 «*Artra* et votre société: un mariage de raison.» Page double et illustrations couleurs d'une brochure adressée aux clients d'*Artra*, imprimeurs et conseils. Les références: la qualité (190), les dates limites (191), les contacts (192), la créativité (193). (FRA)
194 Page double d'une brochure publiée par le Gold Bronze Powder Council afin d'illustrer l'emploi des colorants de bronze d'or. Le «disque» sortant de la pochette est en or. (USA)
195 Elément de publicité d'une papeterie. Cette page est consacrée à l'enfance et présente l'idée qu'en a un illustrateur. (USA)

ART DIRECTOR / DIRECTEUR ARTISTIQUE:
189–193 Alain Pontecorvo
194 Bob Salpeter
195 Jim Witham/Ralph Moxcey

AGENCY / AGENTUR / AGENCE – STUDIO:
189–193 Roux-Seguela-Cayzac
194 Lopez Salpeter, Inc.
195 Humphrey Browning MacDougall

195

196

ARTIST / KÜNSTLER / ARTISTE:

196 Ewald Becker/Grit von Fransecky
197 J. Down/J. Davenport
198–201 Heather Cooper/Tim Saunders (Photo)
202 Heather Cooper

DESIGNER / GESTALTER / MAQUETTISTE:

197 J. Down/J. Davenport
202 Robert Burns/John Speakman
203–205 Wilburn O. Bonnell III

ART DIRECTOR / DIRECTEUR ARTISTIQUE:

196 Ewald Becker/Grit von Fransecky
197 Jack Feldman
198–202 Robert Burns
203–205 Wilburn O. Bonnell III

AGENCY / AGENTUR / AGENCE – STUDIO:

196 Studio Becker + von Fransecky
197 Brewer, Jones & Feldman, Inc.
198–202 Burns & Cooper
203–205 Container Corporation of America

197

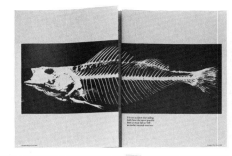

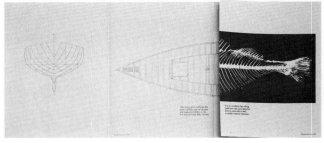

198–201

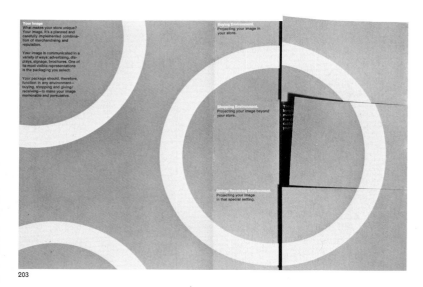

196 Postcard entitled "Yugoslav impressions" sent to printers to illustrate the qualities of *Hartmann* printing inks. (GER)
197 Inside of a black folder containing a bogus loose-sheet quarterly report issued as promotion for the papers of the Beckett Paper Co. One yellow sheet emerges from a slit in the red and orange typewriter. (USA)
198–202 Double spreads and gatefold from a booklet about sailing-boats, and side of a poster-size folder entitled "Wind and Wave", both used as mailers to illustrate the qualities of *Abitibi* papers. (CAN)
203 Cut gatefold in red, white and blue from a brochure about the retail packaging of the Container Corporation of America. (USA)
204, 205 Spreads in red, white and black from a "reporter's handbook" issued as part of employee communications by the Container Corporation of America. (USA)

196 Postkarte mit dem Titel «Jugoslawische Impressionen», herausgegeben von der Firma Hartmann Druckfarben, die solche Karten an alle deutschen Druckereien verschickt. (GER)
197 Innenseite eines Faltprospektes der Papierfabrik Beckett Paper Co. Der Prospekt enthält eine Anzahl loser Blätter, die zusammen einen Vierteljahrsrapport bilden. (USA)
198–202 Faltseite (blau auf Weiss) und zwei Doppelseiten aus einem Prospekt über Segelboote, der die Vorteile eines von der Abitibi Provincial Papers hergestellten Papiers demonstriert. (USA)
203 Innenseite in Rot, Weiss und Blau aus einer Broschüre über Verpackungen für Kleinhändler, herausgegeben von der Container Corporation of America. (USA)
204, 205 Seiten in Rot, Weiss und Schwarz aus einem Handbuch für Angestellte der Container Corporation of America. (USA)

196 Carte postale intitulée «Impressions yougoslaves». Publicité adressée aux imprimeurs afin d'illustrer la qualité des encres d'imprimerie *Hartmann.* (GER)
197 Intérieur d'un dépliant noir contenant un rapport trimestriel feint en feuilles volantes. Elément de publicité d'une papeterie. Une feuille jaune sort de la fente coupée dans la machine à écrire en rouge et orange. (USA)
198–202 Pages doubles et repli d'une brochure consacrée aux bateaux à voiles et recto d'un dépliant au format d'affiche intitulé «Le vent et la vague». Ces deux éléments démontrent la qualité d'une variété de papiers *Abitibi.* (CAN)
203 Repli découpé en rouge, blanc et bleu figurant dans une brochure consacré aux emballages pour la vente au détail, fabriqués par la Container Corporation of America. (USA)
204, 205 Pages doubles en rouge, blanc et noir d'un «manuel pour correspondants». Celui-ci fait partie des communications pour les employés de la Container Corp. (USA)

203

202

204

205

206

208

ARTIST / KÜNSTLER / ARTISTE:

206 Haruo Miyauchi
208 Terry Sharbach
209 Erich Hölle
210 James Barkley

DESIGNER / GESTALTER / MAQUETTISTE:

206, 207 Seymour Chwast
210 B. M. Pederson
211 Luca Häfliger
212 Matilde Contri

ART DIRECTOR / DIRECTEUR ARTISTIQUE:

206, 207 Seymour Chwast
208 Elaine Pollom/F. R. Peters
210 B. M. Pederson
212 Matilde Contri

AGENCY / AGENTUR / AGENCE – STUDIO:

206, 207 Push Pin Studios, Inc.
210 B. M. Pederson
211 Francesco Milani
212 Centro Di

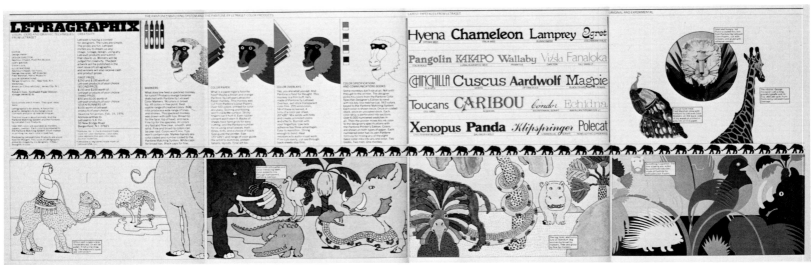

207

206, 207 Cover and complete inside spread of a folder from a series issued by *Letraset.* (USA)
208 Promotion card (with real whistle) for the *Football Magazine* of *The Detroit News.* (USA)
209 Cover in roughly actual size of a catalogue of *Thienemann* books for children. (GER)
210 Colour spread from *The Weather Machine*, a booklet by Champion International Papers. (USA)
211 Organization diagram from a booklet about Cartiera di Locarno SA, papermakers. (SWI)
212 Catalogue of the publications of *Centro Di.* Black print on yellow. (ITA)

206, 207 Umschlag und vollständige Innenseite aus einer Broschüre für *Letraset.* (USA)
208 Werbekarte (mit richtiger Pfeife) für das Fussballmagazin der Zeitung *Detroit News.*
209 Umschlag in Originalgrösse eines Kinderbuch-Katalogs vom Thienemann Verlag, Stuttgart. (GER)
210 Farbige Doppelseite aus einer Broschüre mit dem Titel «Die Wettermaschine», herausgegeben von der Champion International Papers. (USA)
211 Doppelseite aus einem Rapport der Papierfabrik Cartiera di Locarno SA. (SWI)
212 Umschlag des Kunstkatalogs *Centro Di.* Schwarze Schrift auf gelbem Grund. (ITA)

206, 207 Couverture et intérieur d'un dépliant figurant dans une série publiée par *Letraset.* (USA)
208 Carte promotionnelle (sifflet rouge) pour *Football Magazine* publié par *Detroit News.* (USA)
209 Couverture (approx. grandeur nature) du catalogue des livres d'enfant de *Thienemann.* (GER)
210 Page double (en couleur) figurant dans la brochure d'une papeterie. (USA)
211 Organigramme tiré d'une brochure de la Cartiera di Locarno SA, fabricant de papiers. (SWI)
212 Catalogue des publications de *Centro Di.* Impression noir sur fond jaune. (ITA)

210

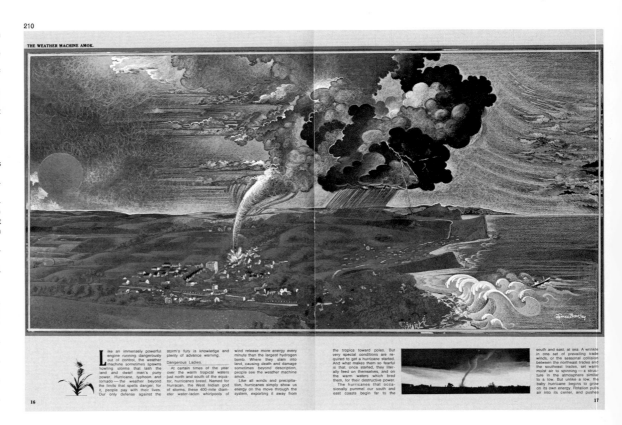

Thienemann

Organigramme

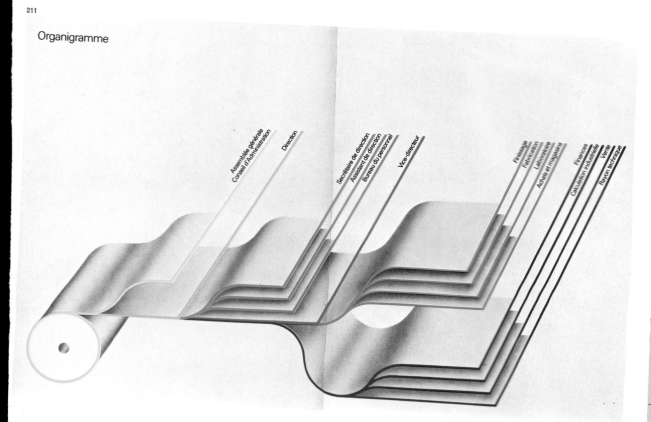

Assemblée générale
Conseil d'Administration
Direction
Secrétaire de direction
Assistant de direction
Bureau du personnel
Vice-directeur
Finissage
Fabrication
Laboratoire
Achats et magasins
Calculation industrielle
Finances
Vente
Rayon technique

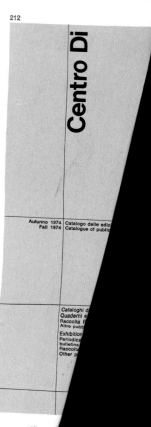

Centro Di

Autunno 1974 — Catalogo delle ediz
Fall 1974 — Catalogue of public

Cataloghi d
Quaderni e
Raccolta P
Altre pubbl

Exhibition
Periodici e
bulletins
Raccolta
Other p

209

211

Organigramme

Assemblée générale
Conseil d'Administration
Direction
Secrétaire de direction
Assistant de direction
Bureau du personnel
Vice-directeur
Finissage
Fabrication
Laboratoire
Achats et magasins
Finances
Calculation industrielle
Vente
Rayon technique

212

Centro Di

Autunno 1974 Catalogo delle edizioni
Fall 1974 Catalogue of publications

Cataloghi di mostre
Quaderni e bollettini di musei
Raccolta Pisana di saggi e studi
Altre pubblicazioni

Exhibition catalogues
Periodical booklets and
bulletins of museums
Raccolta Pisana di saggi e studi
Other publications

ARTIST / KÜNSTLER / ARTISTE:

213 Flavio Costantini
214 Pierre Le-Tan
215, 216 Stan Mack

DESIGNER / GESTALTER / MAQUETTISTE:

213 Pino Milas
214, 216 Andrew Kner
215 Allen Weinberg

ART DIRECTOR / DIRECTEUR ARTISTIQUE:

214–216 Andrew Kner

Booklets
Prospekte
Brochures

213 Full-page illustration from a book about Ravachol and other anarchists published in the series *Quadragono Libri*. (ITA)
214 Cover of a folder about the advantages of job advertising in *The New York Times*. Illustrations in shades of brown, red title. (USA)
215 Cover of a brochure about the school service programme of *The New York Times*. Drawings in black and blue. (USA)
216 Cover of a booklet intended for schools about the range of information supplied by *The New York Times*. Black and white on pale buff ground. (USA)

213 Ganzseitige Illustration aus einem Buch über Ravachol und andere Anarchisten. Diese Publikation ist aus der Serie von *Quadragono Libri*. (ITA)
214 Umschlag eines Faltprospektes über die Vorteile einer Stellenanzeige in der *New York Times*. Illustrationen in Brauntönen, roter Titel. (USA)
215 Umschlag einer Broschüre über die Dienstleistungen der *New York Times* für Schulen. Zeichnungen in Schwarz und Blau. (USA)
216 Titelblatt einer Broschüre, die Schulen auffordert, die *New York Times* zu abonnieren, da sie alle nötigen Informationen für Schüler enthält. (USA)

213 Illustration pleine page figurant dans un livre consacré à Ravachol et d'autres anarchistes. Publication qui a parue dans la série *Quadragono Libri*. (ITA)
214 Couverture d'un dépliant démontrant les avantages du placement d'annonces dans la rubrique des offres et demandes d'emploi du *New York Times*. Tons bruns, titre en rouge. (USA)
215 Couverture d'une brochure en faveur d'un service de distribution scolaire qui offre le *New York Times* à prix réduit. Dessins en noir et bleu. (USA)
216 Couverture d'une brochure destinée aux écoles. Elle met en évidence l'abondance des sujets contenus dans le *New York Times*. Noir et blanc sur fond chamois. (USA)

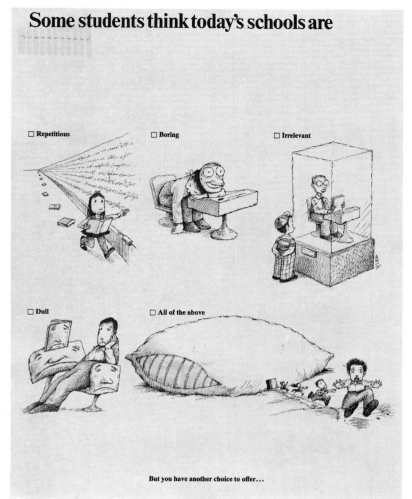

215

214　216

217

219

218

221

217, 218 Covers of space promotion folders for the *Tages-Anzeiger-Magazin*, here referring to its reach and to its first place in its readership area. Fig. 217 in red and yellow, Fig. 218 in blue and green shades. (SWI)
219 Cover of a folder containing the sports programmes of WLS Television, Chicago. Composite sports figure in full colour. (USA)
220 Complete cover of a booklet on the planning of newspaper advertising in Bicentennial year, issued by Newspaper Advertising Bureau, Inc. (USA)
221—223 Complete cover and spreads from a brochure about improvements in record-making technology issued by James B. Lansing Sound Inc. All in full colour. (USA)

ARTIST / KÜNSTLER / ARTISTE:

217, 218 Claus Knézy
219 Roy Carruthers
220 Fred Otnes
221—223 Glen Iwasaki

DESIGNER / GESTALTER / MAQUETTISTE:

217, 218 Robert Hösli
219 Susan Heydt

220

222

223

217, 218 Titelbilder von zwei Faltprospekten des *Tages-Anzeiger-Magazins,* die zur Inseraten-werbung aufmuntern. Abb. 217 in Rot- und Gelbtönen; Abb. 218 in Blau- und Grüntönen. (SWI)
219 Umschlag eines Programms der WLS Television, das die im Fernsehen übertragenen Sport-Reportagen ankündigt. Mehrfarbig. (USA)
220 Vollständiger Umschlag einer Broschüre über das Planen von Inseraten in Zeitungen während des Jahres 1976 – der 200-Jahr-Feier Amerikas –, herausgegeben vom Newspaper Advertising Bureau, Inc. Mehrfarbig. (USA)
221–223 Vollständiger Umschlag und zwei Seiten aus einer Broschüre zur Verkaufsförderung von Schallplatten für Einzelhändler. Mehrfarbig. (USA)

217, 218 Couvertures de dépliants promotionnels pour le *Tages-Anzeiger-Magazin.* Ils se réfèrent à la grande portée et au fait que celui-ci occupe la première place parmi les magazines abonnés dans la région de Zurich, la plus importante du point de vue économique. (SWI)
219 Couverture d'un dépliant contenant les programmes sportifs de WLS Television, Chicago. Figure composée d'un sportif en couleurs. (USA)
220 Couverture d'une brochure consacrée au planning publicitaire des journaux pendant l'an-née du Bicentenaire. Publication du Newspaper Advertising Bureau. (USA)
221–223 Couverture et pages doubles figurant dans une brochure sur le perfectionnement tech-nique de la fabrication de disques. Tous les éléments sont en couleurs. (USA)

ART DIRECTOR / DIRECTEUR ARTISTIQUE:

217, 218 Robert Hösli
219 James Ong
220 Tom Clemente
221–223 Oswald Sosa

AGENCY / AGENTUR / AGENCE – STUDIO:

217, 218 Adata AG/Walther & Leuenberger AG
219 Ong & Associates, Inc.

**Booklets
Prospekte
Brochures**

224, 225 One side of a large folder announcing a performance of *Othello* in Adelaide, and detail of the illustration, chiefly in dark brown and green shades. (AUL)
226 Black-and-white design for the cover of a guide for ABC Radio (unpublished). (AUL)
227 One side of a folder about a graphic design contest organized by the Barcelona Industrial Design Centre. Orange and green. (SPA)
228, 229 Covers of two catalogues issued by Boosey & Hawkes Music Publishers Ltd. Fig. 228 is in black and white. (GBR)
230 Invitation to a multimedia presentation in connection with the Bicentennial celebrations, issued by *Time* magazine. (USA)
231 Cover of a catalogue for an exhibition, "A Decade of Collecting", mounted by the Los Angeles County Museum of Art. White X on muted shades of brown, green, red and blue. (USA)

224, 225 Innenseite und Detail eines grossformatigen Programms für eine Aufführung des Theaterstücks *Othello* von Shakespeare. Dunkelbraune und grüne Töne. (AUL)
226 Schwarzweisse Illustration eines Umschlags für ein Radioprogramm (unveröffentlicht). (AUL)
227 Innenseite einer Einladung für einen Wettbewerb über Graphic Design, organisiert vom Centro de Diseno Industrial, Barcelona. Orange und grün. (SPA)
228, 229 Titelbilder zweier Broschüren, herausgegeben von einem englischen Musikverlag. Abb. 228 ist in Schwarzweiss. (GBR)
230 Einladung zu einer Multimedia-Präsentation der Zeitschrift *Time* aus Anlass der 200-Jahr-Feier von Amerika. (USA)
231 Titelblatt eines grossen Katalogs für eine Ausstellung mit dem Titel «Eine 10jährige Sammlung», organisiert vom Kunstmuseum von Los Angeles. Weisses X auf Braun, Grün, Rot und Blau. (USA)

224, 225 Recto d'un dépliant grand format annonçant une représentation de l'*Othello* à Adelaide et détail de l'illustration (prédominance de tons brun foncé et verts). (AUL)
226 Design en noir et blanc pour la couverture d'un guide pour ABC Radio (inédit). (USA)
227 Recto d'un dépliant pour un concours d'art graphique organisé par le Centre de Création Industrielle de Barcelone. Orange et vert. (SPA)
228, 229 Couvertures de deux catalogues publiés par Boosey & Hawkes Music Publishers Ltd. La fig. 228 est en noir et blanc. (GER)
230 Invitation pour une présentation multimédia organisée dans le cadre des célébrations du Bicentenaire. Publication du magazine *Time*. (USA)
231 Couverture d'un catalogue pour une exposition présentée par le Los Angeles County Museum of Art. X en blanc sur fond en tons bruns, verts, rouges et bleus atténués. (USA)

224

225

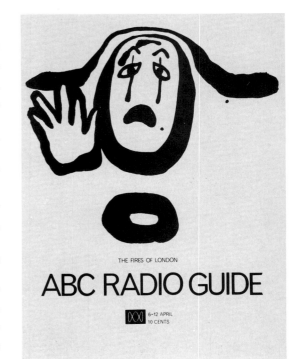

226

227

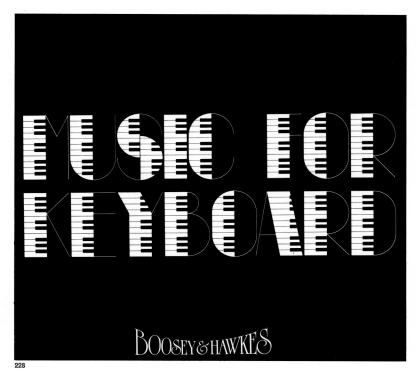

228

229

230

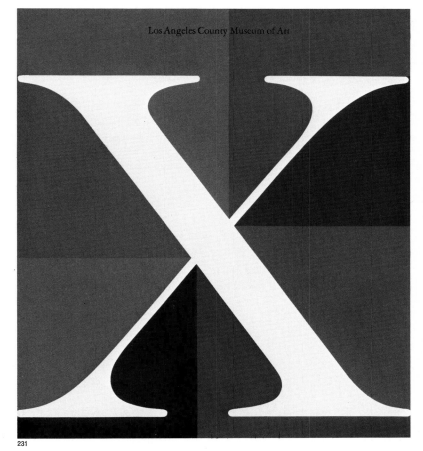

231

ARTIST / KÜNSTLER / ARTISTE:

224, 225 Barrie Tucker
226 Jane Eldershaw
227 Gervasio Gallardo

DESIGNER / GESTALTER / MAQUETTISTE:

224, 225 Barrie Tucker
226 Jane Eldershaw
228, 229 Mervyn Kurlansky
230 Seldon Dix
231 Ken Parkhurst

ART DIRECTOR / DIRECTEUR ARTISTIQUE:

224, 225 Barrie Tucker
226 Jane Eldershaw
227 Albert Isern/J. M. Mir
228, 229 Mervyn Kurlansky
230 Walter Lefmann
231 Jean D'Andrea

AGENCY / AGENTUR / AGENCE – STUDIO:

224, 225 Barrie Tucker
226 Eldershaw Graphics
227 Barcelona Centro de Diseño Industrial
228, 229 Pentagram
231 Ken Parkhurst & Associates, Inc.

232

233

ARTIST / KÜNSTLER / ARTISTE:

232 Geert Setola
233 TIM
236, 237 Barrie Tucker
238 Aubrey Beardsley
239 Walter Grieder

DESIGNER / GESTALTER / MAQUETTISTE:

232 Geert Setola
233 Costa-Gavras
234, 235 Wilburn O. Bonnell III
236, 237 Barrie Tucker
238 Hans Schleger and Associates
239 Walter Grieder

ART DIRECTOR / DIRECTEUR ARTISTIQUE:

232 Geert Setola
233 Jacques Perrin
234, 235 Wilburn O. Bonnell III
236, 237 Barrie Tucker
238 Hans Schleger
239 Walter Grieder

AGENCY / AGENTUR / AGENCE – STUDIO:

233 Artistes Associés
234, 235 Container Corporation of America
236, 237 Barrie Tucker

234

235

238

236

37

239

232 Side of a programme for the play *Magie Rouge* performed in Bruges. (BEL)
233 Cover of a programme booklet about a film by Costa-Gavras, *Section Spéciale*, dealing with the misuse of power through the courts. (FRA)
234, 235 Cover, with detail, of a catalogue published by the Container Corporation for an exhibition of the AGPA (Artes Graficas Panamericanas). (USA)
236, 237 Inside and detail of a theatre programme for a play about prison life by a former convict, presented in Adelaide. Sombre hues, yellow flower. (AUL)
238 Page in black and grey introducing the opera section in the programme of the Edinburgh International Festival. (GBR)
239 Cover of a programme for an autumn bazaar to collect funds for the renovation of a church in Basle. Black and white. (SWI)

232 Seite aus einem Programm für das Theaterstück *Magie Rouge*. (BEL)
233 Titelbild eines Programms für den Kinofilm *Section Spéciale* von Costa-Gavras. Schwarzweiss. (FRA)
234, 235 Umschlag und Detail eines Ausstellungskatalogs, herausgegeben von der Container Corporation of America. (USA)
236, 237 Innenseite und Detail eines Programms für ein Theaterstück über das Leben im Gefängnis. Dunkelbraune Töne und gelbe Blume. (AUL)
238 Seite aus dem Programm für das Festival von Edinburgh. Diese Illustration in Schwarz und Grau ist die Einführungsseite für den Opern-Teil. (GBR)
239 Titelseite, die einen Herbstmarkt zugunsten der Innenrenovation einer Kirche in Basel ankündigt. Schwarzweiss. (SWI)

232 Recto d'un programme pour la pièce *Magie Rouge*, présentée à Bruges. (BEL)
233 Couverture d'un programme contenant des textes sur le film *Section Speciale* de Costa-Gavras. Il retrace les rapports entre l'homme et le pouvoir judiciaire. (FRA)
234, 235 Couverture (avec détail) d'un catalogue publié par la Container Corp. pour une exposition de l'AGPA (Artes Graficas Panamericanas). (USA)
236, 237 Intérieur et détail d'un programme pour une pièce sur la vie en prison, écrite par un ancien détenu. Tons sombres, fleur jaune. (AUL)
238 Page en noir et blanc figurant dans le programme du Festival International d'Edimbourg. Introduction de la section consacrée aux opéras. (GBR)
239 Couverture du programme d'une vente d'automne organisée pour réunir des fonds pour la rénovation d'une église à Bâle. Noir et blanc. (SWI)

Hessischer Rundfunk
März 1975

Hessisches
Fernsehprogramm
3. Programm

Die halbe Eva 3.3. 21.15

240

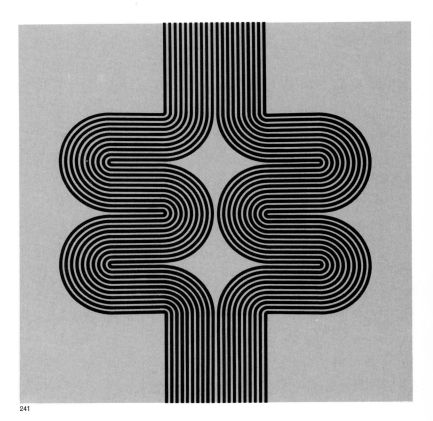

241

240 Cover of a monthly television programme of the Hessian radio authority. (GER)
241 Illustration (in two blues) for a publication on music. (CUB)
242 Illustration for a publication of the School of Geography, Havana, on demography. (CUB)
243 Cover of a booklet on new Cuban architecture published by Ediciones de Arquitectura. (CUB)
244, 245 Cover (pink glass) and double spread in black and white from the programme of a play by Bert Brecht about Mr. Puntila and his servant Matti, performed in Gera. (GDR)
246 Catalogue cover for an exhibition of Polish theatre posters. Black and white. (POL)
247 Cover of a press kit for a dramatic series on the suffragette movement presented by WGBH Television and sponsored by the Mobil Oil Corporation. (USA)

ARTIST / KÜNSTLER / ARTISTE:

240 Eberhard Marhold
241—243 Felix Beltran
244, 245 Rolf-Felix Müller
246 Franciszek Starowieyski
247 Ivan Chermayeff

DESIGNER / GESTALTER / MAQUETTISTE:

241—243 Felix Beltran
244, 245 Rolf-Felix Müller
247 Ivan Chermayeff

ART DIRECTOR / DIRECTEUR ARTISTIQUE:

241—243 Felix Beltran
247 Ivan Chermayeff

AGENCY / AGENTUR / AGENCE – STUDIO:

247 Chermayeff & Geismar Associates, Inc.

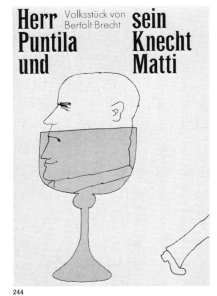

Herr Puntila und sein Knecht Matti
Volksstück von Bertolt Brecht

244

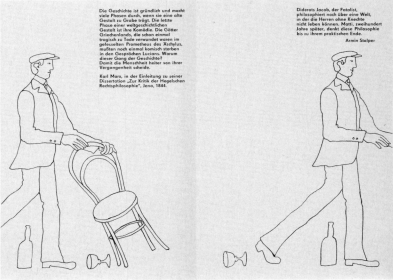

Die Geschichte ist gründlich und macht viele Phasen durch, wenn sie eine alte Gestalt zu Grabe trägt. Die letzte Phase einer weltgeschichtlichen Gestalt ist ihre Komödie. Die Götter Griechenlands, die schon einmal tragisch zu Tode verwundet waren im gefesselten Prometheus des Äschylus, mußten noch einmal komisch sterben in den Gesprächen Lucians. Warum dieser Gang der Geschichte? Damit die Menschheit heiter von ihrer Vergangenheit scheide.

Karl Marx, in der Einleitung zu seiner Dissertation „Zur Kritik der Hegelschen Rechtsphilosophie", Jeno, 1844.

Diderots Jacob, der Fatalist, philosophiert noch über eine Welt, in der die Herren ohne Knechte nicht leben können. Matti, zweihundert Jahre später, denkt diese Philosophie bis zu ihrem praktischen Ende.

Armin Stolper

245

Booklets / Prospekte / Brochures

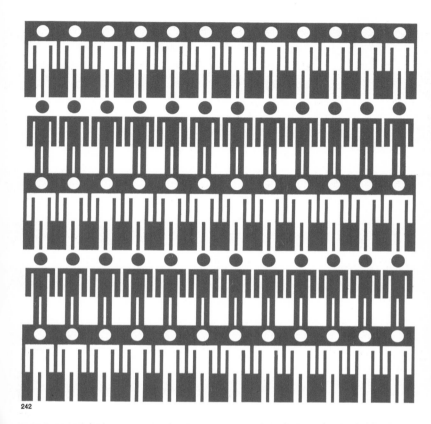

242

243

246

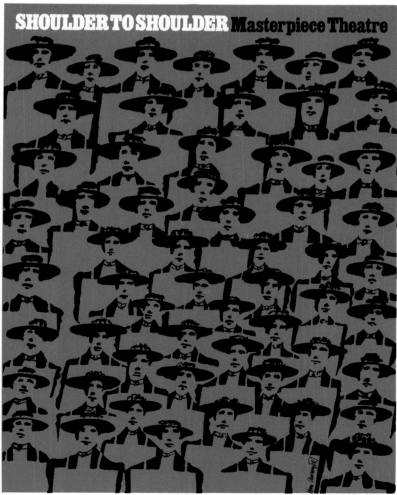

247

93

248

249

250

251

252

94

ARTIST / KÜNSTLER / ARTISTE:

254 Bruce Nauman
255 Jacques Richez
256 Leif F. Anisdahl

DESIGNER / GESTALTER / MAQUETTISTE:

248–251 Bob Ross
253 Ivan Chermayeff
256 Leif F. Anisdahl
257, 258 Charles Eames

ART DIRECTOR / DIRECTEUR ARTISTIQUE:

253 Ivan Chermayeff
256 Leif F. Anisdahl

AGENCY / AGENTUR / AGENCE – STUDIO:

248–251 Ross Design
253 Chermayeff & Geismar Associates, Inc.
256 Anisdahl/Christensen A/S
257, 258 Charles & Ray Eames

253

254

248–252 Panels from a series of folders, and example of one complete folder, announcing the monthly activities of the San Francisco Museum of Art. (USA)
253 Cover (red and white on blue) of an invitation to the opening of an exhibition of American posters in the Corcoran Gallery, sponsored by Mobil Oil. (USA)
254 Announcement of an exhibition in the San Francisco Museum of Art. Black and grey with orange type matter. (USA)
255 Programme cover (black and white, red and orange eye) for a Belgian ceramics and tapestry exhibition in Britain. (BEL)
256 Cover of a theatre programme for a performance of *Macbeth*. (NOR)
257, 258 Cover and spread from the programme of an IBM-sponsored exhibition about Franklin and Jefferson. (USA)

248–252 Seiten. aus einer Serie von Faltprospekten und ein vollständiger Prospekt über die monatlichen Veranstaltungen vom Kunstmuseum von San Francisco. (USA)
253 Umschlag in Blau, Rot und Weiss für eine Einladung an die Eröffnung der Ausstellung von amerikanischen Plakaten 1945–75 in der Corcoran Galerie. (USA)
254 Ankündigung einer Ausstellung im Kunstmuseum von San Francisco. Schwarz und grau mit oranger Schrift. (USA)
255 Umschlag eines Katalogs für eine Ausstellung von belgischem Keramik und Tapisserie in London. (BEL)
256 Programm für *Macbeth*. (NOR)
257, 258 Umschlag und Doppelseite aus dem Katalog für eine von der IBM unterstützten Ausstellung über die Präsidenten Franklin und Jefferson. (USA)

248–252 Panneaux d'une série de dépliants et exemple d'un dépliant. Eléments figurant dans des publications mensuelles du San Francisco Museum of Art. (USA)
253 Couverture (en rouge et blanc sur fond bleu) de l'invitation pour le vernissage d'une exposition d'affiches américaines présentée à la Corcoran Gallery. Exposition patronnée par Mobil Oil. (USA)
254 Carte annonçant une exposition du San Francisco Museum of Art. (USA)
255 Couverture du programme (noir et blanc, œil en rouge et orange) pour une exposition d'artisanat belge (céramique et tapisserie) à Londres. (BEL)
256 Couverture du programme pour une présentation de la pièce *Macbeth*. (NOR)
257, 258 Couverture et page double du catalogue d'une exposition sur Franklin et Jefferson présentée dans le cadre du Bicentenaire. Exposition patronnée par IBM. Illustrations en polychromie. (USA)

255

256

257

258

A message to the Army

259

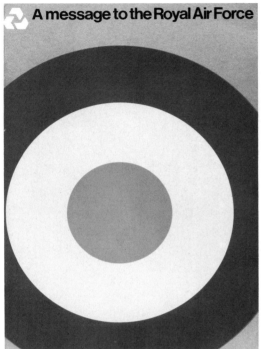

A message to the Royal Air Force

260

A message to the Police

261

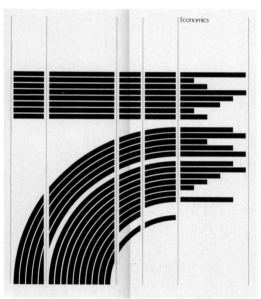

Economics

264

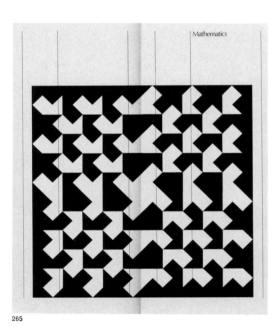

Mathematics

265

266

259–261 Covers of booklets from a series in which the National Westminster Bank recommends its services to various groups of potential clients. Fig. 259, red gun on buff; Fig. 260, red, white and blue target on silver; Fig. 261, black watch on blue. (GBR)
262, 263 Complete cover and closing spread from a savings book for children issued by a bank. Pastel shades. (AUS)
264–266 Three spreads from a tall-format catalogue of studies issued by Wellesley College, Mass. Fig. 264 refers to economics, Fig. 265 to mathematics. Printed in dull red. (USA)
267 Activity calendar issued by Harper College, Chicago. (USA)
268, 269 Cover, with detail of symbol, of a booklet presenting the case of the Indians involved in the Wounded Knee incident. Brown on cream. (USA)

259–261 Umschläge aus einer Serie von Eigenwerbungs-Broschüren der National Westminster Bank. Abb. 259, rote Kanone auf Chamois; Abb. 260, rot-weiss-blauer Kreis auf Silber; Abb. 261, schwarze Uhr auf Blau. (GBR)
262, 263 Vollständiger Umschlag und letzte Seite aus einem kleinen Buch für Kinder, mit dem Titel «Das erste Sparkassenbuch», herausgegeben von der Österr. Sparkasse. (AUS)
264–266 Drei Seiten aus einer grossformatigen Broschüre über verschiedene Studien, herausgegeben vom Wellesley College. Abb. 264 für Ökonomie, Abb. 265 für Mathematik. (USA)
267 Veranstaltungskalender des Harper College. (USA)
268, 269 Umschlag und Detail einer Informations-Broschüre über Wounded Knee. Braun auf Chamois. (USA)

259–261 Couvertures d'une série de brochures d'une banque qui offre ses services à divers groupes de futurs clients. Fig. 259: fusil rouge sur chamois; fig. 260: cible rouge, blanc et bleu sur argent; fig. 261: montre noir sur bleu. (GBR)
262, 263 Couverture complète et dernière page double d'un livret de caisse d'épargne pour enfants. Tons pastel. (AUS)
264–266 Trois pages doubles d'un catalogue grand format contenant les cours du Wellesley College. Fig. 264 se réfère à l'économie, fig. 265 à la mathématique. Tons rouges mats. (USA)
267 Calendrier des manifestations du Harper College. (USA)
268, 269 Couverture (avec détail du symbole) d'une publication défendant la cause des Indiens qui se sont engagés dans les incidents au Wounded Knee. Brun sur fond clair. (USA)

Booklets / Prospekte / Brochures

262

263

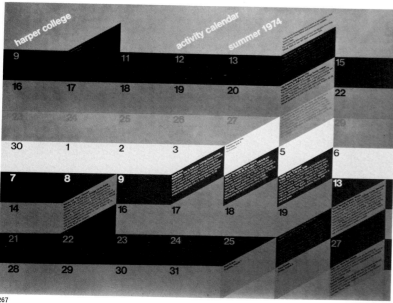

267

268

269

ARTIST / KÜNSTLER / ARTISTE:

259–261 Ken Kirkwood
262, 263 Mark & Nevosad

DESIGNER / GESTALTER / MAQUETTISTE:

259–261 Ken Kirkwood
262, 263 Mark & Nevosad
264–266 Dietmar R. Winkler
267 Frank Ofiana
268, 269 Alternative Media

ART DIRECTOR / DIRECTEUR ARTISTIQUE:

259–261 Ken Kirkwood
262, 263 Hannes Rausch
264–266 Dietmar R. Winkler
267 Al Dunikoski

AGENCY / AGENTUR / AGENCE – STUDIO:

262, 263 Austria 3
264–266 Dietmar R. Winkler
267 LRC-Production Services
268, 269 Owen C. Luck/Alternative Media

270

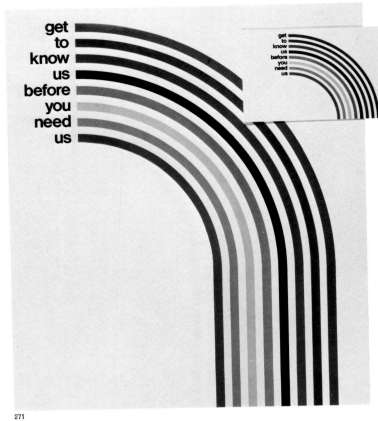

271

272

273

ARTIST / KÜNSTLER / ARTISTE:

271 David Lawrence
272 Joseph Scorsone
274—276 Gunhild Terzenbach

DESIGNER / GESTALTER / MAQUETTISTE:

270 Henry Steiner
271 David Lawrence
272 Joseph Scorsone
273 Gerry Kano
274—276 Helmut Schmid

ART DIRECTOR / DIRECTEUR ARTISTIQUE:

270 Henry Steiner
271 David Lawrence
272 Joseph Scorsone
273 Gerry Kano
274—276 Harry Walter/Nils Johannissohn

AGENCY / AGENTUR / AGENCE – STUDIO:

270 Graphic Communication Ltd.
271 David Lawrence Design
272 Joseph Scorsone
273 Gerry Kano Design
274—276 ARE Kommunikation

274

Beispiel:
Verbaute Seeufer

**Von unseren
schönsten Erholungs-
landschaften
bleiben uns oft nur
ein paar Meter.**

275

276

270 Four coloured brochures in a folder, issued to accompany an exhibition illustrating 133 years of development in Hong Kong. The brochures deal with the history, crafts, products and future of Hong Kong. (HGK)
271 Booklet, folders and cards issued by the American Hospital Association on the occasion of National Hospital Week. (USA)
272 Cover of a folder about school improvement published by Research for Better Schools, Inc., a non-profit organization. Yellow pencils. (USA)
273 Lettering on a booklet for Bicentennial Year Observance issued by the Archdiocese of Los Angeles. (USA)
274–276 Two illustrations and one complete spread from a booklet about land reform issued by the West German Socialist party. (GER)

270 Vier mehrfarbige Broschüren, herausgegeben anlässlich einer Ausstellung über 133 Jahre Entwicklung in Hongkong. Die Broschüren informieren über die Geschichte, Handwerk, Produkte und Zukunft von Hongkong. (HGK)
271 «Lernen Sie uns kennen, bevor Sie uns benötigen.» Broschüren und Karten, die zum Besuch eines Spitals anlässlich des «Tag der offenen Tür» auffordern. (USA)
272 Umschlag einer Broschüre über Verbesserungen am Schulsystem, herausgegeben von einer gemeinnützigen Organisation. Gelbe Bleistifte. (USA)
273 Beschriftung für den Umschlag einer Broschüre, herausgegeben vom Erzbistum von Los Angeles. (USA)
274–276 Zwei Illustrationen und eine vollständige Seite aus der Broschüre «Argumente 2», herausgegeben von der SPD, über Bodenrechtsreform. (GER)

270 Dépliant contenant quatre brochures (en couleurs) publiées lors d'une exposition sur le développement de Hong Kong au cours des dernières 133 ans. Les brochures sont consacrées aux sujets suivants: l'histoire, l'artisanat, la production et les perspectives concernant le développement de Hong Kong. (HGK)
271 Brochure, dépliants et cartes publiés par l'Association américaine des hôpitaux à l'occasion de la Semaine nationale des hôpitaux. (USA)
272 Couverture d'un dépliant sur la réorganisation des écoles. Publication d'une institution non-bénéficiaire qui se propose comme objectif l'amélioration du système scolaire. Crayons jaunes. (USA)
273 Inscription sur la brochure de l'Archevêché de Los Angeles concernant les pratiques religieux à l'occasion de l'année bicentenaire. (USA)
274–276 Deux illustrations et page double figurant dans une brochure du Parti Socialiste de l'Allemagne occidentale sur la réforme foncière. (GER)

Booklets / Prospekte / Brochures

ARTIST / KÜNSTLER / ARTISTE:

279 Thomas Allan Brown (Photos)
280 Jim Johnson
281 Craig Fetzer
282 Larry Winborg

DESIGNER / GESTALTER / MAQUETTISTE:

277, 278 Mike McCarty
279 Inge H. Druckrey
280 Bruce Berkel

ART DIRECTOR / DIRECTEUR ARTISTIQUE:

277, 278 Mike McCarty
279 Inge H. Druckrey
280 Bruce Berkel
281, 282 Larry Winborg

AGENCY / AGENTUR / AGENCE – STUDIO:

277, 278 Communigraphics
279 Inge H. Druckrey
280 The Agency, Inc.
281, 282 Bicentennial Graphics

277

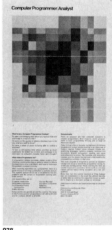

278

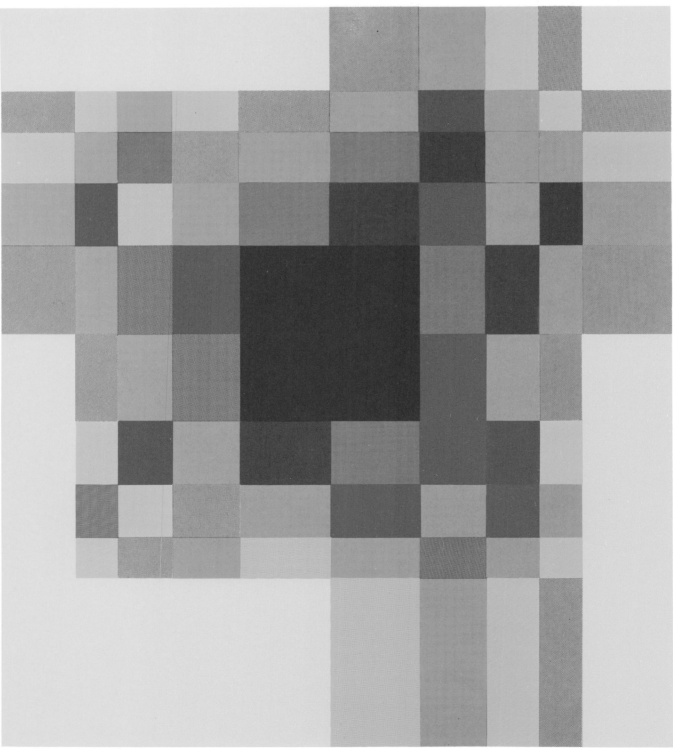

277, 278 Illustration in actual size and complete side of a folder about a training as a computer programmer offered by Pima College, Tucson. (USA)
279 Double spread from a black-and-white fund-raising brochure published by the School of Forestry of Yale University. (USA)
280 Public service press kit portfolio about the arts in the city of Grand Rapids. (USA)
281, 282 From a series of commemorative postcards and posters issued by Bicentennial Graphics; here two American presidents. (USA)

277, 278 Illustration in Originalgrösse und vollständige Seite eines Faltprospekts über die Ausbildung als Computer-Programmierer. (USA)
279 Doppelseite aus einer Broschüre in Schwarzweiss, herausgegeben vom Institut für Forstwirtschaft der Yale Universität. (USA)
280 Umschlag einer Pressedokumentation über die Kunst in der Stadt Grand Rapids. (USA)
281, 282 Aus einer Serie von Erinnerungspostkarten und Plakaten, herausgegeben anlässlich der 200-Jahr-Feier Amerikas von Bicentennial Graphics. Die Beispiele zeigen die Präsidenten Thomas Jefferson und Teddy Roosevelt. (USA)

277, 278 Illustration (en grandeur nature) et panneau du dépliant où elle figure. Elément publicitaire pour un cours de programmeurs tenu au Pima College, Tucson. (USA)
279 Page double d'une brochure en noir et blanc publiée par l'Institut d'économie forestière de l'Université de Yale pour réunir des fonds. (USA)
280 Documentation de presse du service public de Grand Rapids sur les manifestations organisées par la ville. (USA)
281, 282 D'une série de cartes commémoratives et d'affiches publiées par Bicentennial Graphics. Les deux cartes se réfèrent aux présidents Thomas Jefferson et Teddy Roosevelt. (USA)

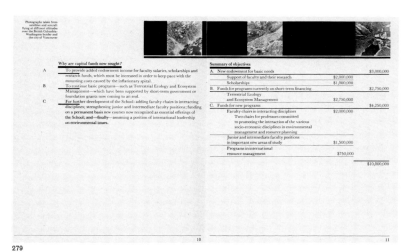

279

281

280

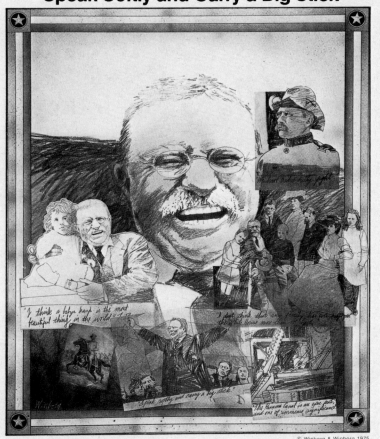

282

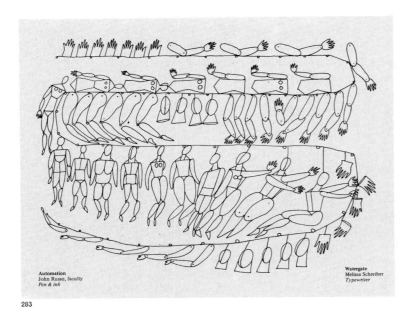

Automation
John Russo, faculty
Pen & ink

283

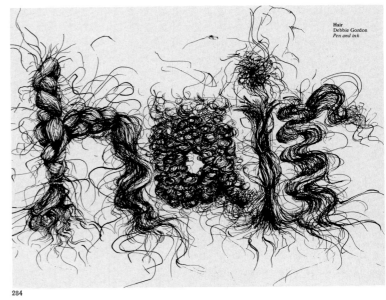

Hair
Debbie Gordon
Pen and ink

Watergate
Melissa Schreiber
Typewriter

284

285

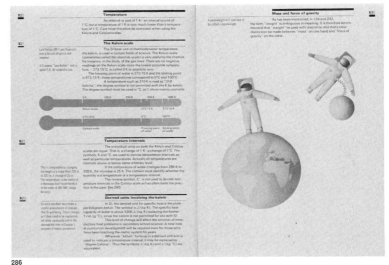

286

ARTIST / KÜNSTLER / ARTISTE:

283 John Russo
284 Debbie Gordon
285, 286 Fredy Jaggi
287 Stanley Wong
291–293 Nicolas Sidjakov

DESIGNER / GESTALTER / MAQUETTISTE:

285, 286 Roslyn Eskind
287 Garry Emery
288 Bob Sherman
289 Peter Adam
290 Ernst Roch
291–293 Nicolas Sidjakov

ART DIRECTOR / DIRECTEUR ARTISTIQUE:

283, 284 Cipe Pineles Burtin
285, 286 Stuard Ash
287 Garry Emery
288 Bob Sherman
290 Ernst Roch
291–293 Gene Dispara

AGENCY / AGENTUR / AGENCE – STUDIO:

285, 286, 289 Gottschalk + Ash Ltd.
287 Interact Communications
288 Brand Advertising
290 Design Collaborative
291–293 Needham, Harper & Steers

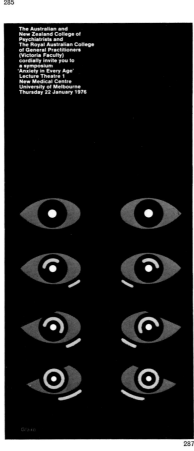

The Australian and
New Zealand College of
Psychiatrists and
The Royal Australian College
of General Practitioners
(Victoria Faculty)
cordially invite you to
a symposium
'Anxiety in Every Age'
Lecture Theatre 1
New Medical Centre
University of Melbourne
Thursday 22 January 1976

287

288

283, 284 Two pen-and-ink drawings from *Since we were born,* an annual student publication of the Parsons School of Design: *Automation* by John Russo, red and blue, and *Hair* by Debbie Gordon, brown. (USA)
285, 286 Page and spread from a guide to the metric system issued by the Council of Ministers of Education. Printed in green and beige. (CAN)
287 Invitation to a symposium on anxiety at Melbourne. (AUL)
288 Folder about travel incentives for dealers issued by Conn Organ. (USA)
289 Cover of a booklet issued by the Ministry of Colleges and Universities, Ontario. Blue and white. (CAN)
290 Cover of a booklet on immigration to Canada (Signum Press). (CAN)
291–293 Spreads from a booklet issued by The Mitsubishi Bank of California, showing a 17th-century coin, a purse and the Japanese emblem. (USA)

283, 284 Zwei Tuschzeichnungen aus einer Studenten-Publikation der Parsons School of Design: *Automation* von John Russo, rot und blau, und *Hair* (Haare) von Debbie Gordon, braun. (USA)
285, 286 Seite und Doppelseite aus einem Lehrbuch des metrischen Systems. Grün und beige. (CAN)
287 Einladung für ein Symposium mit dem Thema «Angst in jedem Alter», organisiert von einer Schule für Psychiatrie. Zwei verschiedene Blau und Rot. (AUL)
288 Prospekt über Flüge als Anreizpreise für das Personal. (USA)
289 Umschlag einer Informationsbroschüre für Techniker, herausgegeben vom Erziehungsministerium. Blau und weiss. (CAN)
290 Umschlag einer Broschüre über die Immigration nach Kanada. (CAN)
291–293 Doppelseiten aus einer Broschüre, herausgegeben von der Mitsubishi Bank of California. (USA)

283, 284 Deux dessins à la plume d'une publication estudiantine de la Parsons School of Design, intitulée *Since we were born.* Les deux dessins: *Automation* (rouge et bleu) par John Russo et *Hair* (brun) par Debbie Gordon. (USA)
285, 286 Page et page double d'un guide discutant le système métrique. Publication du Conseil des ministres de l'éducation nationale. Vert et beige. (CAN)
287 Invitation pour un symposium sur l'anxiété, tenu à Melbourne. (AUL)
288 Dépliant de Conn Organ présentant diverses primes d'encouragement à ses employés. (USA)
289 Couverture d'une brochure publiée par le Ministère de l'éducation nationale d'Ontario. Bleu et blanc. (CAN)
290 Couverture d'une brochure sur l'immigration au Canada. (CAN)
291–293 Pages doubles figurant dans la brochure d'une banque californienne. Les illustrations présentent une pièce de monnaie du 17e siècle, une bourse et l'emblème du Japon. (USA)

290

291

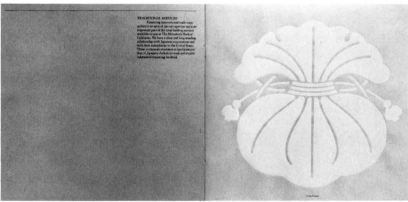
292

289

293

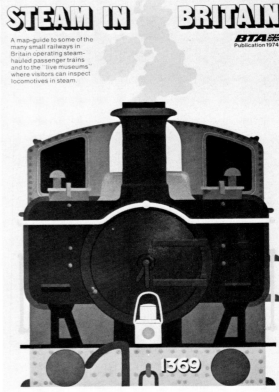

294

295

296

ARTIST / KÜNSTLER / ARTISTE:

296 John Jones
299 Steve Kasloff
300 Carl Kock
302 Helmut Kraft

DESIGNER / GESTALTER / MAQUETTISTE:

294 Dean R. Lindsay
296 Philip Sharland
297 Michael Baviera
298 Harald Gutschow
299 Steve Kasloff
300 Debbie Baker
301 Zisowsky + Oehring
302 Helmut Kraft

ART DIRECTOR / DIRECTEUR ARTISTIQUE:

294 Dean R. Lindsay
297 Michael Baviera
298 Harald Gutschow
299 Steve Kasloff/Dennis Machlica
300 Debbie Baker
301 Zisowsky + Oehring
302 Helmut Kraft

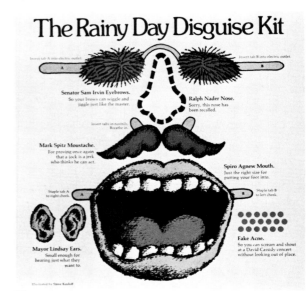

298

299

300

301

302

	Schwarenbach Mountain Hotel, Kandersteg: Alpine Youth Instruction Centre, Arolla and Fafferalp: rock and ice climbing courses, group tours	
June/Sept.	Zermatt	Guided high-altitude mountain tours
June/Oct.	Gstaad	Guided high-altitude mountain tours
June 4/Sept. 3	Wengen	Weekly game-watching excursions
June 13, 20, 27		
June 15/Sept. 15	Mürren	Guided rambles
June 15/Sept.	Pontresina	Daily guided tours, Diavolezza Glacier
June 16/28	Pontresina	Botanical weeks
June 20	Brissago	Guided rambles
June 21	Bergün	Botanical excursion
June 21/29	Poschiavo	
July	Meiringen	Puschlav rambling week
July/Aug.	Château-d'Oex	Riding and rambling weeks
July/Aug.	St. Moritz	Guided excursions to alpine pastures
		Weekly botanical and geological excursions
July/Aug.	Flims	Weekly local lore and botanical excursions
July/Aug.	Pontresina	Weekly botanical excursions
July/Sept.	Braunwald	Weekly guided mountain tours
July/Sept.	Arosa	Guided mountain tours, mycological and game-watching excursions
July/Sept.	Pontresina	Geological excursions
July 4, 11, 18, 25	Wengen	Guided rambles
July 7/12	Engelberg	Engelberg rambling week
July 9	Bergün	Game-watching excursion
July 16, 23, 30	Klosters	Botanical excursions
July 17, 24, 29	Crans	Guided rambles
July 19/20	Bergün	Guided rock-climbing tour
July 20/27	Einsiedeln	Einsiedeln holiday week
Aug. 1, 8, 15	Wengen	Guided rambles
Aug. 1, 7, 14	Crans	Guided rambles
Aug. 5, 12, 19	Crans	Guided mountain tours
Aug. 6, 13, 20	Klosters	Botanical and mycological excursions
Aug. 12	Bergün	Game-watching excursions
Aug. 15, 27	Bergün	Mycological excursions
Aug. 17/24	Klosters	ACS rambling week
Sept.	Meiringen	Bird-watching and botanical excursions
Sept. 20	Brissago	Guided rambles

		Wrestling and alpine herdsmen's festivals
June 6/8	Sargans	Alpine herdsmen's and traditional patriotic festival
June 15	Root	Michaelskreuz wrestling meeting above Root
June 22	Stoos	Wrestling and alpine herdsmen's festival
June 22	Kandersteg	Wrestling and alpine herdsmen's festival on Oeschinen
July 6	Sörenberg	Alpine wrestling meeting
July 6	Rigi-Kulm	Grand wrestling and alpine herdsmen's festival
July 6	Schwarzsee	Schwarzsee wrestling meeting
July 13	Hasliberg	Käserstatt wrestling and alpine herdsmen's festival
July 27	Zugerberg	Zugerberg wrestling meeting
July 27	Brünig	Brünig wrestling meeting
July 27	Grindelwald	Wrestling and alpine herdsmen's festival on the Grosse Scheidegg

24

July 27	Adelboden	Hahnenmoos: mountain fête and wrestling meeting
July 27	Moléson-Village	Wrestling and alpine herdsmen's festival
July 27	Leukerbad	Alpine herdsmen's festival on Alp Maying
Aug. 3	Vevey	Mont-Pèlerin alpine herdsmen's festival
Aug. 10	Morgarten	Morgarten wrestling meeting
Aug. 31	Herisau	Sedel wrestling meeting
Aug. 31	Sempach	Sempach wrestling meeting

		Shooting
May 8/11	Berne	Clay pigeon shooting: Berne international grand prix
May 25/26	Basel	International archery tournament
June 5/8	Berne	International Skeet match
July 26/27	St. Moritz	Clay pigeon shooting at 9,200 ft above sea level
Aug. 1	Leysin	Crossbow shooting
Aug. 1	Leukerbad	1st August shooting match
Aug. 9	Wengen	Small-bore championship: Wengen Cup
Aug. 16/17	Rigi-Klösterli	Rigi shooting contest
Aug., end	Berne	Swiss hunting championships
Aug. 31	St-Cergue	Popular shooting contest
Sept. 9	Scuol-Tarasp	Opening of mountain game season
Sept. 13	Gstaad	Opening of mountain game season
Sept., middle	Leysin	Opening of game season (except deer)

		Show-jumping and horse racing
May 4, 11	Aarau	Race meetings
May 10/11	Biel/Bienne	National show jumping
May 10/11	Buchs SG	Show jumping
May 17/18, 26	Baden	Würenlos: jumping contest
May 18	Frauenfeld	Horse racing and Squadron Cup
May 18	Val-de-Travers	Bovéresse: show jumping
May 18/June 1	Franches-Montagnes	Show jumping
May 24/26	Frauenfeld	Show jumping and race meeting
June 7/8	Schaffhausen	Schaffhausen equestrian meeting
June 8	Aarau	Horse racing
July 4/6	Yverdon	Horse racing and show jumping
July 31/Aug. 3	Tramelan	National show jumping
Aug. 10	Leysin	17th Leysin show jumping
Aug. 10	Verbier	Show jumping
Aug. 16/17	Gstaad	National show jumping
Aug. 23/24	Basel	Show jumping
Aug. 24	Château-d'Oex	Show jumping
Aug. 24	Zinal	Grand alpine meeting
Aug. 24/31	Gstaad	ACS riding week
Aug. 29/31	St. Gall	International equestrian meeting
Aug. 30/31	Les Verrières	Show jumping
Sept. 5/7	Locarno	Tenero: show jumping
Sept. 6/7	Colombier	National show jumping
Sept. 7	Basel	International race meeting
Sept. 13/14	Zurich	Show jumping and Swiss championships
Sept. 14	Lucerne	International race meeting
Sept. 28	Aarau	Race meeting
Oct. 5	Aarau	Race meeting
Oct. 12	Maienfeld	Race meeting

25

297

294 Invitation to an alumni exhibition of the Division of Design, Ohio State University. Black and white. (USA)
295 Folder issued by the Insurance Company of North America and Pacific Employers Insurance Company, describing their rehabilitation scheme for injured employees. Real gauze. (USA)
296 Colour cover of a large folder issued by the British Tourist Authority on small steam railways and rail museums in Britain. (GBR)
297 Spread from a booklet issued by the Swiss National Tourist Office listing summer events in Switzerland. (SWI)
298 Cover of a folder about art and artists in Düsseldorf. Brightly coloured beads. (GER)
299 Page from the "Performing Arts" section of *The Rainy Day Yearbook*, a publication of the Pratt Institute, with some satirical references to famous contemporaries. (USA)
300 Five-foot card from Dial Finance Co., referring to fast-growing children and offering loans to finance them. (USA)
301 Detail of the cover of a list of wines for a ball in the Atrium Hotel, Brunswick. Cream on deep orange. (GER)
302 Cover in actual size of a prospectus about Bad Schwalbach, a watering-place in Hesse. (GER)

294 Einladung zu einer Ausstellung, organisiert von der Design-Fakultät der Ohio State Universität. Schwarzweiss. (USA)
295 Faltprospekt einer Versicherungsgesellschaft, die hier ihren Aufwand zur Rehabilitation von verunfallten Berufstätigen beschreibt. Echte Gaze, blauer Grund und schwarze Schrift. (USA)
296 Mehrfarbiges Titelbild eines Prospekts für englische Verkehrsmuseen, herausgegeben vom englischen Touristenbüro. (GBR)
297 Doppelseite aus einer Broschüre der Schweizerischen Verkehrszentrale, Zürich, in der sämtliche Veranstaltungen während des Sommers in der Schweiz verzeichnet sind. (SWI)
298 Umschlag eines Prospekts über Kunst und Künstler in Düsseldorf. Mehrfarbig. (GER)
299 Seite aus dem Jahrbuch *The Rainy Day Yearbook*, eine Publikation mit satirischen Anspielungen auf berühmte Persönlichkeiten. (USA)
300 1,50 m lange Karte, mit der eine Finanzgesellschaft Darlehen anbietet. Man bezieht sich hier auf die schnell wachsenden Kinder. (USA)
301 Detail des Umschlags einer Weinkarte für den Ball eines Golfklubs im Atrium Hotel. Chamois auf dunklem Orange. (GER)
302 Titelbild in Originalgrösse des Prospekts für das Hessische Staatsbad Bad Schwalbach. (GER)

294 Invitation pour une exposition présentant les œuvres des anciens étudiants de la faculté des arts de la Ohio State University. Noir et blanc. (USA)
295 Dépliant publié par deux grandes compagnies d'assurances qui présentent leurs programmes pour la rééducation professionnelle des employés grièvement blessés. (USA)
296 Couverture (en couleurs) d'un dépliant grand format contenant des informations sur les trains à vapeur et le musées ferroviaires en Grande Bretagne. (GBR)
297 Page double figurant dans une brochure de l'Office National Suisse du Tourisme, contenant le programme des manifestations estivales organisées en Suisse. (SWI)
298 Couverture d'un dépliant consacré aux beaux-arts et aux artistes à Dusseldorf. (GER)
299 Page tirée de la section «Performing Arts» de l'annuaire *The Rainy Day Yearbook* une publication du Pratt Institute. Références satiriques à divers personnages contemporains. (USA)
300 Carte de 1 m 50 de la Dial Finance Co. sur le thème de la croissance rapide des enfants, avec des offres de prêts. (USA)
301 Détail de la couverture de la carte des vins pour un bal à l'Hôtel Atrium à Brunswick. Tons atténués sur fond orange foncé. (GER)
302 Couverture d'un prospectus pour Bad Schwalbach, une station thermale de la Hesse. (GER)

AGENCY / AGENTUR / AGENCE – STUDIO:

294 Lindsay Design
296 Philip Sharland Associates
297 M. + M. Baviera
300 Marvin H. Frank Co. Adv.
301 Udo Zisowsky

Booklets / Prospekte / Brochures

105

303 Cover of a menu in actual size (also used on a street sign) for a restaurant in Böttcherstrasse, a pedestrian mall in Bremen. (GER)
304 Christmas and New Year's card for Arti Grafiche Antonio Mantegazza, a design studio in Milan Black and silver with red type matter. (ITA)
305 Cover of a booklet about the services of Channing Weinberg & Co., technologically oriented business consultants. Red ground, lettering fading from orange through yellow to white. (USA)
306 Cover of a folder specifying the official colours to be used in the symbol of the Calgary Stampede, an annual rodeo and Wild West show. (CAN)
307 Inside spread of an invitation to the fortieth anniversary celebrations of The American Museum, Hayden Planetarium, New York. White on dark blue. (USA)

303 Umschlag in Originalgrösse einer Speise- und Getränkekarte des Restaurants *Kleiner Ratskeller* in Bremen. (GER)
304 Weihnachts- und Neujahrskarte für das Design-Studio Arti Grafiche Antonio Mantegazza, Mailand. Schwarz und Silber, rote Schrift. (ITA)
305 Umschlag einer Broschüre als Eigenwerbung für die Beratungsfirma Channing Weinberg & Co. Roter Grund, Schrift wechselnd von Orange zu Gelb und Weiss. (USA)
306 Umschlag eines Prospekts über die zu verwendenden Farben im Symbol des Calgary-Rodeos, einer jährlichen Wildwestvorführung. (CAN)
307 Innenseiten der Einladung für den fünfzigsten Jahrestag des American Museum, New York. Weiss auf Dunkelblau. (USA)

303 Couverture du menu (grandeur nature), utilisée aussi en tant que plaque dans la rue, pour le restaurant Kleiner Ratskeller à la Böttcherstrasse, une rue piétonnière de Brême. (GER)
304 Carte de vœux de Noël et de Nouvel An d'Arti Grafiche Antonio Mantegazza, un studio de design à Milan. Noir et argent, texte en rouge. (ITA)
305 Couverture d'une brochure de Channing Weinberg & Co., conseillers économiques d'orientation technologique. Fond rouge, texte passant de l'orange par le jaune jusqu'au blanc. (USA)
306 Couverture d'un dépliant sur les couleurs officielles de l'emblème du Calgary Stampede, un rodeo annuel. (CAN)
307 Double page figurant dans l'invitation pour une fête organisée à l'occasion du 40e anniversaire du Hayden Planétarium de l'American Museum à New York. Blanc sur fond bleu foncé. (USA)

Booklets / Prospekte / Brochures

303

ARTIST / KÜNSTLER / ARTISTE:

303 Dietrich Ralle
304 Armando Milani (Photo)
306 Roger Hill

DESIGNER / GESTALTER / MAQUETTISTE:

304 Armando Milani
305 Victor Vizbara/Mauro Filicori
306 Roger Hill
307 Ivan Chermayeff

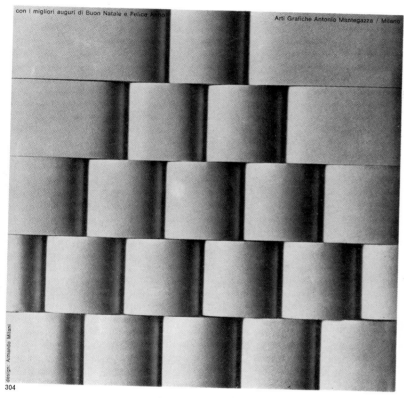
304

305

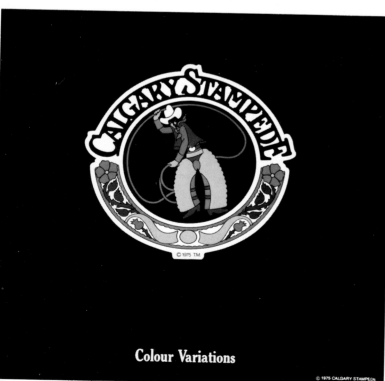
306

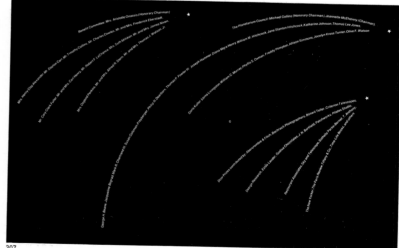
307

ART DIRECTOR / DIRECTEUR ARTISTIQUE:

303 Fritz Haase/Dietrich Ralle
306 Robert Burns
307 Ivan Chermayeff

AGENCY / AGENTUR / AGENCE – STUDIO:

303 Haase & Knels
304 Armando Milani
306 Burns & Cooper
307 Chermayeff & Geismar Associates, Inc.

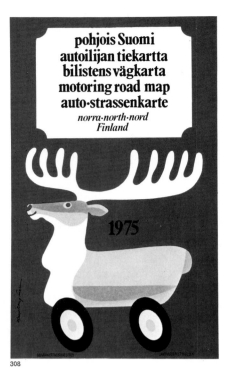

308

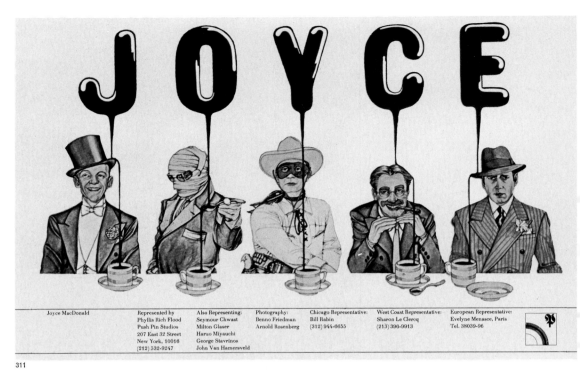

311

309

310

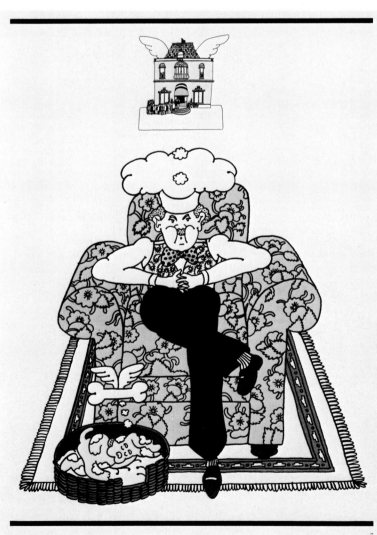

313

Booklets
Prospekte
Brochures

308, 309 Covers of two motoring road maps of the north and south of Finland, Fig. 308 on a red ground, Fig. 309 on a turquoise ground. (FIN)
310 Cover of a wine list for a restaurant in Bremen. Turquoise and brown. (GER)
311 Self-promotion card for the illustrator Joyce MacDonald of the Push Pin Studios. Dull red lettering, full-colour figures. (USA)
312 Double spread with flap from a brochure about Decima Research, a business information service. White, red, mauve and blue frontier on black, grey flap. (USA)
313, 314 Page and spread from a booklet on restaurant design issued by the Canadian Office of Tourism. Illustrations in grey and black: the restaurant manager's dream and his clientele. (CAN)

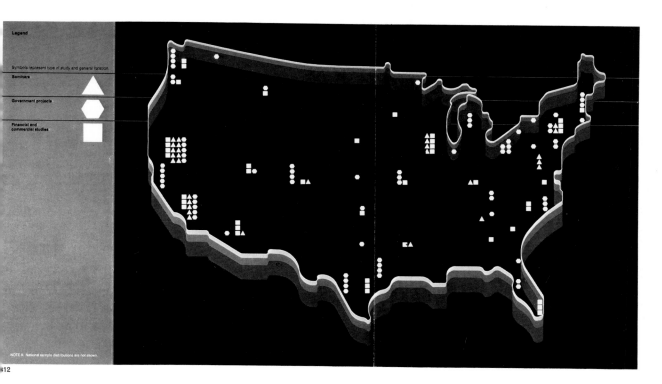

ARTIST / KÜNSTLER / ARTISTE:

308, 309 Kurt Bengtsson
310   Dietrich Ralle
311   Joyce MacDonald
313, 314 John Speakman

DESIGNER / GESTALTER:

308, 309 Kurt Bengtsson
311   Seymour Chwast
312   Jann Church
313, 314 Robert Burns/
          John Speakman

ART DIRECTOR:

308, 309 Kurt Bengtsson
310   Fritz Haase
311   Seymour Chwast
312   Jann Church/Geoff Bjork
313, 314 Robert Burns

AGENCY / AGENTUR:

310   Haase & Knels
311   Push Pin Studios, Inc.
312   Jann Church Graphic Design
313, 314 Burns & Cooper

312

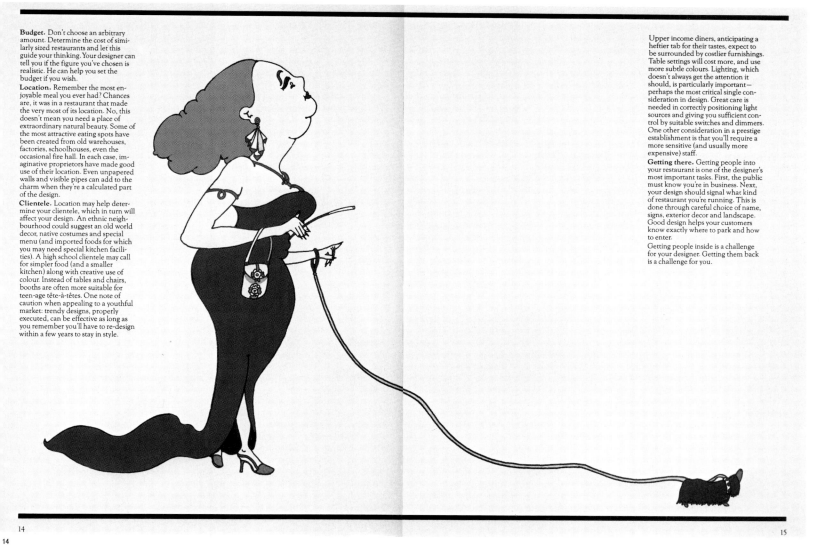

Budget. Don't choose an arbitrary amount. Determine the cost of similarly sized restaurants and let this guide your thinking. Your designer can tell you if the figure you've chosen is realistic. He can help you set the budget if you wish.

Location. Remember the most enjoyable meal you ever had? Chances are, it was in a restaurant that made the very most of its location. No, this doesn't mean you need a place of extraordinary natural beauty. Some of the most attractive eating spots have been created from old warehouses, factories, schoolhouses, even the occasional fire hall. In each case, imaginative proprietors have made good use of their location. Even unpapered walls and visible pipes can add to the charm when they're a calculated part of the design.

Clientele. Location may help determine your clientele, which in turn will affect your design. An ethnic neighbourhood could suggest an old world decor, native costumes and special menu (and imported foods for which you may need special kitchen facilities). A high school clientele may call for simpler food (and a smaller kitchen) along with creative use of colour. Instead of tables and chairs, booths are often more suitable for teen-age tête-à-têtes. One note of caution when appealing to a youthful market: trendy designs, properly executed, can be effective as long as you remember you'll have to re-design within a few years to stay in style.

Upper income diners, anticipating a heftier tab for their tastes, expect to be surrounded by costlier furnishings. Table settings will cost more, and use more subtle colours. Lighting, which doesn't always get the attention it should, is particularly important—perhaps the most critical single consideration in design. Great care is needed in correctly positioning light sources and giving you sufficient control by suitable switches and dimmers. One other consideration in a prestige establishment is that you'll require a more sensitive (and usually more expensive) staff.

Getting there. Getting people into your restaurant is one of the designer's most important tasks. First, the public must know you're in business. Next, your design should signal what kind of restaurant you're running. This is done through careful choice of name, signs, exterior decor and landscape. Good design helps your customers know exactly where to park and how to enter.

Getting people inside is a challenge for your designer. Getting them back is a challenge for you.

14   15

08, 309 Zwei Umschläge von Auto-Strassenkarten von Nord- und Südfinnland. Abb. 308 auf otem Grund, Abb. 309 auf Türkis. (FIN)
10 Umschlag einer Getränkekarte des Restaurants *Amtsfischer-Haus.* Türkis und braun. (GER)
11 Eigenwerbungs-Karte für die Illustratorin Joyce McDonald der Push Pin Studios. Dunkelrote chrift, mehrfarbige Figuren. (USA)
12 Doppelseite aus einer Broschüre über die wissenschaftlichen Forschungen der Decima Re-earch. Weiss, rot, violett und blau auf Schwarz. (USA)
13, 314 Seite und Doppelseite aus einer Design-Anleitung für Restaurants, herausgegeben vom anadischen Verkehrsbüro. Illustrationen in Grau und Schwarz. (CAN)

308, 309 Couvertures de deux cartes routières du Nord et du Sud de la Finlande. Fig. 308: sur fond rouge; fig. 309: sur fond turquoise. (FIN)
310 Couverture de la carte des vins d'un restaurant à Brême. Turquoise et brun. (GER)
311 Carte autopromotionnelle de l'illustrateur Joyce MacDonald des Push Pin Studios. Texte en rouge atténué, figures en couleurs. (USA)
312 Page double avec rabat figurant dans la brochure d'un service d'informations économiques. Frontière en blanc, rouge, mauve et bleu sur fond noir, rabat gris. (USA)
313, 314 Eléments d'une brochure de décorations de restaurants, publiée par l'Office National Canadien du Tourisme. Illustration gris-noir: le rêve du directeur et sa clientèle. (CAN)

315, 316 Invitation, shown closed and opened at first page, to a forum on leveraged leasing, issued by Itel Leasing Corp. Double title blind embossed and printed in gold on flap. (USA)
317, 318 Spreads from a small invitation booklet to the tenth anniversary celebration of the Heritage Press, Dallas. Drawings in colour, blue type matter. (USA)
319 Invitation to a preview of a film issued by the weekly *People*. Black on magenta. (USA)
320 Self-promotion card issued by Graphicsgroup, Inc., represented in New York by Whistl'n Dixie, Inc. Drawing in shades of grey. (USA)
321 Self-promotion piece for a designer in actual size as used in an annual booklet presenting the work of 27 Chicago designers. (USA)

315, 316 Einladung (geschlossen und auf der ersten Seite geöffnet) zu einem Forum mit dem Thema Leasing. Blindgeprägter Titel, Druck in Gold. (USA)
317, 318 Zwei Doppelseiten aus einer Einladung zum 10. Jahrestag einer Druckerei. Illustration mehrfarbig, blaue Schrift. (USA)
319 Einladungskarte für die Vor-Première des Films *Chinatown* von Polanski, organisiert von der Zeitschrift *People*. Schwarz auf Altrosa. (USA)
320 Eigenwerbungs-Karte herausgegeben von Graphicsgroup, Inc., deren Agent in New York Whistl'n Dixie, Inc. ist. Illustration in Grautönen. (USA)
321 Eigenwerbungs-Karte für den Designer Franz Altschuler. Diese Illustration ist in der Jahrespublikation über Werke von 27 Designern von Chicago erschienen. (USA)

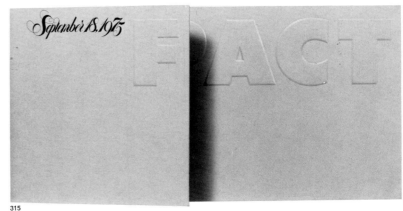

315

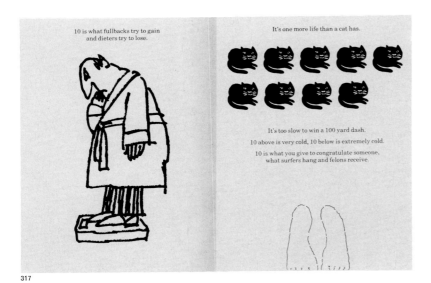

317

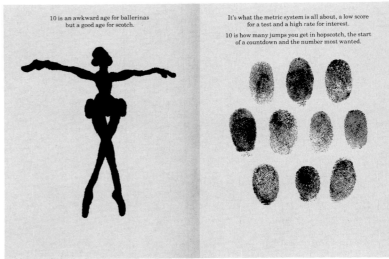

318

319

315, 316 Invitation (fermée et ouverte à la première page) pour un forum discutant le crédit bail. Double titre gaufré, impression en or. (USA)
317, 318 Pages doubles figurant dans une petite brochure publiée en tant qu'invitation pour une fête organisée à l'occasion des dix ans d'existence de *Heritage Press* à Dallas. Dessins en couleurs, texte en bleu. (USA)
319 Invitation pour l'avant-première d'un film, organisée par l'hebdomadaire *People*. Noir sur fond magenta. (USA)
320 Carte autopromotionnelle de Graphicsgroup, Inc., qui est représenté à New York par Whistl'n Dixie, Inc. Dessins en divers tons gris. (USA)
321 Elément autopromotionnel d'un dessinateur. Le format de la reproduction ici correspond à celui utilisé dans la publication annuelle qui présente les créations de 27 designers de Chicago. (USA)

ARTIST / KÜNSTLER / ARTISTE:

315, 316 Hank Barenz
317, 318 Bob Dennard/Larry Sons
320 Bob Boyd
321 Franz Altschuler

DESIGNER / GESTALTER / MAQUETTISTE:

315, 316 Thom LaPerle
317, 318 Bob Dennard
319 Gilbert Lesser
320 Andy Di Martino

Booklets / Prospekte / Brochures

320

The leveraged leasing industry has grown dramatically in the last dozen years. In 1974 alone, $5.7 billion of equipment was financed in this manner. ■ The Internal Revenue Service's recent issuance of guidelines for advance tax rulings on leasing transactions has generated much comment concerning the application and effect they will have on the future of leveraged leasing. ■ The Forum's purpose is to explain, through in-depth analysis and practical recommendations, what the new guidelines are, how they operate and how to apply them; and to discuss their impact on the future of leveraged leasing.

ART DIRECTOR / DIRECTEUR ARTISTIQUE:

317, 318 Bob Dennard
319 Gilbert Lesser
320 Andy Di Martino
321 Franz Altschuler

AGENCY / AGENTUR / AGENCE – STUDIO:

315, 316 LaPerle/Assoc., Inc.
317, 318 The Richards Group
319 Gilbert Lesser/Design
320 Graphicsgroup Inc.

316

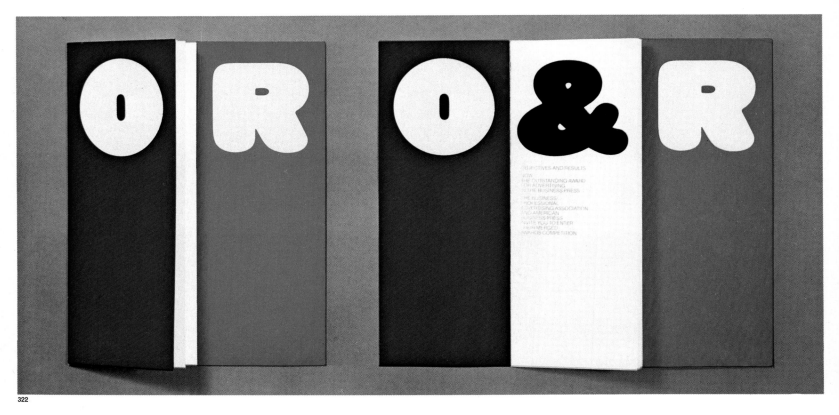

322

Booklets / Prospekte / Brochures

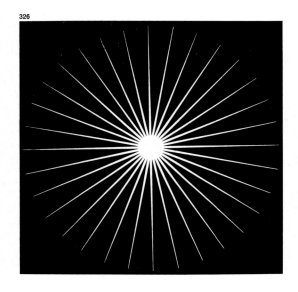

326

327

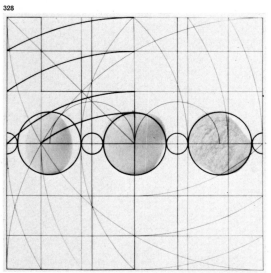

328

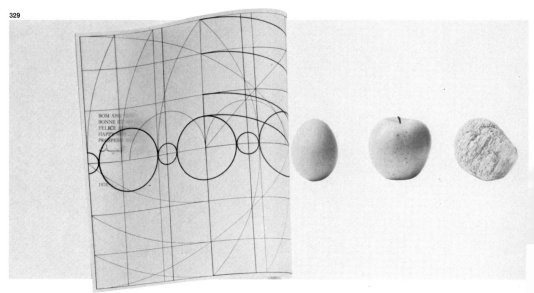

329

ARTIST / KÜNSTLER / ARTISTE:

322 W. Chris Gorman/Cynthia Owczarek
323–325 John McConnell
326 Felix Beltran
327 Jack Summerford
328, 329 Marco Baroni
330 Stanley Wong/Garry Emery
331 John Greiner
332 Crosby Family/Bart Crosby

ART DIRECTOR / DIRECTEUR ARTISTIQUE:

322 W. Chris Gorman
323–325 John McConnell
326 Felix Beltran
327 Jack Summerford
328, 329 Franco Bassi
330 Garry Emery
331 John Greiner
332 Bart Crosby

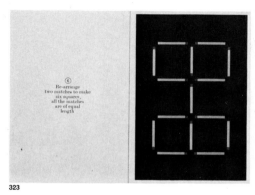

323

324

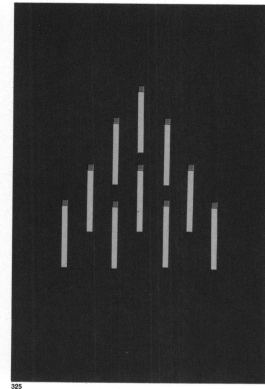

325

330

331

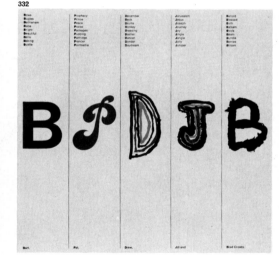

332

322 Call for entries, shown closed and open, for "Objectives and Results", an awards contest for business advertising. (USA)
323–325 Spread and pages from a booklet of match puzzles a Christmas mailing by the Pentagram design studio. (GBR)
326 New Year's card for the designer. White on blue. (CUB)
327 Invitation to a graphics exhibition issued by the Olmsted-Kirk Paper Company. Orange, blue and green shapes. (USA)
328, 329 Page and spread with transparent overlay from a New Year's card from the Italconsult agency. (ITA)
330 Cover of a programme for an asthma symposium in Sydney. Yellow and black figures. (AUL)
331 Change of address for John Greiner & Associates. (USA)
332 Christmas greetings from a family, white initials. (USA)

322 Einladung zu einem Wettbewerb über die besten Arbeiten und Resultate in der Geschäftswerbung. (USA)
323–325 Streichholz-Puzzles aus einer zu Weihnachten herausgegeben Broschüre von Pentagram. (GBR)
326 Neujahrskarte für einen Designer. Weiss auf Blau. (CUB)
327 Einladung zu einer Graphik-Ausstellung, organisiert von einer Papierfabrik. Orange, blau und grün. (USA)
328, 329 Seite und Doppelseite mit transparentem Aufleger aus einer Neujahrskarte der Agentur Italconsult. (ITA)
330 Umschlag eines Programms für ein Symposium über Asthma in Sidney. Gelbe und schwarze Figuren. (AUL)
331 Adressänderung der John Greiner & Assoc. (USA)
332 Weihnachtswünsche einer fünfköpfigen Familie. (USA)

322 Invitation (fermée et ouverte) pour la soumission de travaux pour un concours de la publicité commerciale. (USA)
323–325 Eléments figurant dans une brochure présentant des puzzles d'alumettes, distribuée à Noël par Pentagram. (GBR)
326 Carte de Nouvel An d'un designer. Blanc et bleu. (CUB)
327 Invitation pour une exposition d'art graphique, patronnée par une papeterie. Formes en orange, bleu et vert. (USA)
328, 329 Page et page double d'une carte de Nouvel An d'Italconsult avec feuille transparente intercalée. (ITA)
330 Couverture du programme d'un symposium sur l'asthma tenu à Sydney. Figures en jaune et noir. (AUL)
331 Changement d'adresse de John Greiner & Assoc. (USA)
332 Carte familiale de vœux de Noël, avec initiales. (USA)

AGENCY / AGENTUR / AGENCE – STUDIO:

322 W. Chris Gorman Associates, Inc.
323–325 Pentagram
327 The Richards Group
328, 329 Italconsult
330 Interact Communications
331 John Greiner & Associates
332 Center for Advanced Research in Design

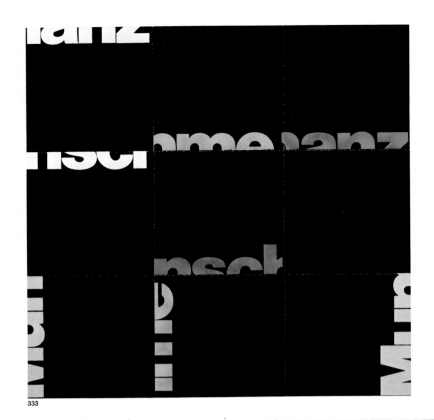

333

334

ARTIST / KÜNSTLER / ARTISTE:

335 John Dolby
337 Jackie L.W. Geyer
338, 339 Don Weller

DESIGNER / GESTALTER:

333 Stan Baker
335 John Dolby
336 Fritz Haase
338, 339 Don Weller

ART DIRECTOR:

333 Stan Baker
335 John Dolby
336 Franz Cesarz/Fritz Haase
337 Jackie L.W. Geyer
338, 339 Don Weller

AGENCY / AGENTUR:

335 BBDM, Inc.
336 Haase & Knels
337 Marini, Climes & Guip
338, 339 Weller Institute

337

338

335

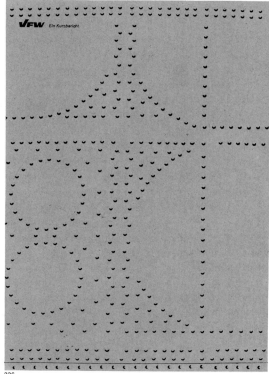

336

339

333 Invitation to a performance by a mime troupe called "Mummenschanz" sponsored by *Ciba-Geigy*, New York. Lettering pale blue, orange, red and yellow. (USA)
334 Programme of a conference on neighbourhood conservation held in New York City. (USA)
335 Invitation to an open house of the BBDM agency in Chicago. Full colour. (USA)
336 Cover of a brochure about the VFW-*Fokker* aircraft works in Bremen. (GER)
337 Cover illustration for a self-promotion booklet presenting the work of a Pittsburgh-born illustrator. (USA)
338, 339 Double spread and illustration (of a retired media director) from a self-promotion booklet of flying-saucer stories issued by the Weller Institute. (USA)

333 Einladung zu einer Aufführung von Mimen mit dem Namen «Mummenschanz», organisiert von *Ciba-Geigy*, New York. Schrift in Blau, Orange, Rot und Gelb auf schwarzem Grund. (USA)
334 Programm für eine Konferenz über die Planung und Konservierung der Stadt und deren Umgebung. (USA)
335 Einladung zum Tag der «offenen Tür» einer Werbeagentur in Chicago. (USA)
336 Prospektumschlag für die Vereinigten Flugtechnischen Werke, VFW-Fokker GmbH, Bremen. (GER)
337 Titelbild-Illustration für eine Eigenwerbungs-Broschüre der Illustratorin Jackie L.W. Geyer. (USA)
338, 339 Vollständige Doppelseite und Illustration aus einer Eigenwerbungs-Broschüre mit Geschichten über fliegende Untertassen, herausgegeben vom Weller-Institute. (USA)

333 Invitation pour la représentation de «Mummenschanz», un groupe de mimes. Représentation patronnée par *Ciba-Geigy* à New York. Texte en bleu pâle, orange, rouge et jaune. (USA)
334 Programme d'une conférence sur la planification et la conservation de la ville et de ses allentours. (USA)
335 Invitation d'une journée de portes ouvertes à l'agence publicitaire BBDM à Chicago. Polychromie. (USA)
336 Couverture d'une brochure consacrée à l'usine d'aviation VWF-*Fokker* à Brême. (GER)
337 Illustration de couverture d'une brochure autopromotionnelle présentant l'œuvre d'un illustrateur né à Pittsburgh. (USA)
338, 339 Page double et illustration (d'un directeur retraité) figurant dans une brochure autopromotionnelle du Weller Institute. Elle présente des histoires de soucoupes volantes. (USA)

3

Magazine Covers
Trade Magazines
Magazine Illustrations
Newspaper Illustrations
Annual Reports
House Organs
Book Covers

Zeitschriften-Umschläge
Fachzeitschriften
Zeitschriften-Illustrationen
Zeitungs-Illustrationen
Jahresberichte
Hauszeitschriften
Buchumschläge

Couvertures de périodiques
Revues professionnelles
Illustrations de périodiques
Illustrations de journaux
Rapports annuels
Journaux d'entreprises
Couvertures de livres

340–342 Covers (in full colour) of the satirical weekly *Nebelspalter*. Fig. 340: a Nazi-inspired Cupid launches the Spring offensive in a March issue; Fig. 341: a reference to the tablet habit; Fig. 342: "Everything totters where faith is lacking" (Schiller). (SWI)
343 Cover (in full colour) for the fortnightly humorous magazine *Okapi*. "They're no fools, the orang-utans." (FRA)
344 A further cover for the *Nebelspalter*. (SWI)
345–347 Three covers for *New York*. The references are to the domino effect in New York's financial predicament (Fig. 345), the possible end of the cult of St. Valentine's Day (Fig. 346) and a murder mystery contained in the issue (Fig. 347). (USA)
348 Cover of the humorous magazine *Szpilki*. Yellow flame, red title. (POL)

340–342 Mehrfarbige Umschläge der satirischen Monatszeitschrift *Nebelspalter*. Abb. 340: ein Nazi-inspirierter Amor nimmt die Frühjahrs-Offensive in einer März-Ausgabe in Angriff; Abb. 341: mit Bezug auf die Tabletten-Abhängigkeit; Abb. 342: Anspielung auf ein Schiller-Zitat. (SWI)
343 Mehrfarbiger Umschlag für das humoristische Magazin *Okapi*: «Sie sind nicht dumm, die Orang-Utans.» (FRA)
344 Ein weiterer Umschlag für den *Nebelspalter*. (SWI)
345–347 Drei Umschläge für *New York*. Diese Illustrationen beziehen sich auf die New Yorker Domino-Finanzpolitik (Abb. 345), auf das mögliche Ende der St.-Valentins-Tradition (Abb. 346) und auf eine Kriminalgeschichte (Abb. 347). (USA)
348 Umschlag des humoristischen Magazins *Szpilki*. Gelbe Flamme, roter Titel. (POL)

340–342 Couvertures (en couleurs) de l'hebdomadaire satirique *Nebelspalter*. Fig. 340: un Cupidon influencé par les Nazis déclenche l'offensif de printemps; fig. 341: référence à la dépendance de pilules; fig. 342: référence à un mot de Schiller suivant lequel tout chancelle si l'homme ne croit pas. (SWI)
343 Couverture (en couleurs) d'un numéro du magazine *Okapi*, un bimensuel satirique. (FRA)
344 Une autre couverture de l'hebdomadaire *Nebelspalter*. (SWI)
345–347 Couvertures du magazine *New York*. Les illustrations se réfèrent à la situation financière de New York, ressemblant à un jeu de dominos, à la fin éventuelle de la culte de la Saint-Valentin et à un meurtre mystérieux. (USA)
348 Couverture de *Szpilki*, un magazine humoristique. Flamme jaune, titre rouge. (POL)

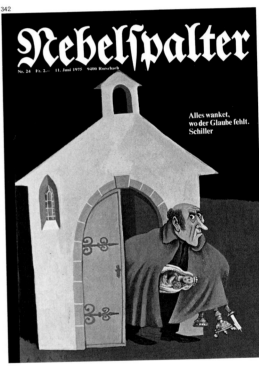

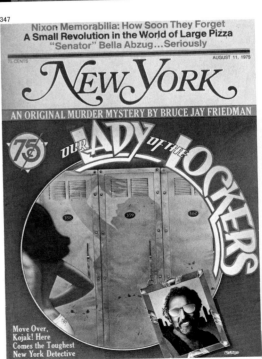

Magazine Covers
Zeitschriftenumschläge
Couvertures de périodiques

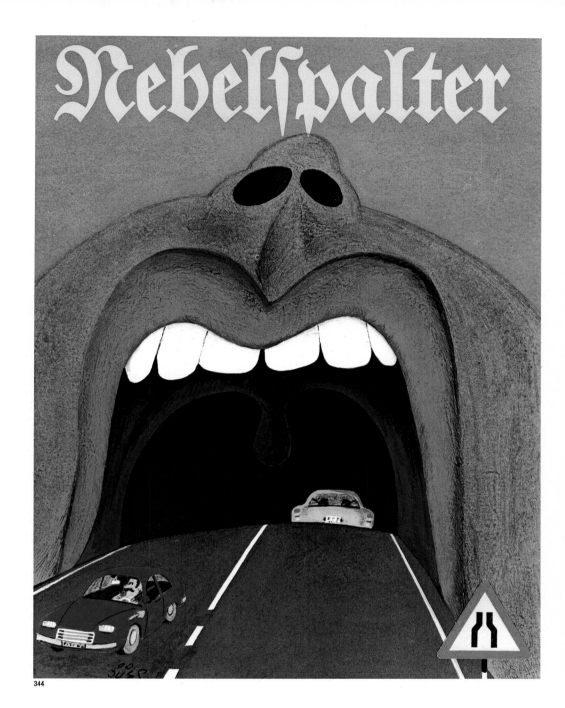

344

343

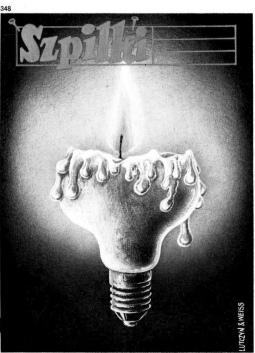

348

ARTIST / KÜNSTLER / ARTISTE:

340 Fredy Sigg
341, 342 Barth
343 Fernando Puig Rosado
344 Jüsp
345 Richard Hess
346 Phil Slagter
347 Charles White III
348 Edward Lutczyn/Janusz Weiss

DESIGNER / GESTALTER / MAQUETTISTE:

343 Michel Rémondière
345, 346 Milton Glaser
347 Walter Bernard/Milton Glaser
348 Marek Goebel

ART DIRECTOR / DIRECTEUR ARTISTIQUE:

340–342, 344 Franz Mächler
343 Denys Prache
345–347 Walter Bernard/Milton Glaser
348 Marek Goebel

PUBLISHER / VERLEGER / EDITEUR:

340–342, 344 Nebelspalter
343 Bayard Presse
345–347 New York Magazine
348 Szpilki

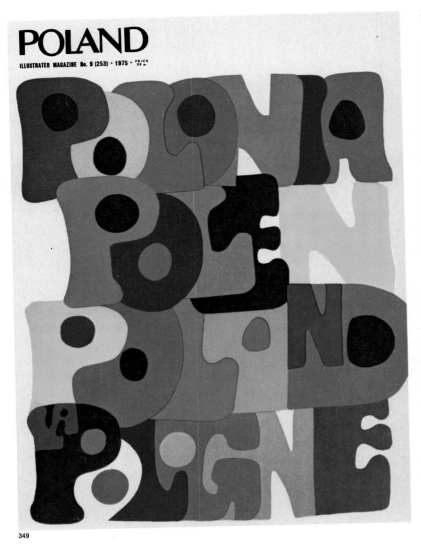

349

352

350

351

35 cents **POLAND**
ILLUSTRATED MAGAZINE   OCTOBER 1971

353

354

349, 352, 353 Two covers and one complete cover (entitled "Spinning") of the illustrated magazine *Poland,* which appears in six language editions. (POL)
350, 351 Covers of *The New York Times Magazine.* Fig. 350 refers to a feature on economics, Fig. 351 to competition on television. (USA)
354 Cover of *The New Yorker* referring to the suburban competition for the best lawn. (USA)

349, 352, 353 Zwei Titelbilder und ein kompletter Umschlag (betitelt «Spinnen») des illustrierten Magazins *Polen,* welches in sechs verschiedenen Sprachen erscheint. (POL)
350, 351 Umschläge von *The New York Times Magazine.* Abb. 350 bezieht sich auf einen Artikel über die wirtschaftliche Situation, Abb. 351 auf den Konkurrenzkampf am Fernsehen. (USA)
354 Umschlag der Zeitschrift *The New Yorker,* der sich auf den vorstädtischen Wettstreit um den schönsten Rasen bezieht. (USA)

349, 352, 353 Deux illustrations de couverture et couverture complète (intitulée «Filage») du magazine illustré *Pologne.* Ce magazine culturel paraît chaque mois en six langues différentes. (POL)
350, 351 Couverture du supplément hebdomadaire *New York Times Magazine.* La fig. 350 se réfère à un article sur l'économie, la fig. 351 à la concurrence à la télévision. (USA)
354 Couverture du magazine *The New Yorker,* dont l'illustration se réfère à la compétition du plus beau gazon de la banlieue. (USA)

ARTIST / KÜNSTLER / ARTISTE:

349 Teresa Wilbik
350 Eugène Mihaesco
351 Seymour Chwast
352, 353 Andrzej Krajewski
354 R. O. Blechman

ART DIRECTOR / DIRECTEUR ARTISTIQUE:

349, 352, 353 Lech Zahorski
350, 351 Ruth Ansel
354 Lee Lorenz

PUBLISHER / VERLEGER / EDITEUR:

349, 352, 353 Polish Interpress Agency
350, 351 The New York Times
354 The New Yorker

Magazine Covers
Zeitschriftenumschläge
Couvertures de périodiques

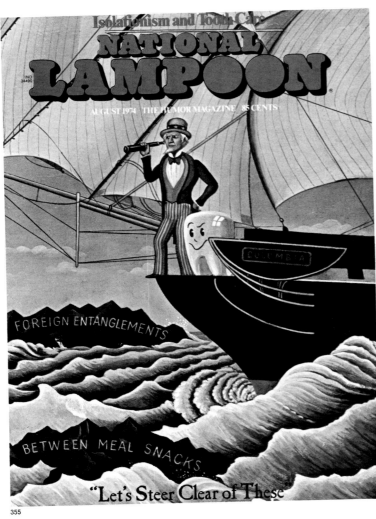

355

356

357

358

355—358 Four covers of the humorous magazine *National Lampoon*. Fig. 355 on the unusual subject combination of isolationism and tooth care, Fig. 356 on food, Fig. 357 for a ''back to college'' issue, Fig. 358 on things to do on a rainy Sunday. (USA)
359 Cover of *Potomac*, the Sunday magazine of *The Washington Post*. (USA)
360, 361 Detail and complete cover of an issue of *Time* magazine containing a feature on the rock musician Elton John. (USA)

355—358 Vier Umschläge des humoristischen Magazins *National Lampoon*. Abb. 355 bringt die beiden Begriffe Isolation und Zahnpflege in unüblicher Weise in Zusammenhang; Abb. 356 bezieht sich auf Nahrung; Abb. 357 plädiert für ein «zurück zur Schule»; Abb. 358 lässt sich Sachen einfallen, die man an einem regnerischen Sonntag tun könnte. (USA)
359 Umschlag der Zeitschrift *Potomac*, des illustrierten Sonntags-Magazins der *Washington Post*. (USA)
360, 361 Detail und kompletter Umschlag einer Ausgabe des *Time* Magazins über den Rock-Musiker Elton John. (USA)

355—358 Quatre couvertures du magazine humoristique *National Lampoon*. La fig. 355 se réfère à un article qui établit un rapport assez bizarre entre l'isolationisme et l'hygiène dentaire; la fig. 356 aux denrées alimentaires; la fig. 357 à un numéro qui plaide pour «un retour à l'école»; la fig. 358 donne quelques propositions de ce qui se prête en tant que passe-temps un dimanche pluvieux. (USA)
359 Couverture de *Potomac*, supplément de fin de semaine du *Washington Post*. (USA)
360, 361 Détail et couverture complète où il figure. Numéro du magazine d'information *Time* contenant un article sur la musique rock d'Elton John. (USA)

ARTIST / KÜNSTLER / ARTISTE:

355 Richard Hess
356 Melinda Bordelon/R. G. Harris
357 Bernie Lettick
358 Edward Gorey
359 John Heinly
360, 361 Don Weller

DESIGNER / GESTALTER / MAQUETTISTE:

355, 356 Michael Gross
358 Peter Kleinman
359 John Heinly
360, 361 Don Weller

ART DIRECTOR / DIRECTEUR ARTISTIQUE:

355, 356 Michael Gross
357, 358 Peter Kleinman
359 David Moy
360, 361 David Merrill

AGENCY / AGENTUR / AGENCE — STUDIO:

355, 356 Pellegrini, Kaestle & Gross, Inc.

PUBLISHER / VERLEGER / EDITEUR:

355—358 21st Century Communications, Inc.
359 The Washington Post
360, 361 Time Inc.

360

359

361

362

364

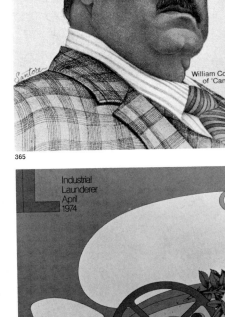

366

363

365

362 Cover of a special issue of the magazine *Pilote* on the subject of the circus. Full colour, white title. (FRA)
363 Cover of the official circus magazine *Manège*. Blue and white. (SWI)
364, 365 Covers of the television programme magazine *TV Guide*. They refer to a new family series and to a famous overweight detective. (USA)
366 Cover of the trade magazine *Industrial Launderer*. (USA)
367, 368 Detail and complete cover of *Publishers Weekly* in which André François makes fun of the laureate author whose laurel leaves begin to change colour and fall. (USA)

362 Umschlag einer Spezialausgabe der Zeitschrift *Pilote* über das Thema Zirkus. Mehrfarbig, weisser Titel. (FRA)
363 Umschlag des offiziellen Zirkus-Magazins *Manège*. (SWI)
364, 365 Umschläge des Programm-Magazins *TV Guide*. Sie beziehen sich auf eine Familien-Serie und einen übergewichtigen Detektiven. (USA)
366 Umschlag der Fachzeitschrift *Industrial Launderer*. (USA)
367, 368 Detail und kompletter Umschlag der Zeitschrift *Publishers Weekly*, in welcher André François sich lustig macht über den lorbeerbekränzten Autoren, dessen Kranz sich verfärbt und verdorrt. (USA)

362 Couverture d'un numéro spécial du magazine *Pilote*, numéro consacré entièrement au cirque. Polychromie, titre en blanc. (FRA)
363 Couverture de *Manège*, revue officielle du cirque. Bleu et blanc. (SWI)
364, 365 Couvertures du télé-magazine *TV Guide*. Elles se réfèrent à une nouvelle série de famille et à un célèbre agent de police. (USA)
366 Couverture du magazine professionnel *Industrial Launderer*. (USA)
367, 368 Détail et couverture où il figure. Numéro de *Publishers Weekly* dans lequel André François se moque de l'auteur-lauréat dont la couronne de laurier commence à se faner et à se dessécher. (USA)

ARTIST / KÜNSTLER / ARTISTE:

362 Solé
363 Walter Grieder
364 Paul Davis
365 Charles Santore
366 Pam + Jack Lefkowitz
367, 368 André François

DESIGNER / GESTALTER / MAQUETTISTE:

363 Walter Grieder
364, 365 Jerry Alton
366 Pam + Jack Lefkowitz

ART DIRECTOR / DIRECTEUR ARTISTIQUE:

363 Walter Grieder
364, 365 Jerry Alton
366 Jack Lefkowitz

AGENCY / AGENTUR / AGENCE – STUDIO:

366 Jack Lefkowitz
367, 368 John Locke Studio

PUBLISHER / VERLEGER / EDITEUR:

362 Dargot Editeur
363 Club der Circus-, Variété- und Artistenfreunde
364, 365 Triangle Publications
366 Institute of Industrial Launderers
367, 368 Arnold Ehrlich

368

367

125

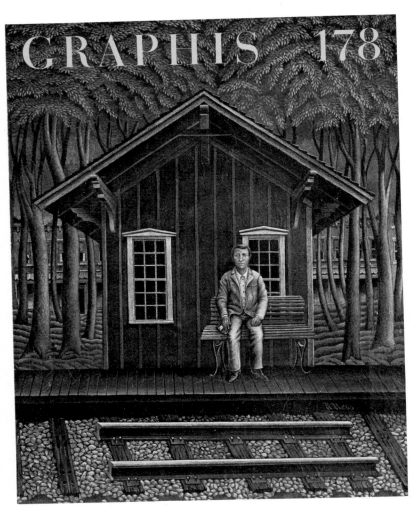
369

ARTIST / KÜNSTLER / ARTISTE:

369 Richard Hess
370, 371 Yoji Kuri
372 Paul Davis

ART DIRECTOR / DIRECTEUR ARTISTIQUE:

369 Walter Herdeg
372 Milton Glaser

PUBLISHER / VERLEGER / EDITEUR:

369 Graphis Verlag/Walter Herdeg
370, 371 Kodansha Ltd.

369 Cover of the graphic design magazine *Graphis*, predominantly in dark brown, green and blue shades. (SWI)
370, 371 Covers of a magazine (spring and summer issues) published by the pharmaceutical company Japan Upjohn Limited. (JPN)
372 Picture painted for George McGovern's presidential campaign, to accompany his statement on Indian rights. (USA)

369 Umschlag der Zeitschrift *Graphis*, einer Zweimonatsschrift für Graphik und angewandte Kunst. Illustration vorwiegend in dunkelbraunen, grünen und blauen Farbtönen. (SWI)
370, 371 Umschläge einer Zeitschrift (Frühjahrs- und Sommerausgabe), die von der Pharmazeutik-Firma Japan Upjohn Ltd. herausgegeben wird. (JPN)
372 Bild, das für die Präsidentschafts-Wahlkampagne George McGoverns gemalt wurde und als Illustration zu seiner Erklärung über die Rechte der Indianer diente. (USA)

369 Couverture de *Graphis*, magazine d'art graphique et d'art appliqué. Prédominance de tons bruns foncé, verts et bleus. (SWI)
370, 371 Couverture d'un magazine (numéro de printemps et d'été) publié par une entreprise de produits pharmaceutiques. (JPN)
372 Illustration d'un exposé sur les droits des Indiens distribué par George McGovern à ses partisans à l'occasion de sa compagne présidentielle. (USA)

370

371

126

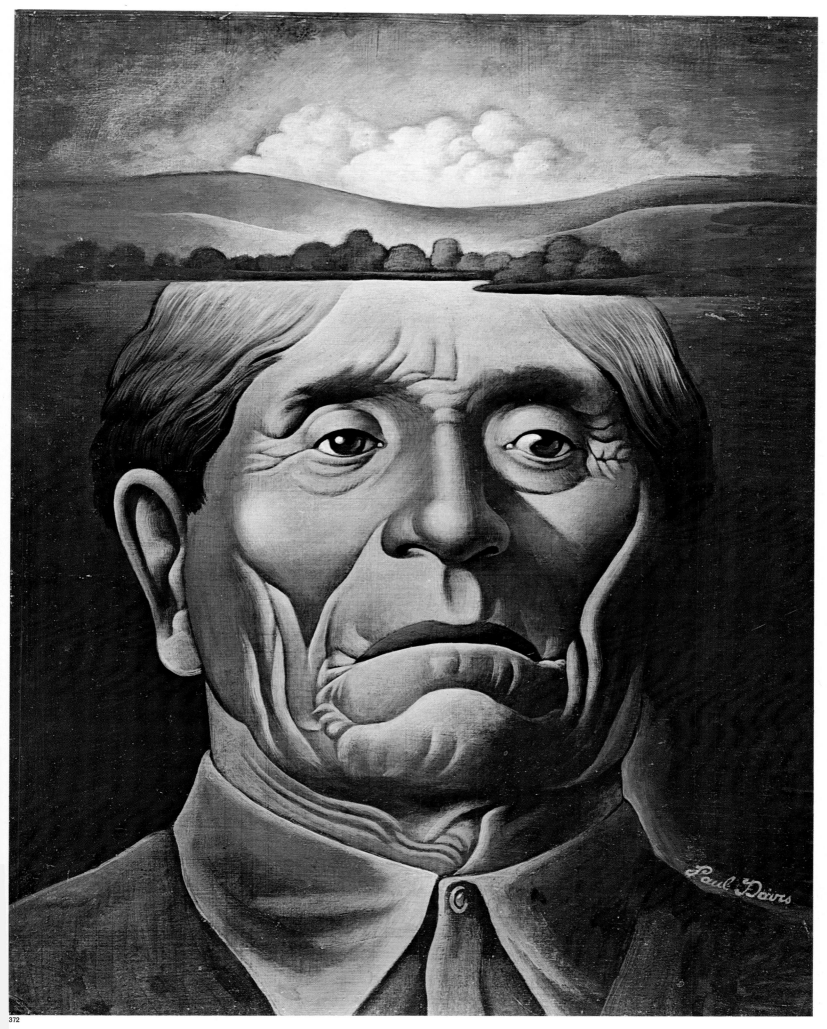

ARTIST / KÜNSTLER / ARTISTE:

373 Heiner H. Hoier
374 Ralph Steadman
375 Tattoo-Studio
376 Don Weller
377 Roland Topor
378 Don Ivan Punchatz

ART DIRECTOR / DIRECTEUR ARTISTIQUE:

373–375 Dietmar Meyer
376–378 Philip F. Dykstra

PUBLISHER / VERLEGER / EDITEUR:

373–375 Adolf Theobald Verlag
376–378 Modern Medicine

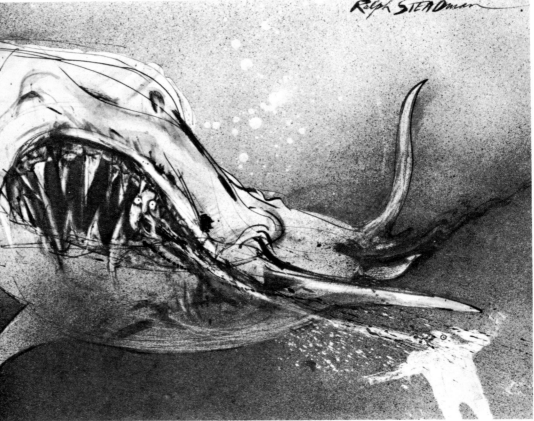

374

373

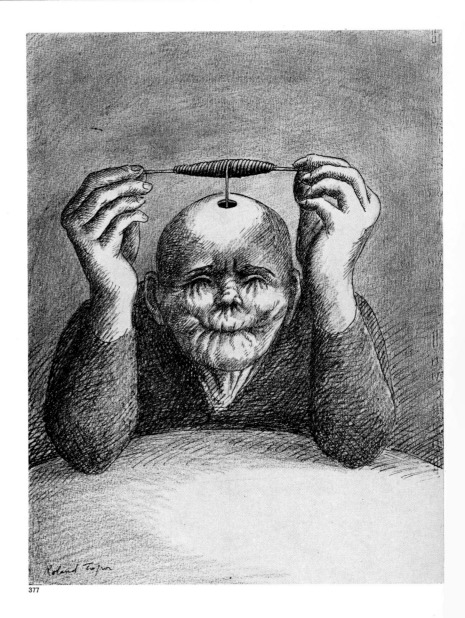

377

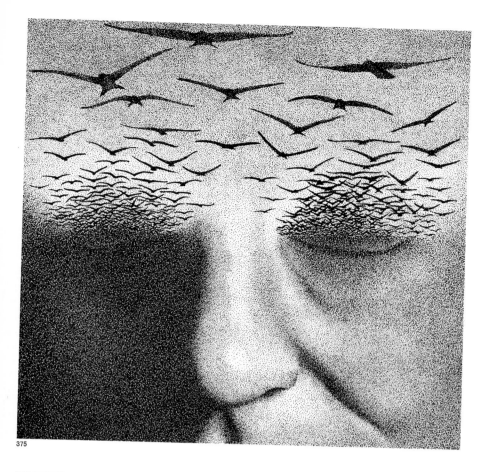

375

376

Monument to Pain   Don Ivan Punchatz

378

373 Vignette from an article in the magazine of popular psychology *Warum!* on the behaviour of the woman boss. (GER)
374 Drawing in black and red illustrating an article in the psychological paper *Warum!* on making money out of human anxiety, here in connection with a film about a white shark. (GER)
375 Illustration for an article in *Warum!* on sleep and dreams. (GER)
376–378 Illustrations by three different artists for a series on the problem of pain published in *Modern Medicine*. Fig. 376 shows the "grip of pain", Fig. 378 a "monument to pain". (USA)

373 Vignette aus dem in *Warum!* — einer populärwissenschaftlichen Zeitschrift für Psychologie — erschienenen Artikel über das Verhalten des weiblichen Boss gegenüber den Untergebenen. (GER)
374 Zeichnung in Schwarz und Rot zu einem Artikel in der psychologischen Zeitschrift *Warum!* Er zeigt am Beispiel des Films «Der weisse Hai» wie aus menschlichen Angstzuständen Profit geschlagen werden kann. (GER)
375 Illustration zu einem Artikel in *Warum!* über Schlaf und Träume. (GER)
376–378 Illustrationen von drei verschiedenen Künstlern zu einer Serie in der Zeitschrift *Modern Medicine* über den Schmerz. Abb. 376: vom Schmerz gepeinigt; Abb. 378: ein Monument zu Ehren des Schmerzes. (USA)

373 Vignette d'un article paru dans le magazine *Warum!*, magazine de psychologie populaire. L'article est consacré à la façon d'agir d'un boss féminin. (GER)
374 Dessin en noir et rouge figurant dans le magazine psychologique *Warum!* Il accompagne un article qui explique en rapport avec le film «Le requin blanc» que l'anxiété peut se révéler être une affaire assez lucrative. (GER)
375 Illustration pour un article de *Warum!* traitant du sommeil et du rêve. (GER)
376–378 Illustrations de trois artistes différents figurant dans une série consacrée à la douleur. Celle-ci a été publiée dans *Modern Medicine*. La fig. 376: la douleur poignante; la fig. 378: un monument érigé à la douleur. (USA)

Trade Magazines
Fachzeitschriften
Revues professionnelles

379

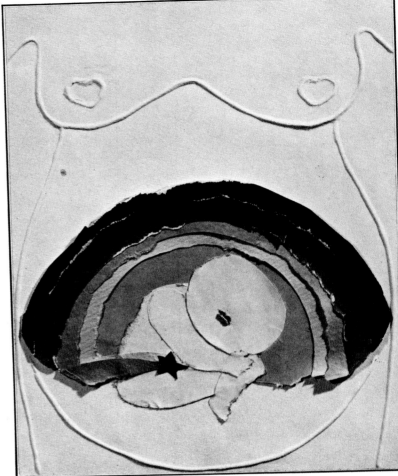

380

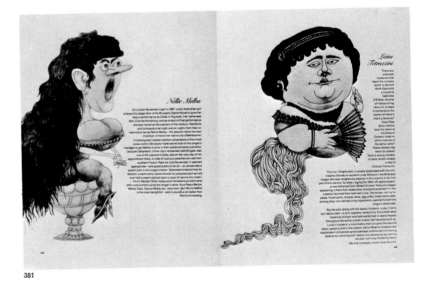

381

379 Illustration on textile fibres for fashion from a publication of the *Bayer* dyeworks. (GER)
380 Illustration in shades of green for a chapter on heredity in the book *Psychology, Explorations in Behavior and Experience* by Mednick, Higgins and Kirschenbaum. (USA)
381 Double spread from *Lithopinion* magazine on the origins of the names of famous dishes. (USA)
382 Double spread from the typographic magazine *U&lc* with an alphabet to which 26 different illustrators contributed a letter. (USA)
383 Double spread from an article in *U&lc* written and illustrated by the late Jerome Snyder on the subject of famous couples linked by an ampersand. (USA)

379 Illustration über Textilfasern für Modeartikel, aus einer Publikation von *Bayer*. (GER)
380 Illustration in Grüntönen zu einem Kapitel über Vererbung aus dem Werk *Psychology, Explorations in Behavior and Experience* von Mednick, Higgins und Kirschenbaum. (USA)
381 Doppelseite aus *Lithopinion*. Artikel über die Herkunft der Namen bekannter Speisen. (USA)
382 Doppelseite aus der Zeitschrift für Typographie *U&lc* mit einem Alphabet, zu welchem 26 Illustratoren je einen Buchstaben beisteuerten. (USA)
383 Aus einem Artikel in *U & lc* über berühmte Paare, deren Namen durch ein Et-Zeichen verbunden sind. Der Artikel wurde vom verstorbenen Jerome Snyder geschrieben und illustriert. (USA)

379 Pour un article sur les fibres textiles figurant dans une publication de *Bayer*. (GER)
380 Illustration en tons verts accompagnant un chapitre sur l'hérédité, publié dans le livre *Psychology, Explorations in Behavior and Experience* par Mednick, Higgins et Kirschenbaum. (USA)
381 Page double de *Lithopinion* sur l'origine des noms de divers mets célèbres. (USA)
382 Page double d'un magazine typographique présentant un alphabet dont chacun des 26 caractères a été créé par un artiste différent. (USA)
383 Page double figurant dans un article d'*U&lc*, écrit et illustré par feu Jerome Snyder. L'article est consacré aux couples célèbres dont les noms s'unient par un 'et' commercial. (USA)

ARTIST / KÜNSTLER / ARTISTE:

379 Elisabeth von Janota-Bzowski
380 Frances Jetter
381, 383 Jerome Snyder

DESIGNER / GESTALTER / MAQUETTISTE:

381 Robert Hallock
382 Herb Lubalin

ART DIRECTOR / DIRECTEUR ARTISTIQUE:

380 Jules Perlmutter
381 Robert Hallock
382, 383 Herb Lubalin

AGENCY / AGENTUR / AGENCE – STUDIO:

382, 383 Lubalin, Smith, Carnase, Inc.

PUBLISHER / VERLEGER / EDITEUR:

379 Bayer AG
380 John Wiley and Sons, Inc.
381 Lithopinion Magazine
382, 383 International Typeface Corporation

Trade Magazines
Fachzeitschriften
Revues professionnelles

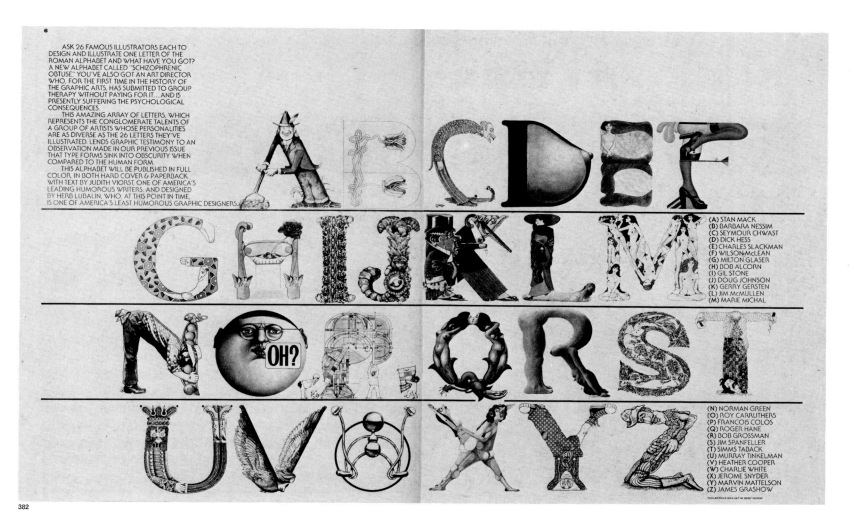

6

ASK 26 FAMOUS ILLUSTRATORS EACH TO DESIGN AND ILLUSTRATE ONE LETTER OF THE ROMAN ALPHABET AND WHAT HAVE YOU GOT? A NEW ALPHABET CALLED "SCHIZOPHRENIC OBTUSE." YOU'VE ALSO GOT AN ART DIRECTOR WHO, FOR THE FIRST TIME IN THE HISTORY OF THE GRAPHIC ARTS, HAS SUBMITTED TO GROUP THERAPY WITHOUT PAYING FOR IT... AND IS PRESENTLY SUFFERING THE PSYCHOLOGICAL CONSEQUENCES.

THIS AMAZING ARRAY OF LETTERS, WHICH REPRESENTS THE CONGLOMERATE TALENTS OF A GROUP OF ARTISTS WHOSE PERSONALITIES ARE AS DIVERSE AS THE 26 LETTERS THEY'VE ILLUSTRATED, LENDS GRAPHIC TESTIMONY TO AN OBSERVATION MADE IN OUR PREVIOUS ISSUE THAT TYPE FORMS SINK INTO OBSCURITY WHEN COMPARED TO THE HUMAN FORM.

THIS ALPHABET WILL BE PUBLISHED IN FULL COLOR, IN BOTH HARD COVER & PAPERBACK, WITH TEXT BY JUDITH VIORST, ONE OF AMERICA'S LEADING HUMOROUS WRITERS, AND DESIGNED BY HERB LUBALIN, WHO, AT THIS POINT IN TIME, IS ONE OF AMERICA'S LEAST HUMOROUS GRAPHIC DESIGNERS.

(A) STAN MACK
(B) BARBARA NESSIM
(C) SEYMOUR CHWAST
(D) DICK HESS
(E) CHARLES SLACKMAN
(F) WILSON McLEAN
(G) MILTON GLASER
(H) BOB ALCORN
(I) GIL STONE
(J) DOUG JOHNSON
(K) GERRY GERSTEN
(L) JIM McMULLEN
(M) MARIE MICHAL

(N) NORMAN GREEN
(O) ROY CARRUTHERS
(P) FRANCOIS COLOS
(Q) ROGER HANE
(R) BOB GROSSMAN
(S) JIM SPANFELLER
(T) SIMMS TABACK
(U) MURRAY TINKELMAN
(V) HEATHER COOPER
(W) CHARLIE WHITE
(X) JEROME SNYDER
(Y) MARVIN MATTELSON
(Z) JAMES GRASHOW

THIS ARTICLE WAS SET IN SERIF GOTHIC

David & Goliath

The way Samuel tells it in The Old Testament (1:17), this match of the millennia came off without much advance promotion. After all, you're not about to find a surplus of volunteers breaking down the gates, ready to do mano a mano with a guy who is 6 cubits and a span high. In case you're puzzled by biblical measurements, a cubit equals 21 inches and a span about 10—the total brings Goliath, our giant of Gath, up around the 11-foot mark; no small potatoes even in The National Basketball Association. No slouch when it comes to chutzpah, David, a mere bantamweight, offered to fight to the finish with the well armored and armed Philistine. To be sure, David with God in his corner had a great manager; but his stone-slinging stratagem seems to be of his own design. As we know, the big fight ended in the first round with a well-slung roundhouse to Goliath's temple. As the biblical report describes it: "And David put his hand in his bag, and took thence a stone, and slang it, and smote the Philistine in his forehead, that the stone sunk into his forehead; and he fell upon his face to the earth." Taking no chances, David followed the knockdown with a couple of whacks of Goliath's sword, lopping off the big fellow's dented noggin. David, who in later life had his share of problems, must have often thought that he who casts the first stone has time to check up after the fact to see if he is without sin.

Abercrombie & Fitch

There isn't much to say about David T. Abercrombie & Ezra H. Fitch, the former a lawyer and the latter a miner, prospector, and inventor. What brought them together was a mutual love of sports and one also concludes that they loved the profit that comes from the sale of sporting goods no less. In 1892 they started up in a tent-covered enterprise at lower Broadway where the merchandise was displayed in a manner closely resembling realistic conditions. Personal history from our sources seems to end there but time has shown that David and Ezra had latched on to something big. The notion of merchandising caught on, and not long after the tents were folded and exchanged for more permanent quarters. There was one move to 36th Street and 5th Avenue, but by 1917 Abercrombie & Fitch was established in the building on 45th Street and Madison Avenue New Yorkers know so well. There were several business acquisitions, city branches established, and on each occasion moving away from the simple ideas of the founders. Corporate history doesn't tell us what happened to Abercrombie & Fitch, how long they stayed around, when they died. Only the names remain on the building plaque which, when you come to think about it, is sort of sporting.

Leda & The Swan

Mythology and fairy tales seem to have a penchant for teaming up women with animals in rather intimate activity. Yet, it would appear that Leda coupling with a swan is about as kinky as you can get. But before you jump to the wrong conclusion, this seeming deviation turns out to be a simple case of top level adultery. First of all, Leda is really Thestias (daughter of Thestius), and she's married to Tyndareus, the King of Sparta. The swan is none other than Zeus in one of his zoomorphic guises, who seduces Leda while she's bathing. The children of the union are Castor and Pollux and/or Helen of Troy. Clytemnestra, the sister, is generally acknowledged as being fathered by Tyndareus. The more orthodox believe that all the children were Tyndareus' issue. It gets even more complicated as Castor and Pollux go on to heroic feats, an account too complicated for description in this short space. Whether it was Thestias and Tyndareus or Leda and The Swan and/or Zeus, the myth has kept a host of painters busy over the years, including Leonardo Da Vinci, a man for all cygnes.

Dempsey & Firpo

This heavyweight championship fight may have been short but it was anything but sweet. Luis Angel Firpo, the challenger, a tough, crude, powerful hombre from Argentina, was billed as the "Wild Bull of the Pampas." Jack Dempsey, the champion, was known as the "Manassa Mauler." The two met on September 14, 1923, before 82,000 people who forked over 1,188,603 dollars, for the spectator privilege, and that was when a dollar was a fully-packed 100 cents. In the first round it looked like the wild bull was going to be mauled to death. Although knocked down seven times, Firpo always managed to get up; then drawing upon a punch that must have started from the pampas, he hung the roundhouse on Jack. The first shot dropped the champ. When he arose, the unangelic Luis Angel tried to send Jack on a quick flight back to Manassa. A terrific shot lifted Dempsey clear out of the ring head first. Only with the aid of some shocked boxing reporters, with a sweat-covered heavyweight on their hands and typewriters, was the champ able to get back in the charmed square before the count of 10. To his credit, sturdy Jack was able to keep the Bull at bay for the rest of the round. Round two started out furiously, but Dempsey was the sharpshooter and Firpo remained the enraged bull. A short, powerful right caught El Toro, and before Firpo hit the canvas he was already dreaming of a white pampas.

The two never fought again. Dempsey went on fighting until the famous Tunney long-count and is still alive but not so well. Firpo also kept on his feet until, at the age of 40, he lost by a knockout in three rounds to Arturo Godoy, another Hispanic. That was only his second and last loss in 17 years of fighting. The wild bull retired to Argentina, became a successful businessman, and died in 1960 with both his ears intact.

THIS ARTICLE WAS SET IN KORINNA

384

386

385

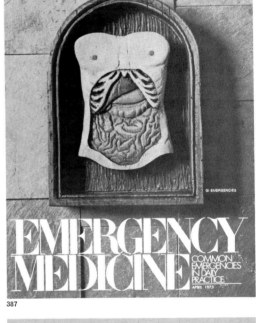

387

384 Double spread from *Emergency Medicine* opening an article on the fluid balance in the body. Ink drawing with pale washes set in a grey frame. (USA)
385 Woodcut illustrating an article on leprosy hazards today in *Emergency Medicine*. (USA)
386, 387 Covers of the monthly magazine *Emergency Medicine*. The issues contain articles on pain and on gastro-intestinal emergencies. (USA)
388 Blue-and-white illustration from *Emergency Medicine* on lesions of knee ligaments. (USA)
389 Double spread opening a feature on drug addiction in *Medical Economics*. (USA)
390 Illustration from an article on thirteen-year-olds in *Eltern*, a magazine for parents. Green landscape, light brown hair, blue sky. (GER)

384 Doppelseite aus *Emergency Medicine*, die einen Artikel über den Flüssigkeitsausgleich im Körper einleitet. Tuschzeichnung mit hellgrüner Lavierung in grauem Rahmen. (USA)
385 Holzschnitt zu einem Artikel über neue Leprafälle in *Emergency Medicine*. (USA)
386, 387 Umschläge der Monatsschrift *Emergency Medicine*. Die Nummern enthalten Artikel über den Schmerz und über Magen-Darm-Erkrankungen. (USA)
388 Illustration in Blau und Weiss zu einem Artikel über Verletzungen der Kniesehnen. (USA)
389 Doppelseite, die einen Artikel über Drogenmissbrauch einleitet. (USA)
390 Illustration aus der Zeitschrift *Eltern* zu einem Artikel über Dreizehnjährige. Grüne Landschaft, hellbraune Haare, blauer Himmel. (GER)

384 Page double d'*Emergency Medicine*, introduisant un article sur la balance des liquides du corps humain. Dessin au lavis vert pâle dans un encadrement gris. (USA)
385 Gravure sur bois pour un article d'*Emergency Medicine* consacré à la lèpre aujourd'hui. (USA)
386, 387 Couvertures du magazine mensuel *Emergency Medicine*. Ces deux numéros comprennent des articles sur la douleur et les affections gastro-intestinales. (USA)
388 Illustration en bleu et blanc figurant dans un article d'*Emergency Medicine* sur les lésions des ligaments du genou. (USA)
389 Page double introduisant un article sur la drogue. Elément de *Medical Economics*. (USA)
390 Illustration figurant dans un article sur les jeunes de treize ans, paru dans *Eltern*, un magazine pour les parents. Paysage vert, cheveux bruns clair, ciel bleu. (GER)

388

390

389

Doctor, could this be your kid?

By JEFF COX

If a child of yours begins experimenting with drugs, he's not necessarily on a one-way road to hell. But as this story of a doctor's son demonstrates, he'll need all the help you can give him.

Because LSD had given him glorious new insight into the mysteries of the universe and himself, Jim Atherby, 21-year-old college dropout and son of the popular Dr. Adrian Atherby, considered himself the luckiest guy in the world. But now the luckiest guy in the world couldn't stop shivering. He was feverish and his neck hurt. He couldn't forget the girl on his sex circuit who'd refused to sleep with him because of the swellings above his pubic area; she'd called them "some sex thing." He forced his eyes away from the wall and rolled them up into his head, thanking God "that your light of heaven is still with me." His last bottle of Southern Comfort was nearly empty, but he had four ounces of marijuana left. He'd been sitting on the couch for four days, sleeping and eating there, moving only to and from the bathroom. He'd been high so long he no longer knew whether he was high or not. And each fresh joint of marijuana only seemed to make his neck and head hurt worse.

Curley, his steady girl, was at work. He was living in her apartment, a neat little place

THE AUTHOR, a newspaperman now working in Pennsylvania, has safeguarded the privacy of his characters. "Except for that," he warrants, "it's all true."

on West 12th Street in New York City's Greenwich Village. Curley was awed by Jim and never told him to do anything, so she hadn't told him to see a doctor. He thought he had the flu and was waiting on the couch for the bug to eat itself into oblivion. But something was wrong — for a week he hadn't had the strength to move, make love, or talk much. These last four days he'd stayed drunk on Southern Comfort.

He thought of eating and it made him nauseous; he fell asleep and woke fitfully, spasms of nightmares and faraway voices flitting through his mind. He forgot where he was.

When he woke his eyes burned and the weak dirty light told him it was late afternoon. He finished the Southern Comfort and rolled a joint. Three puffs made him so dizzy he felt sick. Vomit rose in his throat. He threw off the blanket and rose into the chilly air. His head pounded and throbbed with pain; in the bathroom his knees turned to rubber. He leaned over the sink and, watching the drain grow larger and dimmer, passed out.

He awoke on the floor with a wet face; he'd gashed his head on the sink. He washed off the blood and put on a Band-Aid. Sitting on the toilet, his head dropped from fatigue almost into his underpants and he looked for the crab lice he'd been fighting ever since he came to the city.

"Jim. Jim! Wake up." It was Curley, home from work. He'd fallen asleep on the toilet. Laughing, he staggered up to his feet, grabbed Curley, pulled her into the bedroom, and tried to make love. But he was too feeble. Curley finally stopped him. "Jim, you should see a doctor — shouldn't you?"

"For the flu?" he said. "Never let a little flu get old Jim Atherby down. I'll beat it."

Two days later when the pain in his neck and head was so bad that he cried for an hour in Curley's arms, she called a cab and took him to her family's doctor on Fifth Avenue. The doctor, an internist, took one look at Jim and told him to strip for examination. The internist, let's call him Dr. Avrikos, hadn't seen such a raging case of mononucleosis in years. Jim's lymph glands were

MEDICAL ECONOMICS · SPECIAL ISSUE · APRIL 20, 1970 **23**

Trade Magazines
Fachzeitschriften
Revues professionnelles

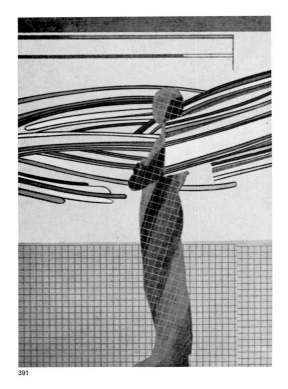

391

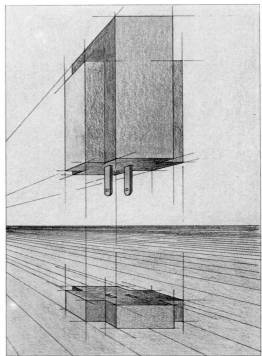

392

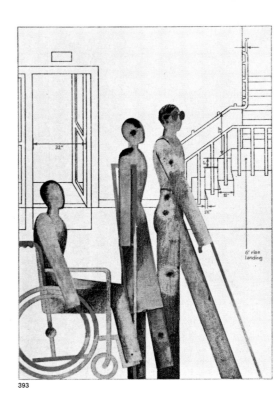

393

395

396

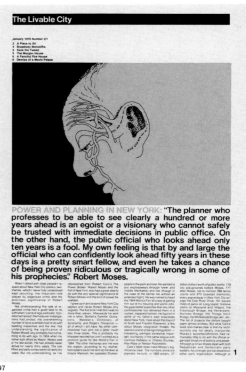

397

Trade Magazines
Fachzeitschriften
Revues professionnelles

391–395 Full-page colour illustrations and one typical double spread from *The Construction Specifier*. The articles deal with the liability of the engineer, building design to accommodate the disabled, the total energy concept and the use of high-performance glass in building. (USA)
396 Cover of *Trèfle/Kim*, magazine of the Swiss girl guides' movement. Black and white. (SWI)
397 Cover of *The Livable City*, a newsletter about the New York environment published by The Municipal Art Society. Blue and black. (USA)
398 Cover of the graphic design magazine *Print*. (USA)
399 Double spread opening an article on medical problems in the wilderness in *Emergency Medicine*. Full colour. (USA)
400 Illustration for an article on meat dishes in the television magazine *TV-Radio Zeitung*. Dark hues. (SWI)

391–395 Mehrfarbige Illustrationen und eine Doppelseite aus *The Construction Specifier*. Die Artikel behandeln die Verantwortung des Ingenieurs, Baupläne für Häuser für Körperbehinderte, Pläne für die Energieverteilung und die Benützung von Glas für Häuserbauten. (USA)
396 Umschlag der schweizerischen Pfadfinder-Zeitschrift *Trèfle/Kim*. Schwarzweiss. (SWI)
397 Titelbild von *The Livable City*, einer Informationszeitschrift über New Yorks Umgebung, herausgegeben von der städtischen Kunstgesellschaft. Blau und schwarz. (USA)
398 Umschlag der Graphic-Design-Zeitschrift *Print*. (USA)
399 Doppelseite aus einem Artikel über medizinische Probleme in der Wüste in *Emergency Medicine*. Mehrfarbig. (USA)
400 Illustration für einen Artikel über Fleischgerichte, in der Fernsehzeitschrift *TV-Radio Zeitung*. (SWI)

391–395 Illustrations pleines pages et page double figurant dans *The Construction Specifier*. Les articles traitent de la responsabilité des ingénieurs, de la conception de maisons pour les handicappés, du plan général pour la répartition d'énergie et de l'usage de verre pour la construction de maisons. (USA)
396 Couverture de *Trèfle/Kim*, magazine officiel des éclaireuses suisses. Noir et blanc. (SWI)
397 Couverture de *The Livable City*, un bulletin d'information sur la banlieue de New York. Ce bulletin est publié par la Municipal Art Society. Bleu et noir. (USA)
398 Couverture de *Print*, magazine d'art graphique. (USA)
399 Page double introduisant un article sur les problèmes médicaux dans le désert. En polychromie. (USA)
400 Illustration pour un article consacré aux plats de viande. Article du télé-magazine *TV-Radio Zeitung*. Tons foncés. (SWI)

399

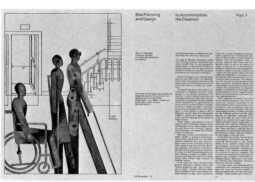

394

398

400

401

402

403

404

401 Illustration (a murderer goes free) from an article on criminal informants in *New York*. (USA)
402 Black-and-white illustration from a feature in *New York* on the city's financial plight. (USA)
403 Full-page illustration in black and blue for an article in *New York* magazine on rock music and the Rolling Stones. (USA)
404 Full-page illustration in full colour for an article in *New York* magazine on Muhammad Ali as a black racist. (USA)
405, 406 Illustration in actual size and complete double spread from an article in *New York* on the secret deals of oil cartels. Sheik Abdullah Sulaiman counts gold sovereigns. (USA)

401 Illustration (ein Mörder in der Freiheit) aus einem Artikel über Spitzel. (USA)
402 Illustration aus einem Artikel über die finanziellen Schwierigkeiten der Stadt New York. (USA)
403 Ganzseitige Illustration in Schwarz und Blau aus der Zeitschrift *New York* über Rock-Musik und die Rolling Stones. (USA)
404 Ganzseitige, mehrfarbige Illustration für einen Artikel in *New York* über Muhammad Ali, der als schwarzer Rassist dargestellt wird. (USA)
405, 406 Illustration in Originalgrösse und vollständige Doppelseite aus einem Artikel in *New York* über geheime Verhandlungen der Öl-Kartelle. (USA)

401 Illustration (un assassin en liberté) d'un article sur les délateurs criminels. (USA)
402 Illustration noir-blanc d'un article de *New York* sur la faillite de la ville de New York. (USA)
403 Illustration pleine page (noir et bleu) faisant partie d'un article du magazine *New York*; cet article est consacré à la musique rock et aux Rolling Stones. (USA)
404 Illustration pleine page (en couleur) figurant dans un article du magazine *New York* sur Muhammad Ali, qui est caractérisé comme raciste noir. (USA)
405, 406 Illustration (en grandeur nature) et page double où elle figure. Article du magazine *New York*, consacré aux affaires secrètes des cartels pétroliers. (USA)

Trade Magazines
Fachzeitschriften
Revues professionnelles

405

ARTIST / KÜNSTLER / ARTISTE:

401 James McMullan
402 David Levine
403 Christian Piper
404 John O'Leary
405, 406 David Wilcox

DESIGNER / GESTALTER / MAQUETTISTE:

405, 406 Walter Bernard/Milton Glaser

ART DIRECTOR / DIRECTEUR ARTISTIQUE:

401–406 Walter Bernard/Milton Glaser

PUBLISHER / VERLEGER / EDITEUR:

401–406 New York Magazine

406

407

407–409 Illustration and two double spreads from a feature in *New York* magazine on the secret deals of the oil cartels. Illustrated here are the crashing of Enrico Mattei's private plane, Dayan reaching the Suez Canal in 1967, and Egyptian tanks crossing the Suez Canal on the eve of Yom Kippur, 1973. All in full colour. (USA)
410 Vertical gatefold for use as a poster from *New York* magazine. It gives a select list of events taking place during the American Bicentennial Celebrations in New York. The frame and vignettes are mainly in brown, yellow and green shades. (USA)
411 Gatefold poster listing seafood restaurants in New York, from *New York* magazine. Illustrations: coloured ink drawings. (USA)
412 Illustration from *New York* for a news item about a restaurant which now serves mako, a man-eating shark. (USA)

Trade Magazines
Fachzeitschriften
Revues professionnelles

407–409 Illustration und zwei Doppelseiten aus einem Artikel der Zeitschrift *New York* über die geheimen Übereinkünfte der Ölkartelle. Die Illustrationen zeigen den Absturz von Enrico Matteis Privatflugzeug, General Dayan, als er 1967 den Suezkanal erreichte und ägyptische Panzer, die am Vorabend des Yom-Kippur-Krieges, 1973, den Suezkanal überqueren. (USA)
410 Seite mit quergefalztem Ausleger aus der Zeitschrift *New York*. Auf diesem Poster sind alle im Rahmen der amerikanischen 200-Jahr-Feierlichkeiten stattfindenden Manifestationen aufgeführt. Rahmen und Vignetten hauptsächlich in Braun-, Gelb- und Grüntönen. (USA)
411 Poster mit Ausleger aus der Zeitschrift *New York*. Es werden hier die Namen von newyorker Fischspezialitäten-Restaurants aufgeführt. Kolorierte Tuschzeichnungen. (USA)
412 Illustration aus den Lokal-Nachrichten der Zeitschrift *New York*, hier zu einem Artikel über ein Restaurant, in welchem Mako, ein menschenfressender Hai, serviert wird. (USA)

407–409 Illustration et deux doubles pages d'un article de *New York* sur les affaires secrètes des cartels pétroliers. Les illustrations se réfèrent à l'écrasement de l'avion privé d'Enrico Mattei, à Dayan qui arrive au Canal de Suez en 1967 et aux chars égyptiens traversant le Canal de Suez à la veilles de la guerre Yom Kippur en 1973. En polychromie. (USA)
410 Illustration à replis vertical publiée sous forme d'affiche par le magazine *New York*. Elle présente une liste détaillée de tous les événements et manifestations ayant lieu à l'occasion de l'année bicentenaire à New York. Prédominance de tons bruns, jaunes et verts quant à l'encadrement et aux vignettes. (USA)
411 Affiche à replis figurant dans le magazine *New York*. Elle présente les noms des restaurants newyorkais qui servent des fruits de mer. Illustrations: dessins à la plume coloriés. (USA)
412 Illustration tirée de la rubrique des faits divers du magazine *New York*. Elle se réfère à un restaurant où l'on sert du mako, un requin féroce. (USA)

408

409

410

411

412

ARTIST / KÜNSTLER / ARTISTE:

407, 409 Richard Hess
408 Melinda Bordelon
410 John O'Leary
411 Mel Furukawa
412 Seymour Chwast

DESIGNER / GESTALTER / MAQUETTISTE:

408, 411 Walter Bernard/Milton Glaser
410 Tom Bentkowski

ART DIRECTOR / DIRECTEUR ARTISTIQUE:

407—412 Walter Bernard/Milton Glaser

PUBLISHER / VERLEGER / EDITEUR:

407—412 New York Magazine

413

La nuova professione di Dorothy Grannis

Racconto di Sally Benson illustrato da Adelchi Galloni

414

415

416

ARTIST / KÜNSTLER / ARTISTE:

413 Pietro Bestetti
414 Adelchi Galloni
415 John O'Leary
416 Robert Grossman
417 Eugène Mihaesco
418 Barbara Nessim
419 Georges Lacroix

ART DIRECTOR / DIRECTEUR ARTISTIQUE:

414 Anita Klinz
415 Carolyn Buckley
416–418 Walter Bernard/Milton Glaser
419 David Hillman

PUBLISHER / VERLEGER / ÉDITEUR:

413 Corriere della Sera
414 Arnoldo Mondadori
415 New Times Magazine
416–418 New York Magazine
419 IPC Magazines Ltd.

413 Black-and-white illustration on the subject of letters to the newspapers, published in the magazine *Il Mondo*. (ITA)
414 Double spread opening a short story in the magazine *Duepiù*. Black outlines, objects and persons in colour. (ITA)
415 Full-page illustration in *New Times* magazine for an article on the art of acting in television spots. Full colour. (USA)
416 Full-page illustration for an article in *New York* on Arab oil and the big oil companies. (USA)
417 Full-page illustration, black on olive, for an article in *New York* on a therapy group. (USA)
418 Full-page illustration for an article in *New York* on the human sexual life cycles—here happy eighteen in pastel shades. (USA)
419 Full-page illustration for a story in *Nova* entitled "The Rescue". Black and white. (GBR)

413 Schwarzweisse Illustration, die sich auf Leserbriefe in der Zeitschrift *Il Mondo* bezieht. (ITA)
414 Doppelseite zu einer Kurzgeschichte, erschienen in der Zeitschrift *Duepiù*. Schwarze Konturen, Objekte und Personen mehrfarbig. (ITA)
415 Ganzseitige Illustration in *New Times* für einen Artikel über das schauspielerische Können in Werbe-Spots. Mehrfarbig. (USA)
416 Ganzseitige Illustration für einen Artikel in der Zeitschrift *New York* über arabisches Öl und die grossen Öl-Firmen. (USA)
417 Ganzseitige Illustration (schwarz auf Olive) für einen Artikel über Gruppentherapien, erschienen in *New York*. (USA)
418 Ganzseitige Illustration für einen Artikel in *New York* über die Zyklen im Sexualleben des Menschen – hier die glückliche Zeit mit 18 Jahren. Pastelltöne. (USA)
419 Ganzseitige Illustration für eine Geschichte mit dem Titel «Die Rettung», erschienen in *Nova*. Schwarzweiss. (GBR)

413 Illustration en noir et blanc se référant aux lettres que les lecteurs adressent aux journaux. Article publié dans le magazine *Il Mondo*. (ITA)
414 Page double introduisant une nouvelle dans le magazine *Duepiù*. Contours noirs, objets et personnes en couleurs. (ITA)
415 Illustration pleine page du magazine *New Times* pour un article sur l'art dramatique et la télévision commerciale. En polychromie. (USA)
416 Illustration pleine page figurant dans un article consacré au pétrol arabe et aux grandes compagnies pétrolières. (USA)
417 Illustration pleine page (noir et olive) tirée d'un article qui traite de la psychothérapie en groupes. (USA)
418 Illustration pleine page figurant dans un article du magazine *New York* sur les cycles de la vie sexuelle de l'homme – ici la vie heureuse à dix-huit ans. Tons pastel. (USA)
419 Illustration pleine page pour une histoire intitulée «le sauvetage». Noir-blanc. (GBR)

23

424

420 Double spread from an article on intelligence tests in *The Sunday Times Magazine*. (GBR)
421, 422 Double spread, with detail of one illustration, from an article on American snakes published in the magazine *Travel & Leisure*. (USA)
423 Illustration for a short story in *Ms.* magazine. Full page, full colour. (USA)
424 Full-page illustration, in full colour, for a reportage about a not-so-vicious German sheepdog in *Chicago* magazine. (USA)
425 Portrait of a collector of birds' eggs from *Westways* magazine. Brown shades. (USA)

420 Doppelseite aus einem Artikel über Intelligenz-Tests im *Sunday Times Magazine*. (GBR)
421, 422 Doppelseite mit Detail einer Illustration, aus einem Artikel über amerikanische Schlangen, erschienen in der Zeitschrift *Travel & Leisure*. (USA)
423 Illustration für eine Kurzgeschichte in der Zeitschrift *Ms.* Ganzseitig, mehrfarbig. (USA)
424 Ganzseitige Illustration für eine Reportage über einen nicht so boshaften deutschen Schäferhund, aus der Zeitschrift *Chicago*. (USA)
425 Portrait eines Vogeleier-Sammlers, erschienen in der Zeitschrift *Westways*. Brauntöne. (USA)

420 Page double figurant dans un article sur les tests d'intelligence, article publié dans le supplément hebdomadaire du *Sunday Times*. (GBR)
421, 422 Page double et détail de l'illustration qui y figure. Elément d'un article sur les serpents américains publié dans le magazine *Travel & Leisure*. (USA)
423 Illustration pour une nouvelle publiée dans le magazine *Ms.* Pleine page en couleurs. (USA)
424 Illustration sur page double (en couleurs) figurant dans un reportage sur un berger allemand qui n'était pas trop vicieux. Article du magazine *Chicago*. (USA)
425 Portrait d'un collectionneur d'œufs d'oiseaux, figurant dans le magazine *Westways*. (USA)

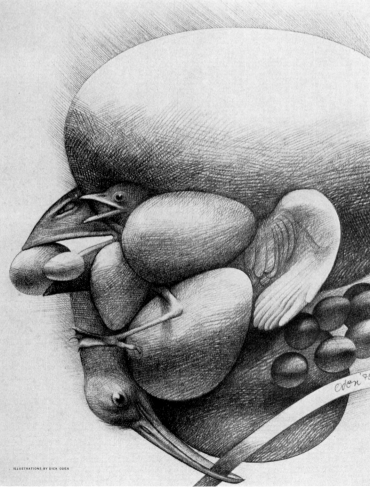

25

Magazine Illustrations
Zeitschriften-Illustrationen
Illustrations de périodiques

426

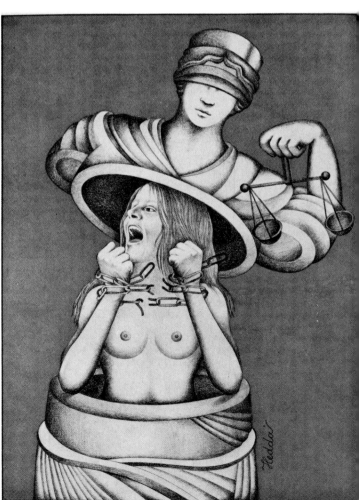

428

427

426 Full-page illustration for an article about cigars published in *Audience* magazine. Ochre shadow with black, green grass. (USA)
427 Black-and-white double spread from a magazine against the war in Vietnam published by Pax Forlag, Oslo. (NOR)
428 Illustration from *Evergreen* magazine. Black and white. (USA)
429, 430 Full-page black-and-white illustrations from articles in *Esquire* on Jimmy Carter, peanut farmer from Georgia, and Ronald Reagan, former Hollywood star, during the 1975/76 Presidential campaign. (USA)
431 Full-page colour illustration from an article on dinners that will wait till afterwards in *Playgirl* magazine. (USA)
432 Full-page illustration from *Human Behavior* magazine. Advice from both places. (USA)

426 Ganzseitige Illustration für einen Artikel über Cigarren, erschienen in der Zeitschrift *Audience*. Ockertöne mit Schwarz, grüner Rasen. (USA)
427 Schwarzweisse Doppelseite aus einer Zeitschrift gegen den Krieg in Vietnam, herausgegeben vom Pax Forlag, Oslo. (NOR)
428 Illustration aus der Zeitschrift *Evergreen*. Schwarzweiss. (USA)
429, 430 Ganzseitige, schwarzweisse Illustrationen aus Artikeln in *Esquire*, über Jimmy Carter, Erdnuss-Farmer in Georgia, und Ronald Reagan, ehemaliger Hollywood-Star. (USA)
431 Ganzseitige, farbige Illustration aus einem Artikel über verschiedene Gerichte, erschienen in der Zeitschrift *Playgirl*. (USA)
432 Ganzseitige Illustration aus der Zeitschrift *Human Behavior*. (USA)

426 Illustration pleine page pour un article sur les cigars, publié dans le magazine *Audience*. Tons ochre et noirs, pré vert. (USA)
427 Page double en noir et blanc figurant dans un magazine contre la guerre au Viêt-nam. Publication des Editions Pax Forlag, Oslo. (NOR)
428 Illustration tirée du magazine *Evergreen*. Noir et blanc. (USA)
429, 430 Illustrations pleines pages (noir et blanc) figurant dans deux articles du magazine *Esquire*. L'un présente Jimmy Carter en tant que propriétaire d'une plantation d'arachides en Géorgie, l'autre Ronald Reagan en tant qu'ancienne vedette de Hollywood. (USA)
431 Illustration pleine page en couleurs tirée d'un article consacré aux mets qui attendront jusqu'à plus tard. Publié dans le magazine *Playgirl*. (USA)
432 Illustration pleine page du magazine *Human Behavior*. (USA)

ARTIST / KÜNSTLER / ARTISTE:

426 Paul Davis
428 Hedda Johnson
429, 430 Robert Pryor
431 Mick Haggerty
432 Roseanne Litzinger

DESIGNER / GESTALTER / MAQUETTISTE:

427 Bruno Oldani

ART DIRECTOR / DIRECTEUR ARTISTIQUE:

426 Milton Glaser/Seymour Chwast
427 Bruno Oldani
428 Ken Deardoff
429, 430 Bob Ciano
431 Lloyd Ziff
432 Annemarie Clark

AGENCY / AGENTUR / AGENCE – STUDIO:

426, 428 Push Pin Studios, Inc.
427 Designstudio Bruno Oldani
429, 430 John Locke Studio
431 Salisbury-Ziff

PUBLISHER / VERLEGER / EDITEUR:

426 Hill Publishing
427 Pax Forlag
429, 430 Esquire, Inc.
431 Playgirl Magazine
432 Manson Western Corporation

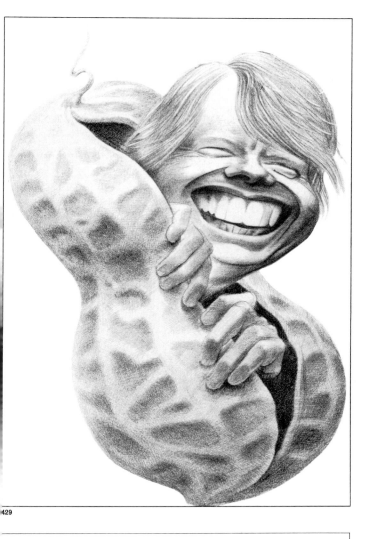

429

431

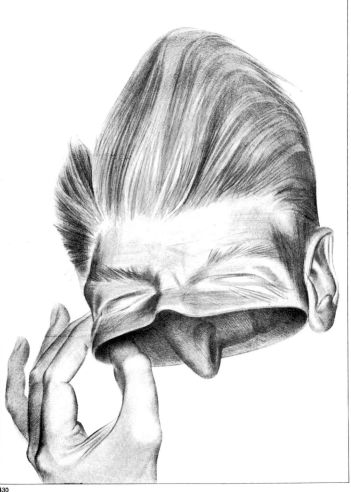

430

432

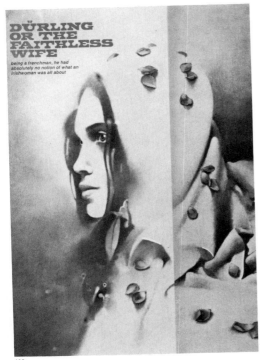

433

434

435

433 Page opening a short story in *Playboy* magazine. (USA)
434 Page opening a fiction feature about a man with a voice in his head in *Playboy* magazine. (USA)
435, 436 Illustration and complete corresponding double spread opening a feature in *Playboy* magazine about a man who suffers from hallucinations. (USA)
437 Full-page illustration in full colour from a feature in *Playboy* about a man who caught flies for Howard Hughes. (USA)
438 Illustration from a feature in *Playboy* magazine. Full page, full colour. (USA)
439 Double spread from a profile on Charles Bronson in *Playboy* magazine. Bulldog in dark brown shades. (USA)
440 Double spread from a profile on Henry Kissinger in *Playboy*. (USA)

433 Erste Seite einer Kurzgeschichte, die in der Zeitschrift *Playboy* erschien. (USA)
434 Titelseite einer Kurzgeschichte aus *Playboy* über einen Mann, der Stimmen hörte in seinem Kopf. (USA)
435, 436 Illustration und entsprechende Doppelseite aus der Zeitschrift *Playboy*. Titelseite zu einem Artikel über einen Mann, der unter Halluzinationen leidet. (USA)
437 Ganzseitige Illustration in Farbe aus einem Artikel in *Playboy* über einen Mann, der für Howard Hughes Fliegen fing. (USA)
438 Illustration zu einem Artikel in der Zeitschrift *Playboy*. Mehrfarbig. (USA)
439 Doppelseite aus einem Artikel in *Playboy* über Charles Bronson. Bulldogge in dunklen Brauntönen. (USA)
440 Doppelseite aus einem Artikel über Henry Kissinger, der in der Zeitschrift *Playboy* erschien. (USA)

433 Page introduisant une nouvelle publiée dans le magazine *Playboy*. (USA)
434 Première page d'un roman traitant d'un homme qui entend parler une voix dans sa tête. Elément du magazine *Playboy*. (USA)
435, 436 Illustration et page double introduisant un article du magazine *Playboy* sur un homme qui souffre de hallucinations. (USA)
437 Illustration pleine page en couleurs figurant dans un article du magazine *Playboy*. Il raconte l'histoire d'un homme qui attrape des mouches pour Howard Hughes. (USA)
438 Illustration pour un article du magazine *Playboy*. Pleine page en couleurs. (USA)
439 Page double figurant dans un article sur Charles Bronson, publié dans *Playboy*. Bouledogue en tons bruns foncé. (USA)
440 Page double introduisant un portrait sur Henry Kissinger qui a paru dans le magazine *Playboy*. (USA)

Magazine Illustrations
Zeitschriften-Illustrationen
Illustrations de périodiques

436

ARTIST / KÜNSTLER / ARTISTE:

433 Martin Hoffman (Photo)
434 Dan Morrill
435, 436 Jean Michel Folon
437 Eraldo Carugati
438 Ignacio Gomez
439 Melinda Bordelon
440 Bill Utterback

DESIGNER / GESTALTER / MAQUETTISTE:

433 Roy Moody
434 Kerig Pope
435, 436 Gordon Mortensen
439, 440 Len Willis

ART DIRECTOR / DIRECTEUR ARTISTIQUE:

433–440 Arthur Paul

PUBLISHER / VERLEGER / EDITEUR:

433–440 Playboy Enterprises, Inc.

437

438

439

440

147

I'M SITTING in my office on 34th Street, cleaning the blood and part of my aunt's large intestine out of my .38, when this sharp sheila comes in and sashays on over to my desk. She's got a pair of galoshes on her that sure look waterproof. After we size each other up, she tells me her name is Myrna Leroy and that her sister Gesundheit is missing.

"How long has she been missing, toots?" I asks, taking out a flask.

"Seventeen years," she says, weeping into her hankie.

"Maybe you better sit down," I says, "and tell me about it."

III

"Oh, you haven't heard anything yet, Mr. Monroe," she says sweetly.

"Call me Elsie," I says.

So she continues. Seems this Esprit fellow had big plans for Gesundheit. He was part owner of a circus and since Gesundheit was brought up by apes, she'd be a whiz on the trapeze. So he kidnaped her and took her off to a dark cave somewhere west of the Jersey Turnpike. One day she breaks a milk bottle over his noodle and tries to escape.

"Then what?" I asks.

"She went to the store to get another bottle of milk."

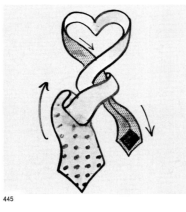

II

So she tells me this crazy story about how her sister was kidnaped by the vicious cad and ex-president of France, Lord Axel Esprit; how he carried her off to a Kenya motel, where he planned to ravish her and drink an iced coffee; how she'd been shipwrecked and brought up by a bunch of apes. . . .

"Wait a minute," I says. "You don't expect me to believe any of this salami, do you, sister?"

But her big brown eyes tell me that she's on the level. Since this is the first time I've ever heard a pair of big brown eyes talk, I decide to listen.

IV

Well, none of this is making much sense to me, but I let the dame go on. Being a private eye, you meet all kinds of crazy dames and the best thing to do is humor them and then take all their dough.

"So," I says, putting out my cigarette on my chin, "keep talking, baby."

So she goes on with the story, telling me how Esprit has a whole covey of dames locked in his basement, how he likes to dress up in skeleton suits on Saturday afternoons and scare people, how he always tucks his necktie into his pants——

441

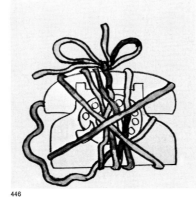

445

446

447

448

ARTIST / KÜNSTLER / ARTISTE:

441, 442 Robert Andrew Parker
443 Victor Hubbard
444 Peter Palombi
445–448 T. A. Lewandowski
449 Donna Brown

DESIGNER / GESTALTER / MAQUETTISTE:

441 Gordon Mortensen
444 Kerig Pope

ART DIRECTOR / DIRECTEUR ARTISTIQUE:

441–444 Arthur Paul
445–448 Peter Knapp
449 David Hillman

PUBLISHER / VERLEGER / EDITEUR:

441–444 Playboy Enterprises, Inc.
445–448 Elle/France Editions et Publications
449 IPC Magazines Ltd.

Magazine Illustrations
Zeitschriften-Illustrationen
Illustrations de périodiques

442

443

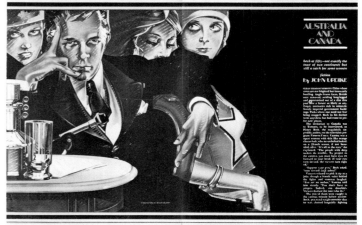

444

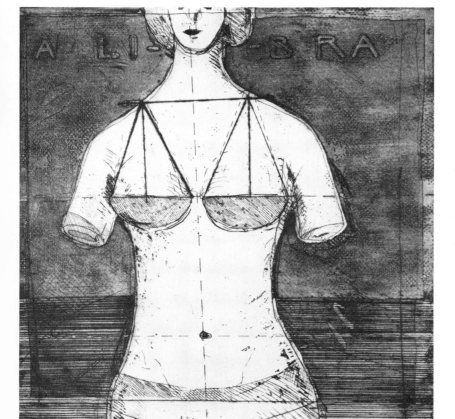

449

441, 442 Double spread from an old-style dime mystery published in an issue of *Playboy*. Full colour illustrations on yellowish paper, as shown in Fig. 442. (USA)
443 Colour illustration from an article in *Playboy* magazine on how to make money when other people are losing theirs. (USA)
444 Colour illustration opening a story in *Playboy* magazine. (USA)
445—448 From a series of drawings used to illustrate a column in the women's magazine *Elle* in which readers recount stories of the heart. (FRA)
449 Black-and-white drawing interpreting the sign Libra, from an astrological feature published in *Nova* magazine. (GBR)

441, 442 Eine im Stil der früheren Groschen-Romane aufgemachte Doppelseite aus einer Nummer von *Playboy*. Mehrfarbige Illustrationen auf gelblichem Papier. (USA)
443 Mehrfarbige Illustration zu einem Artikel in der Zeitschrift *Playboy*. Er klärt die Leser darüber auf, wie sie Geld machen können in einer Zeit, in welcher andere Leute ihr Geld verlieren. (USA)
444 Mehrfarbige Illustration zu einer Geschichte in *Playboy*. (USA)
445—448 Aus einer Serie von Zeichnungen, die in der Frauenzeitschrift *Elle* zur Illustrierung der Rubrik dienen, in welcher Leserinnen ihre Schicksale erzählen. (FRA)
449 Schwarzweiss-Zeichnung als Interpretation des Sternzeichens Waage. Aus einem Artikel über Astrologie, der in der Zeitschrift *Nova* erschien. (GBR)

441, 442 Page double s'inspirant des anciens romans de quatre sous. Elle figure dans un numéro du magazine *Playboy*. Illustrations en couleurs sur papier jaunâtre (voir la fig. 442). (USA)
443 Illustration en couleur accompagnant un article du magazine *Playboy* sur les possibilités de gagner de l'argent pendant que les autres le perdent. (USA)
444 Illustration en couleurs introduisant une histoire dans le magazine *Playboy*. (USA)
445—448 Exemples d'une série de dessins illustrant la rubrique «Courrier du cœur» du magazine féminin *Elle*. (FRA)
449 Dessin en noir et blanc interprétant le signe de la Balance. Il figure dans un article du magazine *Nova* sur l'astrologie. (GBR)

ARTIST / KÜNSTLER / ARTISTE:

450 Günther Blum
451 Gilbert Stone/Roger Hane
452 Ignacio Gomez
453 Karin Welponer
454 Jan Peter Tripp
455, 456 Katrin Lindley

DESIGNER / GESTALTER / MAQUETTISTE:

450, 453 Angelika Bronder
451 Tom Staebler
455, 456 George Guther

ART DIRECTOR / DIRECTEUR ARTISTIQUE:

450, 453–456 Rainer Wörtmann
451, 452 Arthur Paul

PUBLISHER / VERLEGER / EDITEUR:

450, 453–456 Heinrich Bauer Verlag
451, 452 Playboy Enterprises, Inc.

**Magazine Illustrations
Zeitschriften-Illustrationen
Illustrations de périodiques**

453

454

455

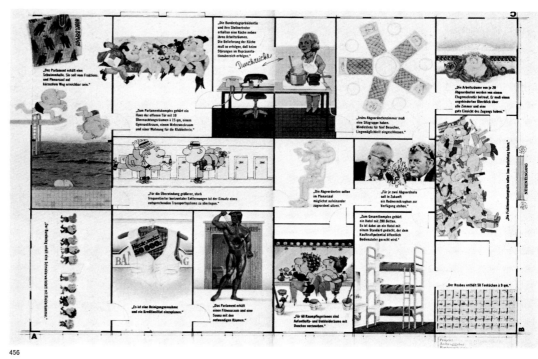

456

459

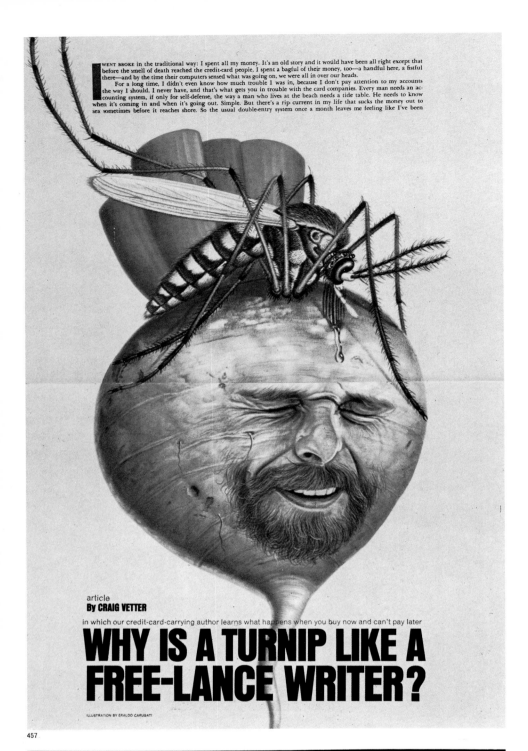

WENT BROKE in the traditional way: I spent all my money. It's an old story and it would have been all right except that before the smell of death reached the credit-card people, I spent a bagful of their money, too—a handful here, a fistful there—and by the time their computers sensed what was going on, we were all in over our heads.

For a long time, I didn't even know how much trouble I was in, because I don't pay attention to my accounts the way I should. I never have, and that's what gets you in trouble with the card companies. Every man needs an accounting system, if only for self-defense, the way a man who lives at the beach needs a tide table. He needs to know when it's coming in and when it's going out. Simple. But there's a rip current in my life that sucks the money out to sea sometimes before it reaches shore. So the usual double-entry system once a month leaves me feeling like I've been

article
By CRAIG VETTER

in which our credit-card-carrying author learns what happens when you buy now and can't pay later

WHY IS A TURNIP LIKE A FREE-LANCE WRITER?

ILLUSTRATION BY ERALDO CARUGATI

457

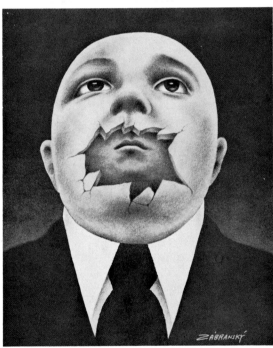

462

458

457 Double spread with full-colour illustration opening an article in *Playboy* about a credit-card owner who got into debt. (USA)
458 Page opening an article on the experiences of a homicide squad in Boston. From *Playboy*. (USA)
459 Illustration for a book published in Milan. Black and blue. (ITA)
460 Page opening a feature in the women's magazine *Vogue*. Figure in pastel shades. (USA)
461 Black-and-white illustration for an article on the communications revolution in the *Saturday Review*. (USA)
462 Satirical drawing from the catalogue of an exhibition staged in Marostica. (CSR)
463 Full-page illustration for an article published in *Business Week* about coping with shortages. (USA)
464 Illustration from the magazine *Perspectives*. (CAN)

460

461

463

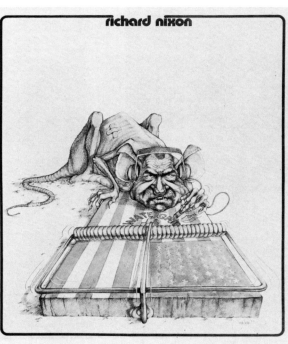

464

ARTIST / KÜNSTLER / ARTISTE:

457 Eraldo Carugati
458 Alex Ebel
459 Emanuele Luzzati
460 Rodica Prato
461 Cathy Hull
462 Vlasta Zabransky
463 Pierre Le-Tan
464 Serge Chapleau

DESIGNER / GESTALTER / MAQUETTISTE:

457 Gordon Mortensen
458 Fred Nelson

ART DIRECTOR / DIRECTEUR ARTISTIQUE:

457, 458 Arthur Paul
459 Cappelletti
460 Alexander Liberman
461 Judy Adele
463 Robert N. Essman
464 Gilles Daigneault

AGENCY / AGENTUR / AGENCE – STUDIO:

460 Jane Lander Associates
462 Gruppo Grafico Marosticense

PUBLISHER / VERLEGER / ÉDITEUR:

457, 458 Playboy Enterprises, Inc.
459 Adelphi Edizioni
460 Condé Nast Publications, Inc.
461 Saturday Review, Inc.
462 Gruppo Grafico Marosticense
463 Business Week
464 Perspectives

457 Doppelseite mit farbiger Illustration aus einem Artikel in *Playboy*, über einen Kreditkarten-Besitzer, der sich verschuldete. (USA)
458 Seite aus einem Artikel in *Playboy* über die Erfahrungen des Morddezernats in Boston. (USA)
459 Illustration für ein Buch. Schwarz und blau. (ITA)
460 Seite aus einem Artikel in der Frauenzeitschrift *Vogue*. Pastelltöne. (USA)
461 Schwarzweisse Illustration für einen Artikel über die Revolution im Fernmeldewesen, erschienen in der *Saturday Review*. (USA)
462 Satirische Zeichnung aus einem Ausstellungskatalog. (CSR)
463 Ganzseitige Illustration aus einem Artikel in *Business Week* über die Schwierigkeiten während der Rezession und wie man am besten damit fertig wird. (USA)
464 Illustration aus der Zeitschrift *Perspectives*. (CAN)

457 Première page double (illustration en couleurs) d'un article de *Playboy* sur un homme qui a une carte de crédit et qui est criblé de dettes. (USA)
458 Page introduisant un article consacré aux expériences d'une brigade qui s'occupe des homicides à Boston. Du magazine *Playboy*. (USA)
459 Illustration pour un livre publié à Milan. Noir et bleu. (ITA)
460 Première page d'un article du magazine féminin *Vogue*. Figure en tons pastel. (USA)
461 Illustration en noir et blanc figurant dans un article sur la révolution dans le domaine des communications. De la *Saturday Review*. (USA)
462 Dessin satirique publié dans le catalogue d'une exposition présentée à Marostica. (CSR)
463 Illustration pleine page d'un article de *Business Week* sur les crises en période de récession et comment ils peuvent être surmontées. (USA)
464 Illustration figurant dans le magazine *Perspectives*. (CAN)

Magazine Illustrations
Zeitschriften-Illustrationen
Illustrations de périodiques

465

466

ARTIST / KÜNSTLER / ARTISTE:

465 Mercer Mayer
466 Patrick Byrne
467 Elizabeth Wilson
468 Dickran Palulian
469 Gene Szafran
470 Don Ivan Punchatz

DESIGNER / GESTALTER / MAQUETTISTE:

466 Peter Kleinman
470 David Kaestle

ART DIRECTOR / DIRECTEUR ARTISTIQUE:

465, 468, 469 Joe Brooks
466 Peter Kleinman
467, 470 Michael Gross

468

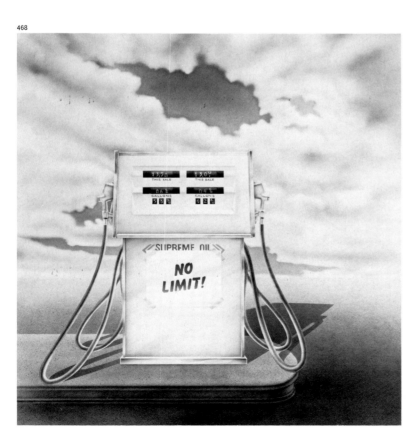

469

467

AGENCY / AGENTUR / AGENCE – STUDIO:

467, 470 Pellegrini Kaestle & Gross Inc.

PUBLISHER / VERLEGER / EDITEUR:

465, 468, 469 Penthouse International
466, 467, 470 21st Century Communications Inc.

Magazine Illustrations
Zeitschriften-Illustrationen
Illustrations de périodiques

465 Full-page illustration from an article on the Irish in *Penthouse*. Full colour. (USA)
466 From a series of malicious wishes for famous figures, from *National Lampoon*. Here tennis ace Jimmy Connors. Full colour. (USA)
467 Double spread opening a Bicentennial article on guns in *National Lampoon*. (USA)
468 Illustration from *Penthouse*. (USA)
469 Illustration in dull hues opening an article in *Penthouse* on jail wardens. (USA)
470 Opening spread of an article on the beaver in *National Lampoon*. (USA)

465 Ganzseitige Illustration aus einem Artikel über die Iren. Mehrfarbig. (USA)
466 Aus einer Serie boshafter Wünsche an berühmte Personen, hier Tennis-Ass Jimmy Connors. Aus *National Lampoon*. Mehrfarbig. (USA)
467 Doppelseite aus *National Lampoon*, die einen Artikel über Pistolen einführt. (USA)
468 Ganzseitige Illustration aus der Zeitschrift *Penthouse*. (USA)
469 Illustration in matten Farben zu einem Artikel in *Penthouse* über Gefängniswärter. (USA)
470 Doppelseite aus *National Lampoon*, die einen Artikel über Biber einführt. (USA)

465 Illustration pleine page d'un article consacré aux Irlandais. En polychromie. (USA)
466 D'une série de vœux malicieux adressés à de célèbres personnages (ici Jimmy Connors) du magazine *National Lampoon*. (USA)
467 Page double introduisant un article de *National Lampoon* sur des pistolets. (USA)
468 Illustration de *Penthouse*. (USA)
469 Illustration en tons atténués introduisant un article consacré aux geôliers. (USA)
470 Première page double d'un article de *National Lampoon* consacré aux castors. (USA)

470

155

471

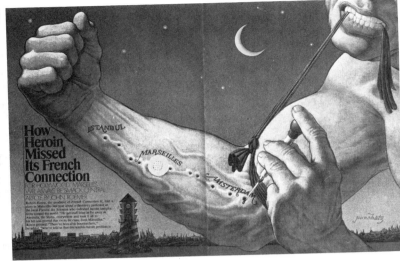

472

ARTIST / KÜNSTLER / ARTISTE:

471, 472 Don Ivan Punchatz
473—475 Erhard Göttlicher
476 Christian Piper

DESIGNER / GESTALTER / MAQUETTISTE:

471, 476 Jean-Pierre Holley
473—475 Michael Brock

ART DIRECTOR / DIRECTEUR ARTISTIQUE:

471 Jean-Pierre Holley/Don Menell
472 Jean-Pierre Holley
473—476 Don Menell

AGENCY / AGENTUR / AGENCE – STUDIO:

471, 472 Sketchpad Studio

PUBLISHER / VERLEGER / EDITEUR:

471—476 Playboy Publications, Inc.

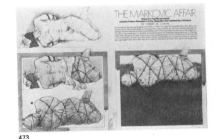

473

MURDER MOST FOUL

A VIOLENT ACT
JOLTS THE SERENITY
OF THE
PEACE-PREACHING
CHILDREN OF GOD

BY JEROME DOOLITTLE

The Victory Monu-
ment in Bangkok sits
in the middle of a
huge traffic circle. All
around the circle are
bus stops. Vendors sit
on the sidewalks
in the heat, sell-
ing mangoes
and durians

475

474

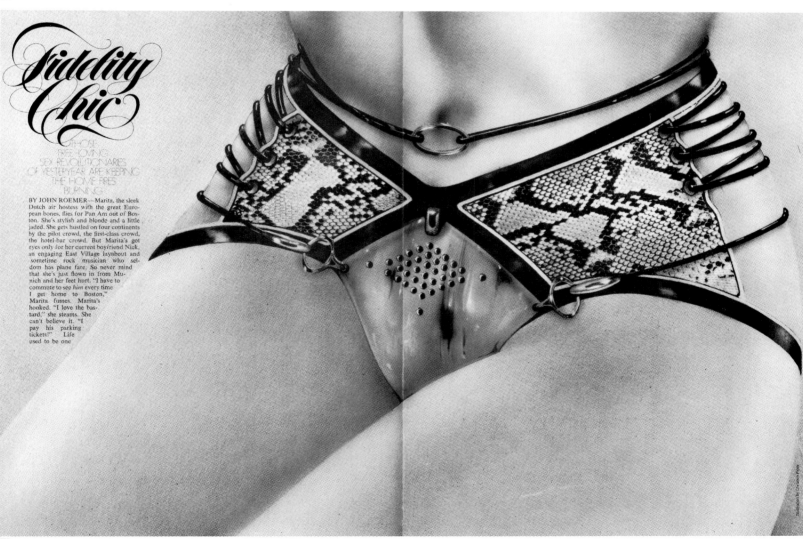

Fidelity Chic

THOSE FREE-LOVING SEX REVOLUTIONARIES OF YESTERYEAR ARE KEEPING THE HOME FIRES BURNING

BY JOHN ROEMER—Marita, the sleek Dutch air hostess with the great European bones, flies for Pan Am out of Boston. She's stylish and blonde and a little jaded. She gets hustled on four continents by the pilot crowd, the first-class crowd, the hotel-bar crowd. But Marita's got eyes only for her current boyfriend Nick, an engaging East Village layabout and sometime rock musician who seldom has plane fare. So never mind that she's just flown in from Munich and her feet hurt. "I have to commute to see *him* every time I get home to Boston," Marita fumes. Marita's hooked. "I love the bastard," she steams. She can't believe it. "I pay his parking tickets!" Life used to be one

476

478

479

477

477 Drawing in black and grey from the magazine *Pardon*. (GER)
478–481 Four sheets from a satirical weekly calendar published in the magazine *Pardon*. The examples poke fun in verse and drawings at promiscuous sex, Communism, young love and xenophobia. Fig. 478 in black and white, others in colour. (GER)
482, 483 Illustrations from a feature in the magazine *Pardon*, a "nostalgic retrospect" on the fading of the flower children. (GER)

477 Zeichnung in Schwarz und Grau aus der Zeitschrift *Pardon*. (GER)
478–481 Vier Blätter aus dem satirischen Wochenkalender der Zeitschrift *Pardon*. In Versen und durch Zeichnungen mokiert man sich über oberflächliche Sexbekanntschaften, Kommunismus, junge Liebe und Xenophobie. Abb. 478 in Schwarzweiss. (GER)
482, 483 Illustrationen zu einem Artikel in der Zeitschrift *Pardon* – eine nostalgische Retrospektive über das Abflauen der Bewegung der Blumenkinder. (GER)

477 Dessin en noir et gris figurant dans le magazine *Pardon*. (GER)
478–481 Quatre feuilles du calendrier satirique publié chaque semaine dans le magazine *Pardon*. On se moque – en vers ou à l'aide d'illustrations – de la promiscuité, du communisme, du premier amour et de la xénophobie. La fig. 478 en noir-blanc. (GER)
482, 483 Illustrations figurant dans un article du magazine *Pardon*: c'est une rétrospective nostalgique sur le mouvement des hippies. (GER)

Magazine Illustrations
Zeitschriften-Illustrationen
Illustrations de périodiques

480

482

481

ARTIST / KÜNSTLER / ARTISTE:

477 Jacques Cardon
478, 480, 481 Hans Arnold
479 Bengt Nyström
482, 483 Aoi Fujimoto

PUBLISHER / VERLEGER / EDITEUR:
477–483 Pardon Verlagsgesellschaft mbH

483

484

485

486

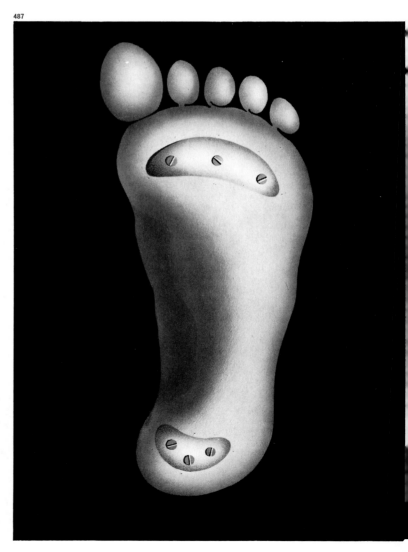

487

ARTIST / KÜNSTLER / ARTISTE:

484, 485 Marek Goebel
486 Jan Sawka
487 Edward Lutczyn
488–491 Günther Blum

PUBLISHER / VERLEGER / EDITEUR:

484–487 Szpilki
488–491 Pardon Verlagsgesellschaft mbH

ART DIRECTOR / DIRECTEUR ARTISTIQUE:

484–487 Marek Goebel

484, 485 "The autumn collection." Cartoon in two scenes from the satirical weekly *Szpilki*. (POL)
486 "To be a bird." Drawing from the weekly *Szpilki*. (POL)
487 Drawing for a cover of the satirical weekly *Szpilki*. (POL)
488–491 Two complete covers of the humorous monthly *Pardon* and details of the caricatures of two politicians—Genscher as a "slit-eared cactus" and Wehner with "hair on his tongue". (GER)

484, 485 «Die Herbstkollektion.» Karikatur aus der satirischen Wochenschrift *Szpilki*. (POL)
486 «Ein Vogel zu sein…» Zeichnung aus der Wochenzeitschrift *Szpilki*. (POL)
487 Umschlagzeichnung für eine Nummer der Wochenzeitschrift *Szpilki*. (POL)
488–491 Vollständige Umschläge der humoristischen Monatsschrift *Pardon* und Details der Karikaturen von zwei Politikern – Genscher als der schlitzohrige Kaktus und Wehner mit Haaren auf der Zunge. (GER)

484, 485 «La collection d'automne.» Dessin animé en deux scènes tiré de l'hebdomadaire satirique *Szpilki*. (POL)
486 «Etre un oiseau.» Dessin figurant dans l'hebdomadaire *Szpilki*. (POL)
487 Dessin de couverture de l'hebdomadaire satirique *Szpilki*. (POL)
488–491 Deux couvertures complètes du magazine mensuel humoristique *Pardon* et détails des illustrations qui y figurent. Elle représentent deux hommes politiques allemands – Genscher est caricaturé en tant que cactus «aux oreilles fourchues» et Wehner en tant que personne qui ne se laisse pas marcher sur les pieds. (GER)

489

490

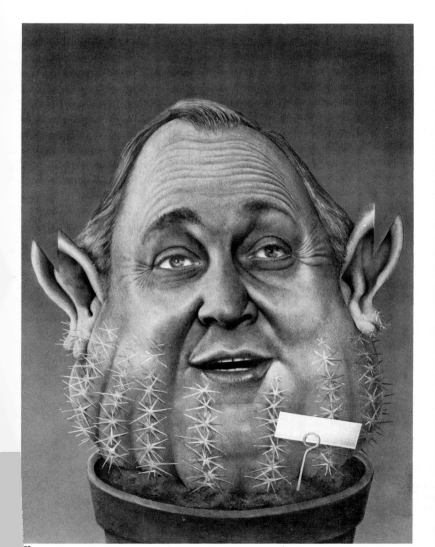
488

491

492

ARTIST / KÜNSTLER / ARTISTE:

492 Georges Lemoine
493, 494 Etienne Delessert
495 Colman Cohen
496, 498 Paul André Perret
497 Tina Mercie

DESIGNER / GESTALTER / MAQUETTISTE:

493, 494 Martin Berthommier

ART DIRECTOR / DIRECTEUR ARTISTIQUE:

492, 497 Denys Prache
493–496, 498 Etienne Delessert

PUBLISHER / VERLEGER / EDITEUR:

492–498 Bayard Presse

493

JE M'ORIENTE

Que feras-tu plus tard? Tout le monde vous pose cette question et vous vous croyez parfois obligés de répondre alors que vous n'en savez rien. Vous avez beaucoup d'idées mais vous n'avez aucune envie de choisir maintenant. Pourtant l'orientation scolaire vous y pousse mais n'est-ce pas trop tôt puisque vous ne connaissez encore ni vos possibilités, ni la réalité des métiers dont on vous parle? Alors pas de panique! Lisez soigneusement ce dossier. Vous verrez que l'avenir n'est pas si noir.

495

494

496

497

498

492 Illustration for a story about beans published in the French magazine for young people, *Record*. (FRA)
493, 494 Complete cover of the young people's magazine *Record* and detail of the portrait of Helder Camara. (FRA)
495 Cover of a dossier about the choice of a career published as part of *Record*. (FRA)
496 Portrait of Les Charlots, a French comic group, from *Record*. Full colour. (FRA)
497 Illustration for a fantastic story published in *Record*. (FRA)
498 Portrait of Gilbert Trigano of the Club Méditerannée on the opening page of *Record*. Face in pink shades on blue. (FRA)

492 Mehrfarbige Illustration zu einer Geschichte über Bohnen, die in der französischen Jugendzeitschrift *Record* publiziert wurde. (FRA)
493, 494 Vollständiger Umschlag des französischen Jugendmagazins *Record* und Detail des Portraits von Helder Camara. (FRA)
495 Titelseite eines Dossiers über Berufswahl, das als Teil des Jugendmagazins *Record* herausgegeben wird. (FRA)
496 Zu einem Artikel über die französische Komik-Gruppe Les Charlots. Aus *Record*. (FRA)
497 Illustration zu einer fantastischen Geschichte aus dem Jugendmagazin *Record*. (FRA)
498 Portrait von Gilbert Trigano, dem Gründer des Club Méditerannée, aus dem Jugendmagazin *Record*. Gesicht in Rosatönen auf blauem Grund. (FRA)

492 Illustration en couleurs accompagnant une histoire sur les harícots, publiée dans *Record*, un magazine français pour la jeune génération. (FRA)
493, 494 Couverture complète d'un numéro de *Record*, magazine pour les jeunes, et détail du portrait de Helder Camara. (FRA)
495 Couverture d'un dossier qui fait partie de chaque numéro du magazine *Record*. Celui-ci est consacré au choix des professions. (FRA)
496 Portrait d'un groupe de comiques français qui s'apelle Les Charlots. Illustration en couleurs figurant dans le magazine *Record*. (FRA)
497 Illustration pour une histoire fantastique publiée dans le magazine *Record*. (FRA)
498 Portrait de Gilbert Trigano du Club Méditerannée figurant sur la première page du magazine *Record*. Visage en tons roses sur fond bleu. (FRA)

Magazine Illustrations
Zeitschriften-Illustrationen
Illustrations de périodiques

499

502

ARTIST / KÜNSTLER / ARTISTE:

499, 502, 503 Fernando Puig Rosado
500 Hasan Fazlic
501 Jochen Widmann
504 Heinz Stieger

ART DIRECTOR / DIRECTEUR ARTISTIQUE:

499, 500, 502–504 Franz Mächler
501 Rolf Gillhausen/Franz Kliebhan

PUBLISHER / VERLEGER / EDITEUR:

499, 500, 502–504 Nebelspalter
501 Gruner & Jahr GmbH & Co.

Magazine Illustrations

503

499 ''Your papers!'' Humorous drawing from the satirical weekly *Nebelspalter*. (SWI)
500 A Yugoslav cartoonist's conception of dictatorship, from the *Nebelspalter*. (SWI)
501 Illustration (full colour) from an article in *Stern* on the brains of cats. (GER)
502 Humorous drawing (in colour, no caption) from the *Nebelspalter*. (SWI)
503 From a series on animal life in the *Nebelspalter*. The newly hatched bird has a green beak, those below it have yellow beaks that gradually turn red, the expiring bird (bottom right) has a completely red beak. (SWI)
504 Black-and-white humorous drawing from the *Nebelspalter*, without caption. (SWI)

499 «Ihre Papiere.» Humoristische Zeichnung aus der satirischen Wochenzeitschrift *Nebelspalter*. (SWI)
500 Ansicht eines jugoslawischen Karikaturisten über die Diktatur. Aus dem *Nebelspalter*. (SWI)
501 Mehrfarbige Illustration zu einem Artikel im *Stern* über das Katzengehirn. (GER)
502 Humoristische Zeichnung (in Farbe), die ohne Kommentar im *Nebelspalter* erschien. (SWI)
503 Aus einer Serie über das Tierleben im *Nebelspalter*. Der eben ausgeschlüpfte Vogel hat einen grünen Schnabel. Die Schnäbel der anderen Vögel röten sich langsam; der Schnabel des sterbenden Vogels ist rot. (SWI)
504 Humoristische Zeichnung, ohne Kommentar, aus dem *Nebelspalter*. Schwarzweiss. (SWI)

499 Dessin humoristique figurant dans l'hebdomadaire satirique *Nebelspalter*. (SWI)
500 Voilà la conception de la dictature illustré par un caricaturiste yougoslave. Du *Nebelspalter*. (SWI)
501 Illustration (en couleurs) d'un article du magazine *Stern* sur le sens de l'orientation des chats. (GER)
502 Dessin humoristique (en couleurs, sans commentaire) de l'hebdomadaire *Nebelspalter*. (SWI)
503 D'une série sur la vie animale, de *Nebelspalter*. Le petit oiseau a un bec vert, les oiseaux d'en bas ont des becs jaunes passant graduellement au rouge, l'oiseau mourant (en bas, à droite) a un bec tout rouge. (SWI)
504 Dessin humoristique noir-blanc (sans commentaire) figurant dans l'hebdomadaire *Nebelspalter*. (SWI)

500

501

504

Magazine Illustrations
Zeitschriften-Illustrationen
Illustrations de périodiques

ARTIST / KÜNSTLER / ARTISTE:

505, 506 Ivan Chermayeff
507, 509 Guy Billout
508 Seymour Chwast
510 Simms Taback
511 Marvin Mattelson
512 Isadore Seltzer

DESIGNER / GESTALTER / MAQUETTISTE:

510–512 Gary Schenk

ART DIRECTOR / DIRECTEUR ARTISTIQUE:

505–509, 511, 512 Henry Wolf
510 Gary Schenk

AGENCY / AGENTUR / AGENCE – STUDIO:

505–512 Henry Wolf Prod.

PUBLISHER / VERLEGER / EDITEUR:

505–512 Children's Television Workshop, Inc.

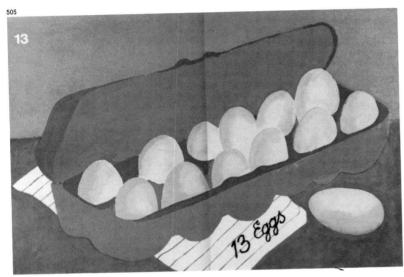

507

510

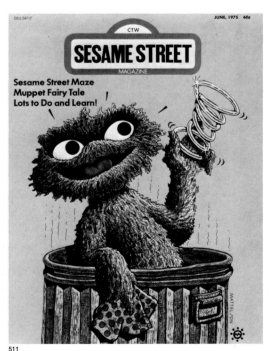

511

512

505 A counting spread (full colour) from the children's magazine *Sesame Street*. (USA)
506 Another counting spread from *Sesame Street*. Blue mice with red eyes, yellow ground. (USA)
507 A spread of hidden letters, from *Sesame Street*. (USA)
508 "Mixed-up-animals" in bright colours to be cut out and permuted, from *Sesame Street*. (USA)
509 Illustration for the letter T for tiger, small and capital, from *Sesame Street*. (USA)
510 Drawing exercise from *Sesame Street*, full colour. (USA)
511, 512 Colour covers for issues of *Sesame Street*, with two of the familiar characters that people it. (USA)

505 Mehrfarbige Doppelseite mit Zählspiel aus der Kinderzeitschrift *Sesame Street*. (USA)
506 Ein weiteres Zählspiel aus der Kinderzeitschrift *Sesame Street*. Blaue Mäuse mit roten Augen, gelber Grund. (USA)
507 Seite aus *Sesame Street* mit versteckten Buchstaben. (USA)
508 Wenn diese Seite auseinandergeschnitten wird, können die buntfarbenen Tiere beliebig kombiniert werden. (USA)
509 Illustration zum Buchstaben T wie Tiger aus der Zeitschrift *Sesame Street*. (USA)
510 Zeichenspiel aus der Kinderzeitschrift *Sesame Street*. (USA)
511, 512 Mehrfarbige Umschläge von *Sesame Street* mit zwei den Kindern wohlbekannten Figuren. (USA)

505 Page double (en couleurs) avec un jeu numérique, figurant dans le magazine *Sesame Street* pour enfants. (USA)
506 Un autre jeu numérique de *Sesame Street*. Souris bleus aux yeux rouges, fond jaune. (USA)
507 Page double de *Sesame Street*: lettres cachées. (USA)
508 Page à couper horizontalement pour ainsi permuter les animaux en couleurs vives. De *Sesame Street*. (USA)
509 Illustration pour la lettre T pour tigre, majuscule et minuscule, figurant dans le magazine *Sesame Street*. (USA)
510 Dessin à compléter en suivant les points numérotés. (USA)
511, 512 Couvertures couleurs du magazine *Sesame Street* avec deux caractères bien connus aux petits lecteurs. (USA)

ARTIST / KÜNSTLER / ARTISTE:

513 Adelchi Galloni
514 Eugène Mihaesco
515 Dickran Palulian
516, 517 Oscar de Meyo

ART DIRECTOR / DIRECTEUR ARTISTIQUE:

513 Adelchi Galloni
514 Sheila Berger
515 Martin Nathan/Harvey Grut
516, 517 Richard Gangel

AGENCY / AGENTUR / AGENCE – STUDIO:

516, 517 John Locke Studio

PUBLISHER / VERLEGER / EDITEUR:

513 Arnoldo Mondadori
514 Harper's Magazine, Inc.
515–517 Time Inc.

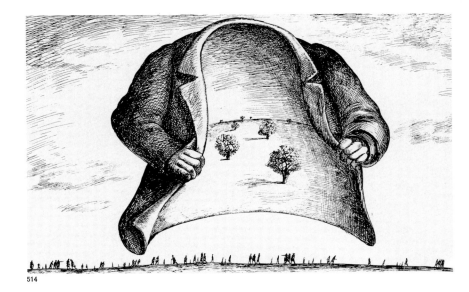

514

513 Illustration for a story published in the monthly magazine *Cosmopolitan*. Full colour. (ITA)
514 Black-and-white drawing illustrating an article in *Harper's* on the lack of leadership in modern America. (USA)
515 Opening spread in full colour of an article in *Sports Illustrated* on the football player Mean Joe Greene. (USA)
516, 517 Colour illustrations from an article on travel reports about pre-Revolutionary America published in *Sports Illustrated*. (USA)

513 Illustration zu einer Geschichte, die im Wochenmagazin *Cosmopolitan* erschien. Mehrfarbig. (ITA)
514 Schwarzweiss-Zeichnung als Illustration zu einem Artikel in *Harper's* über das Fehlen von Führerpersönlichkeiten in Amerika. (USA)
515 Erste Doppelseite zu einem Artikel in *Sports Illustrated* über den Fussballspieler Mean Joe Greene. Mehrfarbig. (USA)
516, 517 Mehrfarbige Illustrationen zu Reiseberichten aus dem vorrevolutionären Amerika, die in *Sports Illustrated* erschienen. (USA)

513 Illustration pour un récit publié dans le magazine mensuel *Cosmopolitan*. En polychromie. (ITA)
514 Dessin en noir et blanc illustrant un article du magazine *Harper's* sur le manque de personnages dirigeants aux Etats-Unis d'aujourd'hui. (USA)
515 Première page double en couleurs pour un article du magazine *Sports Illustrated* sur le footballeur Mean Joe Greene. (USA)
516, 517 Illustrations en couleurs accompagnant des récits de voyages en Amérique pré-révolutionnaire. De *Sports Illustrated*. (USA)

In his dreams, Pittsburgh's Mean Joe Greene pushes and pulls his way past a guard, jumps six feet over the center, slaps aside another blocker, deflects the pass, catches the ball and runs 99 yards for a touchdown

HE DOES WHAT HE WANTS OUT THERE

by ROY BLOUNT JR.

515

513

516

Magazine Illustrations
Zeitschriften-Illustrationen
Illustrations de périodiques

517

518

519

518 Full-page illustration for an article on rape in *Viva* magazine. (USA)
519 Double spread opening a fiction feature in *Viva* magazine. Pale shades of flesh, blue-grey and grey-green. (USA)
520 Colour illustration for a story in *McCall's* magazine. (USA)
521, 522 Full-page illustration (pink body, red apple) and complete spread opening a feature in *Viva* on how men lose their virginity. (USA)

518 Ganzseitige Illustration zu einem Artikel über Vergewaltigung in *Viva*. (USA)
519 Erste Doppelseite zu einer Erzählung in der Zeitschrift *Viva*. Helle Rosatöne mit Blaugrau- und Graugrüntönen. (USA)
520 Mehrfarbige Illustration zu einer Geschichte in der Zeitschrift *McCall's*. (USA)
521, 522 Ganzseitige Illustration (rosa Körper, roter Apfel) und entsprechende Doppelseite zu einem Artikel in *Viva* über Männer, die zum ersten Mal verführt werden. (USA)

518 Illustration pleine page pour un article du magazine *Viva* consacré au viol. (USA)
519 Page double introduisant une nouvelle dans le magazine *Viva*. Tons roses, bleus gris et gris verts atténué. (USA)
520 Illustration en couleurs tirée d'une histoire du magazine *McCall's*. (USA)
521, 522 Illustration pleine page (corps rose, pomme rouge) et page double où elle figure. Introduction d'un article de *Viva:* comment les hommes perdent leur virginité. (USA)

HELP,
THE NEWSBOY HOLLERED,

520

521

ARTIST / KÜNSTLER / ARTISTE:

518 Richard Hess
519 Heather Cooper
520 Paul Davis
521, 522 John Holmes

DESIGNER / GESTALTER:

522 Rowan Johnson

ART DIRECTOR:

520 Otto Storch
521, 522 Rowan Johnson

PUBLISHER / VERLEGER / EDITEUR:

518, 519, 521, 522 Viva International Ltd.
520 McCall Corporation

522

Magazine Illustrations

523

524

525

523, 524 Complete opening spread and detail of the colour illustration from a feature in *Rolling Stone* magazine on a hidden treasure. (USA)
525 Colour page facing the opening of a feature on the science-fiction novelist Philip K. Dick, published in *Rolling Stone* magazine. (USA)
526 Full-page, full-colour illustration from *Rolling Stone* magazine. (USA)
527 Full-page colour portrait of Bob Dylan from *Rolling Stone* magazine. (USA)
528 Page from a feature on summer fashions in *Avenue* magazine. Black and white. (NLD)
529 Illustration in pink and black from an article in *Avenue* on why we work. (NLD)
530 Full-page illustration from an astrological feature in *Avenue* about people born in the Sign of the Ram (Aries). (NLD)

523, 524 Erste Doppelseite und Detail der Illustration zu einem Artikel in *Rolling Stone* über verborgene Schätze. (USA)
525 Farbseite gegenüber der Titelseite eines Artikels über den Science-Fiction-Autor Philip K. Dick, erschienen in der Zeitschrift *Rolling Stone*. (USA)
526 Ganzseitige Farbillustration aus der Zeitschrift *Rolling Stone*. (USA)
527 Ganzseitiges Portrait von Bob Dylan, das in der Zeitschrift *Rolling Stone* erschien. (USA)
528 Seite aus einem Artikel über Sommermode. Aus der Zeitschrift *Avenue*. (NLD)
529 Illustration in Rosa und Schwarz zur Frage warum wir arbeiten. In *Avenue*. (NLD)
530 Ganzseitige Illustration zu einem Artikel über Astrologie in der Zeitschrift *Avenue*, hier über Personen, die im Sternzeichen des Widders geboren sind. (NLD)

523, 524 Page double et détail de l'illustration qui y figure. Introduction d'un article du magazine *Rolling Stone* sur des trésors cachés. (USA)
525 Page couleur face à la première page d'un article consacré à Philip K. Dick, auteur de livres de science-fiction. Du magazine *Rolling Stone*. (USA)
526 Illustration pleine page (en couleurs) du magazine *Rolling Stone*. (USA)
527 Portrait de Bob Dylan (en couleurs). Pleine page du magazine *Rolling Stone*. (USA)
528 Page d'un article sur les modes d'été du magazine *Avenue*. Noir-blanc. (NLD)
529 Illustration (en rose et noir) d'un article sur le pourquoi de notre travail. (NLD)
530 Illustration pleine page d'un article du magazine *Avenue* sur l'astrologie. Celui-ci est consacré aux personnes nées sous le signe d'Ariës. (NLD)

ARTIST / KÜNSTLER / ARTISTE:

523, 524 Bruce Wolfe
525 G. K. Bellows
526 Richard Hess
527 Kim Whitesides
528 Marnix von Freyburg
529, 530 Heinz Edelmann

DESIGNER / GESTALTER / MAQUETTISTE:

523, 524 Tony Lane/Suzy Rice/Roger Black

ART DIRECTOR / DIRECTEUR ARTISTIQUE:

523–527 Tony Lane
528–530 Dick De Moei

PUBLISHER / VERLEGER / EDITEUR:

523–527 Rolling Stone Magazine
528–530 De Geïllustreerde Pers N.V.

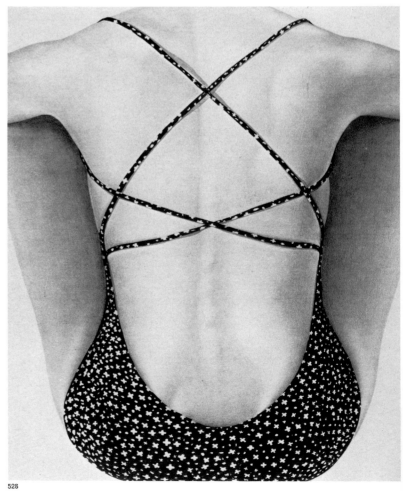

528

526

527

529

530

173

531 Illustration for a macabre story by Roald Dahl set in the desert of Sinai, from *Shock!* magazine. (GER)
532, 533 Full-page colour illustration and corresponding spread from a story ("The Poisoned Letter") in *Freundin* magazine. (GER)
534 Portrait of Charles Bronson (in black and red) from a profile on him in *Shock!* magazine. (GER)
535 Opening spread of an article on the artist Fred Hobbs in the weekly magazine *City*. Full colour. (USA)
536 Etching by Hans-Georg Rauch published in a "Gallery" section of *Shock!* magazine. (GER)

531 Illustration zu einer makabren Geschichte von Roald Dahl, die in der Wüste Sinai spielt. Aus der Zeitschrift *Shock!* (GER)
532, 533 Ganzseitige Illustration (mehrfarbig) und entsprechende Doppelseite. Diese eröffnet eine Kurzgeschichte, die in der Frauenzeitschrift *Freundin* publiziert wurde. (GER)
534 Portrait von Charles Bronson (in Schwarz und Rot) aus einem Artikel über diesen Schauspieler in der Zeitschrift *Shock!* (GER)
535 Erste Doppelseite zu einem Artikel über den Künstler Fred Hobbs. Dieser erschien im Wochenmagazin *City*. Mehrfarbig. (USA)
536 Radierung von Hans-Georg Rauch, die in der Rubrik «Gallerie» der Zeitschrift *Shock!* erschien. (GER)

531 Illustration pour une histoire macabre se déroulant dans le désert du Sinaï, écrite par Roald Dahl et publiée dans *Shock!* (GER)
532, 533 Illustration pleine page (en couleurs) et page double où elle figure. D'un récit (La lettre empoisonnée) de *Freundin*. (GER)
534 Portrait de Charles Bronson (en noir et rouge) figurant dans un article du magazine *Shock!* (GER)
535 Première page double d'un article sur l'artiste Fred Hobbs publié dans l'hebdomadaire *City*. En polychromie. (USA)
536 Gravure à l'eau-forte de Hans-Georg Rauch publiée dans la rubrique «Galerie» du magazine *Shock!* (GER)

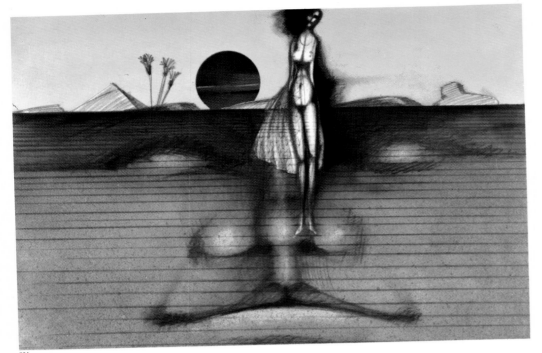

531

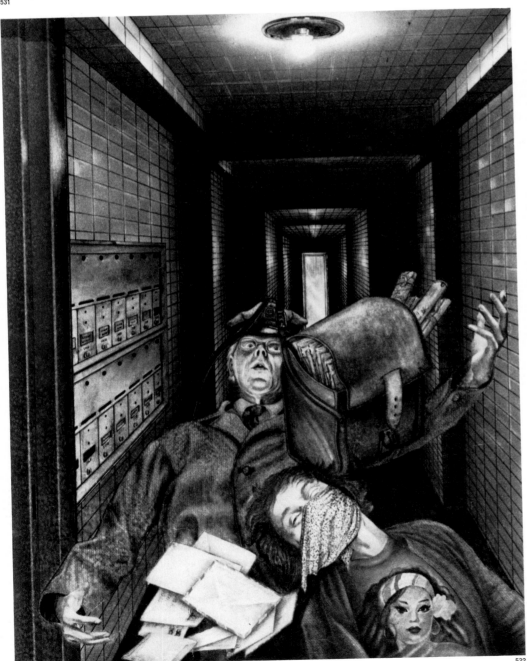

532

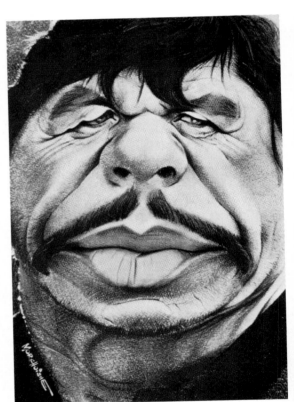

534

533

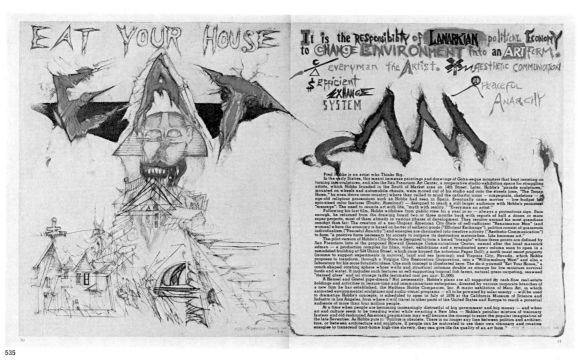

535

536

Newspaper Illustrations
Zeitungs-Illustrationen
Illustrations de journaux

ARTIST / KÜNSTLER / ARTISTE:

537 Haruo Miyauchi
538 Cathy Hull
539 Eugène Mihaesco
540 James Grashow
541 Sue Coe
542 Philip Weisbecker

DESIGNER / GESTALTER / MAQUETTISTE:

540 Ruth Ansel

ART DIRECTOR / DIRECTEUR ARTISTIQUE:

537, 539–542 Ruth Ansel
538 George Cowan

PUBLISHER / VERLEGER / EDITEUR:

537–542 The New York Times

537

538

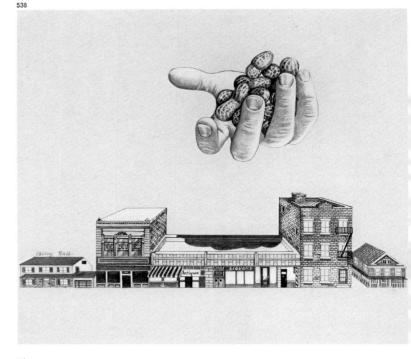

540

541

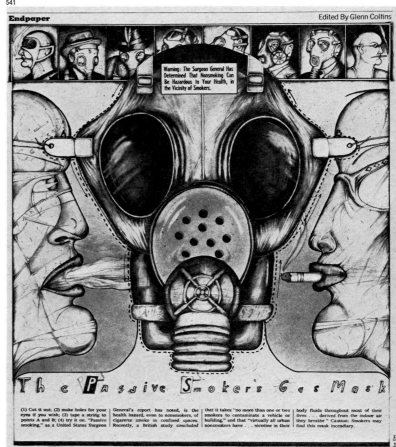

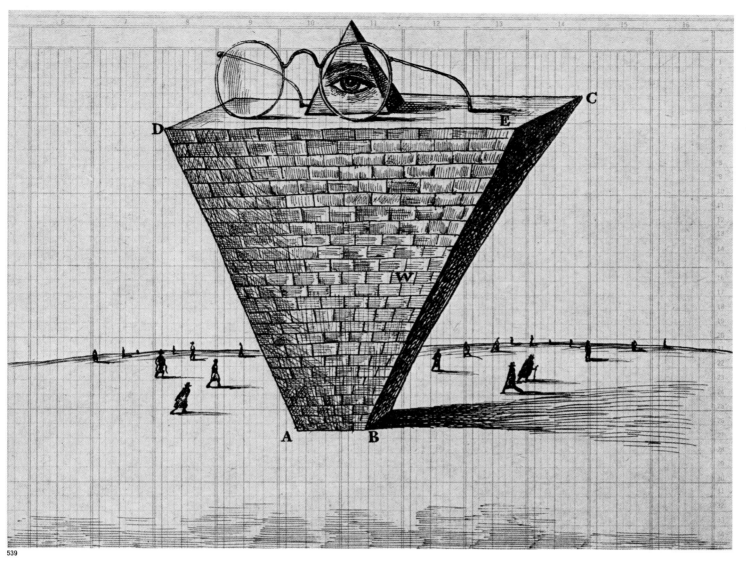

539

542

543

545

544

546

543 Black-and-white drawing illustrating an article on rehumanizing medicine in *The New York Times*. (USA)
544 Illustration in full colour for an article on Dashiell Hammett in *City* magazine, San Francisco. (USA)
545, 546 Complete Op-Ed page from *The New York Times* and detail of the illustration, which relates to an article on the subject of guerrilla tactics. (USA)
547, 548 Two black-and-white drawings used as illustrations in *The New York Times*. (USA)

543 Schwarzweiss-Zeichnung als Illustration zu einem Artikel über eine menschlichere Medizin. (USA)
544 Mehrfarbige Illustration zu einem Artikel über Dashiell Hammet in der Zeitschrift *City*. (USA)
545, 546 Vollständige Op-Ed-Seite (gegenüber dem Leitartikel) und Detail der Illustration zu einem Artikel über die Guerilla-Taktik in der *New York Times*. (USA)
547, 548 Schwarzweiss-Zeichnungen, die in der *New York Times* erschienen. (USA)

543 Dessin noir-blanc illustrant un article du *New York Times* sur la ré-humanisation de la médicine. (USA)
544 Illustration (en couleurs) accompagnant un article du magazine *City* sur Dashiell Hammett. (USA)
545, 546 Page Op-Ed (face à l'éditorial) du *New York Times* et illustration qui y figure. Pour un article sur la tactique de guérilla. (USA)
547, 548 Deux dessins en noir et blanc publiés dans le *New York Times*. (USA)

ARTIST / KÜNSTLER / ARTISTE:

543, 545, 546 Eugène Mihaesco
544 Paul Pratchenko
547, 548 Jean-Claude Suares

DESIGNER / GESTALTER / MAQUETTISTE:

545 Steve Heller

ART DIRECTOR / DIRECTEUR ARTISTIQUE:

543, 545–548 Steve Heller
544 Michael Salisbury

AGENCY / AGENTUR / AGENCE – STUDIO:

544 Salisbury Design Group

PUBLISHER / VERLEGER / EDITEUR:

543, 545–548 The New York Times
544 City of San Francisco

547

548

549 Illustration for an article in *The New York Times* on the employment of women in academic posts. (USA)
550 Illustration for the Op-Ed page of *The New York Times*. (USA)
551 From *The New York Times*. The drawing refers to Israel's determination to strike at terrorists. Black and white. (USA)
552 Complete Op-Ed page from *The New York Times*. The illustration relates to articles on the growing of opium poppies. (USA)
553 Illustration for an article on the oil crisis published in *Newsday*. (USA)
554 From *The New York Times*. The drawing illustrates an article on the Op-Ed page in which the author says what he would do if he were king. (USA)

549 Illustration zu einem Artikel in der *New York Times* über die Beschäftigung von Frauen in akademischen Berufen. (USA)
550 Illustration, die auf der Op-Ed-Seite der *New York Times* erschien. (USA)
551 Illustration aus der *New York Times*. Die Zeichnung bezieht sich auf die Entschlossenheit Israels, den Terrorismus zu bekämpfen. (USA)
552 Vollständige Op-Ed-Seite (gegenüber dem Leitartikel) aus der *New York Times*. Die Illustration bezieht sich auf einen Artikel über den Anbau von Opium-Mohn. (USA)
553 Illustration zu einem Artikel in der Zeitschrift *Newsday* über die Ölkrise. (USA)
554 Illustration zu einem Artikel in der *New York Times* (Op-Ed-Seite), in welchem der Autor beschreibt, was er alles tun würde, wenn er König wäre. (USA)

549 Illustration accompagnant un article du *New York Times* consacré aux professions académiques féminines. (USA)
550 Illustration de la page Op-Ed (face à l'éditorial) du *New York Times*. (USA)
551 Illustration du *New York Times*. Le dessin accompagne un article sur la lutte antiterroriste énergiquement mené par Israël. (USA)
552 Page Op-Ed du *New York Times*. L'illustration accompagne un article consacré à la culture du pavot somnifère. (USA)
553 Illustration figurant dans un article sur la crise pétrolière. De *Newsday*. (USA)
554 Dessin du *New York Times* illustrant un article de la page Op-Ed discutant de ce que l'auteur ferait s'il était roi. (USA)

Newspaper Illustrations
Zeitungs-Illustrationen
Illustrations de journaux

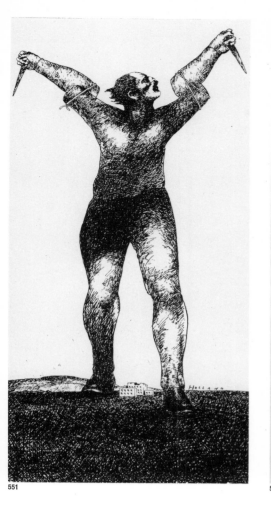

551

552

ARTIST / KÜNSTLER / ARTISTE:

549 Robert Pryor
550 Jean-Claude Suares
551, 552 Brad Holland
553 Gary Viskupic
554 Ralph Steadman

DESIGNER / GESTALTER / MAQUETTISTE:

552 Steve Heller

ART DIRECTOR / DIRECTEUR ARTISTIQUE:

549, 550, 552, 554 Steve Heller
551 Eric Seidman
553 Paul Back

PUBLISHER / VERLEGER / EDITEUR:

549–552, 554 The New York Times
553 Newsday

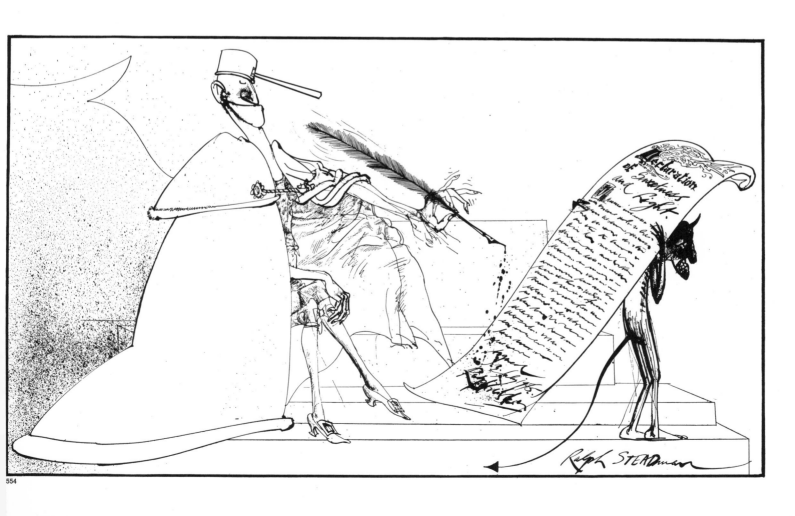

554

555

556

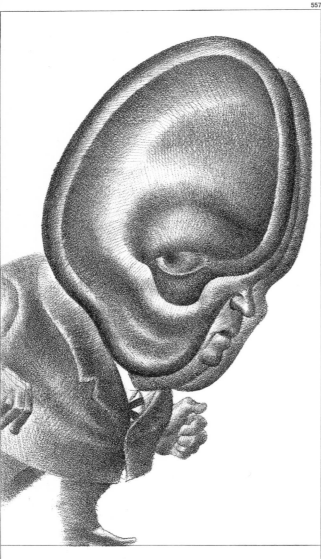

557

Gahan Wilson

528

ARTIST / KÜNSTLER / ARTISTE:

555 Jean-Claude Suares
556 Ralph Steadman
557 Robert Pryor
558 Gahan Wilson
559, 560 Eugène Mihaesco

DESIGNER / GESTALTER / MAQUETTISTE:

560 Steve Heller

ART DIRECTOR / DIRECTEUR ARTISTIQUE:

555, 556, 558–560 Steve Heller
557 Eric Seidman

PUBLISHER / VERLEGER / EDITEUR:

555–560 The New York Times

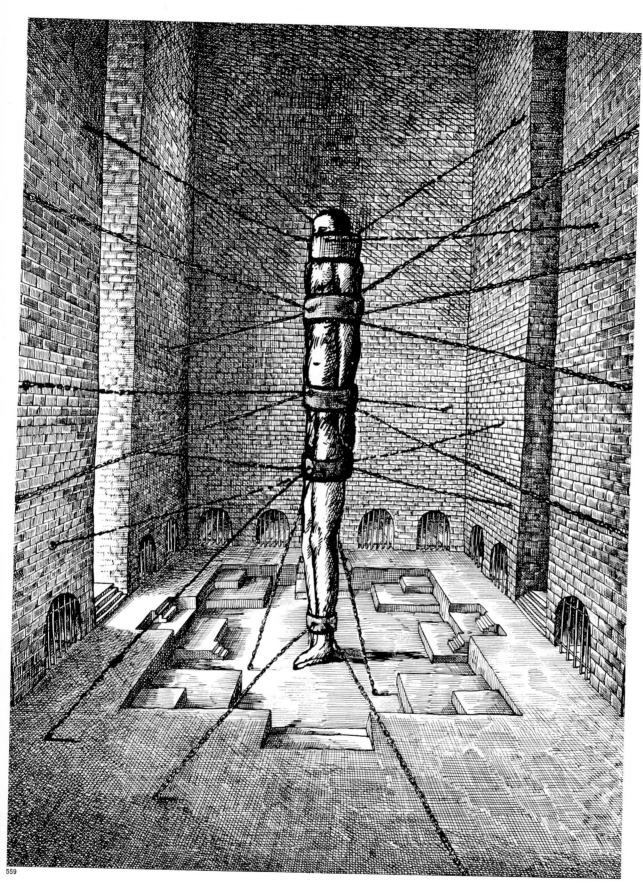

555 Pen-and-ink illustration from *The New York Times.* (USA)
556—560 Black-and-white illustrations from the Op-Ed (opposite editorial) page of *The New York Times,* with one example of a complete page (Fig. 560). The drawings accompany articles on the power of the multinationals (Fig. 556), the activities of the FBI (Fig. 557), recruitment to the CIA (Fig. 558), the grip of Communism (Figs. 559/560). (USA)

555 Tuschzeichnung aus einer Ausgabe der *New York Times.* (USA)
556—560 Schwarzweiss-Illustrationen der Op-Ed-Seite (gegenüber dem Leitartikel) der *New York Times,* und eine komplette Op-Ed-Seite (Abb. 560). Die Zeichnungen beziehen sich auf Artikel über die Macht der multinationalen Konzerne (Abb. 556), die Tätigkeit des FBI (Abb. 557), die Anwerbung von Personal für den CIA (Abb. 558) und die wachsende Einflussnahme des Kommunismus (Abb. 559/560). (USA)

555 Dessin à la plume figurant dans le *New York Times.* (USA)
556—560 Illustrations en noir et blanc de la page Op-Ed (face à l'éditorial) du *New York Times* et l'une des pages complètes (fig. 560). Les dessins accompagnent des articles consacrés au pouvoir des sociétés multinationales (fig. 556), à l'activité du FBI (fig. 557), au recrutement de personnes au sein de la CIA (fig. 558) et à la prise d'influence du communisme (fig. 559/560). (USA)

560

Newspaper Illustrations
Zeitungs-Illustrationen
Illustrations de journaux

561

562

ARTIST / KÜNSTLER / ARTISTE:

563 Richard Brown
564 Michèle Théorêt
565 Heinz Edelmann
566 Marcus Hodel

ART DIRECTOR / DIRECTEUR ARTISTIQUE:

561, 562 Félix Riano
563 Dick Whitson
564 André Coutu
565 Heinz Edelmann
566 Jacques Hauser

PUBLISHER / VERLEGER / EDITEUR:

561, 562 IBM S.A.E.
563 Armstrong Cork Company
564 Hydro-Québec
565 Verkehrsamt der Stadt Köln
566 F. Hoffmann-La Roche

561, 562 Full-page illustrations for an article on aeronautics in *Informatica IBM*, an IBM magazine published in Spain. (SPA)
563 Cover of *Tone*, a journal of interior design published by the Armstrong Cork Company, here referring to ceiling systems in schools. (USA)
564 Complete cover in full colour for *Forces*, house organ of Hydro-Québec, Montreal. (CAN)
565 Complete cover of a brochure issued by the Tourist Office of the city of Cologne. (GER)
566 Composition entitled "Dream", an insert in the *Roche* house magazine *Hexagon*. Pink, black. (SWI)

563

564

561, 562 Ganzseitige Illustrationen zu einem Artikel über Aeronautik in *Informatica IBM*, die in Spanien veröffentlicht wird. (SPA)
563 Umschlag von *Tone*, einer Zeitschrift für Inneneinrichtung, hier über neue Deckenplatten für Schulen. (USA)
564 Vollständiger Umschlag von *Forces*, der Hauszeitschrift von Hydro-Québec, Montreal. (CAN)
565 Geöffneter Umschlag einer Werbeschrift, die vom Verkehrsamt der Stadt Köln regelmässig herausgegeben wird. (GER)
566 Komposition mit dem Titel «Traum», die der *Roche*-Hauszeitschrift *Hexagon* beigelegt wurde. Rosa und schwarz. (SWI)

561, 562 Illustrations pleines pages d'un article sur la technique aéronautique. De *Informatica IBM*, publié en Espagne. (SPA)
563 Couverture de *Tone*, journal de création intérieure. Elle se réfère à un nouveau revêtement de plafond pour écoles. (USA)
564 Couverture complète (en couleurs) de *Forces*, journal d'entreprise de Hydro-Québec à Montréal. (CAN)
565 Couverture complète d'une brochure publiée par l'Office du Tourisme de la ville de Cologne. (GER)
566 Composition intitulée «Rêve». Cette feuille fait partie de *Hexagon*, journal d'entreprise de *Roche*. Rose et noir. (SWI)

House Organs / Hauszeitschriften
Journaux d'entreprise

565

567, 568 Inside spread and cover of an issue of *The Five Minute Hour* devoted to the subject of "Bio feedback and Yoga". The quarterly newspaper is sent to psychiatrists by *Geigy*. This issue is on brown stock with colour sparingly used in the illustrations. (USA)
569, 570 Cover of another issue of *The Five Minute Hour* with detail of the illustration. The subject is the influence of music on human moods. (USA)
571 Embossed envelope containing a copy of *The Five Minute Hour*. (USA)
572 Illustration for an article on art therapy in *The Five Minute Hour*. (USA)
573–575 Illustration in pale hues, complete opening page on which it appears, and following page, from an issue of *The Five Minute Hour*. The subject is the role of the housewife. (USA)

567, 568 Innenseiten und Umschlag einer Nummer von *The Five Minute Hour* zum Thema «Bio-Feedback und Yoga». Diese vierteljährlich erscheinende Zeitung von *Geigy* ist für Psychiater bestimmt. Diese Nummer wurde auf braunes Papier gedruckt; spärlich verwendete Farben. (USA)
569, 570 Umschlag einer anderen Ausgabe von *The Five Minute Hour* und Detail der Illustration. Thema dieser Nummer: der Einfluss der Musik auf die Gemütsverfassung des Menschen. (USA)
571 Blindgeprägter Briefumschlag mit einer Ausgabe von *The Five Minute Hour*. (USA)
572 Illustration zu einem Artikel über Therapiemethoden mit Hilfe der bildenden Kunst. (USA)
573–575 Illustration in matten Farben, entsprechende Seite und nachfolgende Seite aus einer Ausgabe von *The Five Minute Hour*. Thema: die Rolle der Hausfrau. (USA)

567, 568 Page double et couverture d'un numéro de *The Five Minute Hour* consacré au sujet «Le feed-back biologique et le Yoga». Cette publication trimestrielle de *Geigy* s'adresse aux psychiatres. Ce numéro est imprimé sur papier brun; emploi sobre de couleurs. (USA)
569, 570 Couverture d'un autre numéro de *The Five Minute Hour* avec détail de l'illustration qui y figure. Sujet: l'influence de la musique sur le moral de l'homme. (USA)
571 Enveloppe gaufrée contenant un numéro de *The Five Minute Hour*. (USA)
572 Illustration pour un article sur une méthode thérapeutique à l'aide des beaux-arts. (USA)
573–575 Illustration en tons atténués, page où elle figure et page suivante d'un numéro de *The Five Minute Hour*. Sujet: le rôle de la femme dans le ménage. (USA)

567

568

569

572

573

570

571

ARTIST / KÜNSTLER / ARTISTE:

567–575 Alan E. Cober

DESIGNER / GESTALTER:

567–575 Bob Paganucci

ART DIRECTOR:

567–575 Bob Paganucci

PUBLISHER / VERLEGER / EDITEUR:

567–575 Geigy Pharmaceutical

574

575

**House Organs
Hauszeitschriften
Journaux d'entreprise**

576

578

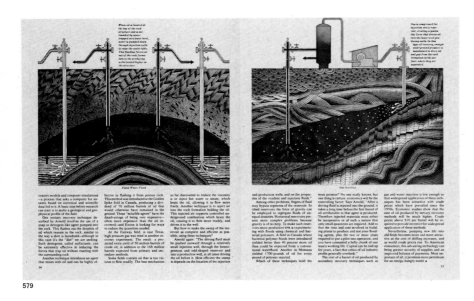

579

Introductions

Betty Bennett pushed her pink plastic reading glasses up on her forehead. Her eyes rose from the "Adventures of the Russian Revolution" to the silhouette of her brother standing[1] in front of her. To leave the great historical figures and come back to an American country doctor was a real effort but she smiled with amusement.

So this was the great Summerville doctor, the country's ex-golf champion, an explorer of the national parks, a traveler obsessed by "Gay Paris", "Gay Berlin", "Gay Brussels"; a 50 years old man living the dreams of the 102 Mayflower pilgrims since childhood. She pictured an American, content with set habits inherited from the Quaker morality and a schoolboy imagination, resemblances to a hamburger in a bun with ketchup to give it taste[2].

ARTIST / KÜNSTLER / ARTISTE:

576–578 Marvin Rubin
579 Pasternak-Londinsky
580 Jean-Charles Rousseau
581, 582 Jerome Snyder

DESIGNER / GESTALTER / MAQUETTISTE:

580 Jean-Charles Rousseau
581, 582 Harry O. Diamond

**House Organs / Hauszeitschriften
Journaux d'entreprise**

580

577

ART DIRECTOR / DIRECTEUR ARTISTIQUE:
576–579, 581, 582 Harry O. Diamond

AGENCY / AGENTUR / AGENCE – STUDIO:
580 Dupuy-Compton Medical

PUBLISHER / VERLEGER / EDITEUR:
576–579, 581, 582 Exxon Corporation
580 Cétrane/Unilabo

581

576–578 Illustrated charts from an article in the *Exxon* magazine *The Lamp* on the metric system. The charts show the metric sizes of familiar objects, here in cubic centimetres and kilograms. (USA)
579 Double spread with full-colour illustrations of water or gas injections from an article in *The Lamp* on how to get more oil out of wells. (USA)
580 Spread with colour illustrations from a brochure incorporating an English lesson issued by the *Schering* laboratories in France. (USA)
581, 582 Double spread from the house magazine *The Lamp* and detail of the illustration. The article deals with the many different products in the manufacture of which petroleum derivatives are used. (USA)

576–578 Illustrierte Diagramme aus einem Artikel über das metrische System, der in *The Lamp,* der Hauszeitschrift von *Exxon* erschien. An vertrauten Objekten werden die metrischen Einheiten aufgezeigt, hier Kubikzentimeter und Kilogramm. (USA)
579 Doppelseite mit mehrfarbigen Illustrationen über Wasser- oder Gasinjektionen aus einem Artikel der Hauszeitschrift *The Lamp* über eine erhöhte Ausbeutung der Ölquellen. (USA)
580 Doppelseite mit mehrfarbigen Illustrationen aus einer Broschüre der Firma *Schering* in Frankreich. Die Zeichnungen illustrieren eine Lektion in Englisch. (USA)
581, 582 Doppelseite aus der Hauszeitschrift *The Lamp* und Detail der Illustration. Im Artikel wird über diejenigen Produkte berichtet, für deren Herstellung Nebenprodukte der Erdölverarbeitung verwendet werden. (USA)

576–578 Diagrammes illustrés figurant dans un article sur le système métrique publié dans *The Lamp,* journal d'entreprise d'*Exxon.* Les différentes unités métriques sont illustrées à l'aide d'objets familiers, dans ce cas en centimètres cubes et en kilogrammes. (USA)
579 Page double avec des illustrations en couleurs sur le forage pétrolier à l'aide d'injections de gaz ou de l'eau. Article de *The Lamp* sur l'exploitation augmentée des puits. (USA)
580 Page double avec des illustrations en couleurs figurant dans une brochure qui contient une leçon d'anglais. Publication des laboratoires *Schering* en France. (USA)
581, 582 Page double du journal d'entreprise *The Lamp* et détail de l'illustration qui y figure. L'article traite des différents produits pour la fabrication desquels on utilise des dérivés pétroliers. (USA)

582

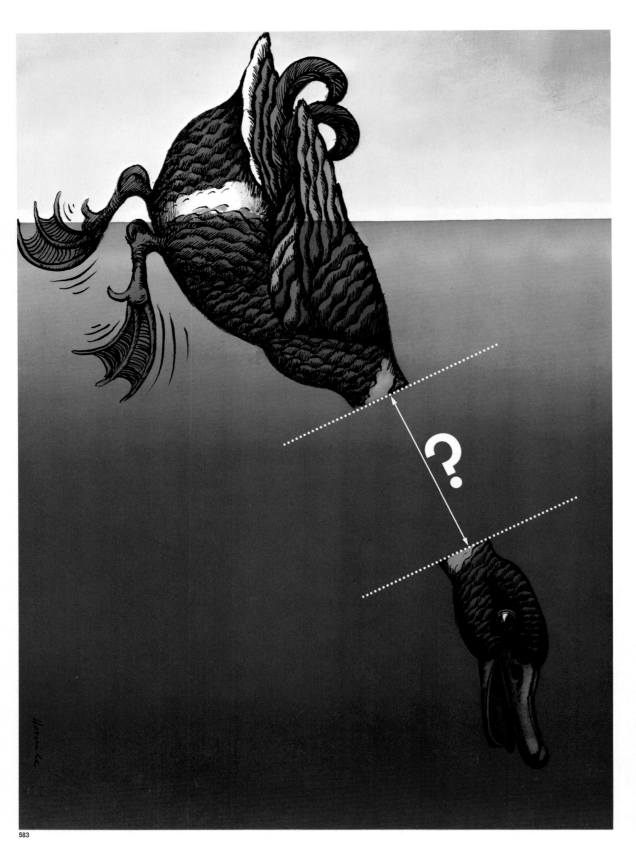

583

583, 584 Detail of the illustration and complete cover of *Pétrole Progrès,* house magazine of *Esso* in France. The issue contains an article on the eating habits of ducks. (FRA)
585 Illustration for an article in *Pétrole Progrès* on anti-pollution measures on board oil tankers. Shades of brown. (FRA)
586–588 Covers (colour) and double spread (black and white) from *Epicurean,* magazine of the Wine and Food Society of Australia. (AUL)
589 Cover of *Le Double Chevron,* house organ of *Citroën.* The coloured drawing refers to the appearance of the 2 CV on racing circuits. (FRA)
590 Cover of *Journal,* house organ of Broken Hill Proprietary Co. Ltd. The issue contains an article on the future of the media. Dark blue and purple, red title. (AUL)

583, 584 Detail der Illustration und vollständiger Umschlag von *Pétrole Progrès,* der Hauszeitschrift von *Esso* Frankreich. Die Nummer bringt einen Artikel über die Essgewohnheiten der Enten. (FRA)
585 Illustration zu einem Artikel in *Pétrole Progrès* über die für Tanker angeordneten Massnahmen gegen Wasserverschmutzung. (FRA)
586–588 Zwei Titelblätter (mehrfarbig) und Doppelseite (schwarzweiss) aus der Hauszeitschrift *Epicurean.* (AUL)
589 Titelblatt von *Le Double Chevron,* der Hauszeitschrift von *Citroën.* Die Zeichnungen beziehen sich auf den neuerdings an Autorennen mitfahrenden 2 CV. (FRA)
590 Titelblatt der Hauszeitschrift *Journal.* Die Nummer enthält einen Artikel über die Zukunft der Medien. Mehrfarbig. (AUL)

583, 584 Détail de l'illustration et couverture complète de *Pétrole Progrès,* journal d'entreprise d'*Esso* France. Numéro avec un article sur la manière de manger des canards. (FRA)
585 Illustration pour un article de *Pétrole Progrès* sur la lutté contre la pollution et la sécurité à bord des pétroliers. Tons bruns. (FRA)
586–588 Couvertures (en couleurs) et page double (noir et blanc) du magazine *Epicurean* de la Wine and Food Society d'Australie. (AUL)
589 Couverture de *Le Double Chevron,* journal d'entreprise de *Citroën.* Le dessin couleurs se réfère à la 2 CV qui fait son début dans les courses automobiles. (FRA)
590 Couverture du journal d'entreprise *Journal.* Le numéro contient un article sur l'évolution future des médias. En polychromie. (AUL)

584

ARTIST / KÜNSTLER / ARTISTE:

583, 584 Jörg Hermle
585 Guiré Vaka
586–588 Leslie L. Mason
589 George Popovitch
590 Barrie Tucker

DESIGNER / GESTALTER / MAQUETTISTE:

583–585 Any Dubois
586–588 Leslie L. Mason
590 Cato Hibberd Hawksby Design Pty Ltd.

ART DIRECTOR / DIRECTEUR ARTISTIQUE:

583–585 Jacques Tribondeau
586–588 Leslie L. Mason
590 Ken Cato

AGENCY / AGENTUR / AGENCE – STUDIO:

583–585 McCann Erickson S.A.
586–588 Les Mason Graphic Design
589 Delpire Advico S.A.
590 Cato Hibberd Hawksby Pty Ltd.

PUBLISHER / VERLEGER / EDITEUR:

583–585 Esso Standard S.A.F.
586–588 Lawrence Publishing Co. Pty Ltd.
589 Citroën S.A.
590 Broken Hill Proprietary Company Ltd.

House Organs / Hauszeitschriften
Journaux d'entreprise

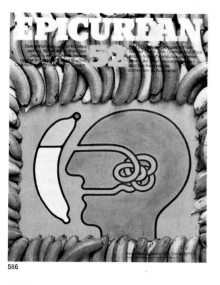

586

587

588

589

585

590

591

ARTIST / KÜNSTLER / ARTISTE:

591 William Bryan Park
593, 594 Giovanni Grasso Fravega

DESIGNER / GESTALTER / MAQUETTISTE:

592 Margrit Stutz

ART DIRECTOR / DIRECTEUR ARTISTIQUE:

591 Caroline Despard
592 Margrit Stutz
593, 594 Giorgio Soavi

AGENCY / AGENTUR / AGENCE – STUDIO:

591 John Locke Studio
592 Gottschalk & Ash Ltd.

PUBLISHER / VERLEGER / EDITEUR:

591 Smithsonian Magazine
592 Central Mortgage and Housing Corp.
593, 594 Ing. C. Olivetti & C. S.p.A.

592

591 Cover of the *Smithsonian*, house organ of the Smithsonian Institution. The issue contains an article on colonial travel. Full colour. (USA)
592 Double spread (black and white) opening an article on citizen participation in urban planning published in *habitat*, house organ of the Central Mortgage and Housing Corporation, Ottawa. (CAN)
593, 594 Two of the full-page illustrations from a gift book published by *Olivetti*, which contains watercolours by Giovanni Grasso Fravega inspired by *The Little Prince* of Antoine de Saint-Exupéry. (ITA)

591 Umschlag des Magazins *Smithsonian*, Hauszeitschrift der Smithsonian Institution. Die Ausgabe beinhaltet einen Artikel über eine Reise in der Kolonialzeit. Mehrfarbig. (USA)
592 Doppelseite (schwarzweiss), die einen Artikel über die Beteiligung der Bevölkerung an der städtischen Planung einleitet, erschienen in *habitat*, der Hauszeitschrift der Central Mortgage and Housing Corporation, Ottawa. (CAN)
593, 594 Zwei der ganzseitigen Illustrationen eines Geschenkbandes, erschienen bei *Olivetti*. Dieser Band enthält Aquarelle von Giovanni Grasso Fravega, der durch *Den kleinen Prinz* von Antoine de Saint-Exupéry inspiriert wurde. (ITA)

591 Couverture de *Smithsonian*, journal d'entreprise de la Smithsonian Institution. Ce numéro contient un article sur le voyage au temps du colonialisme. (USA)
592 Page double (noir et blanc) introduisant un article sur la participation des citoyens au planning urbain, publié dans *habitat*, journal d'entreprise de la Central Mortgage and Housing Corporation, Ottawa. (CAN)
593, 594 Deux illustrations pleines pages d'un livre qu'*Olivetti* a publié en guise de cadeau. Les aquarelles de Giovanni Grasso Fravega s'inspirent du *Petit Prince* d'Antoine de Saint-Exupéry. (ITA)

House Organs
Hauszeitschriften
Journaux d'entreprise

593

Advanced Micro Devices, Inc.

Annual Report 1975

595

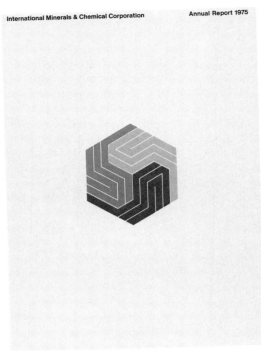

596

The Mother Goose Annual Report of 1838

598

ARTIST / KÜNSTLER / ARTISTE:

595 Mark Wallin
596, 597 Norman Perman

DESIGNER / GESTALTER / MAQUETTISTE:

596, 597 Norman Perman
600, 601 Ronald Jefferies
602, 603 Jerry Rothstein

ART DIRECTOR / DIRECTEUR ARTISTIQUE:

595 Lawrence Bender
596, 597 Paul Faberson
600–603 Robert Miles Runyan

AGENCY / AGENTUR / AGENCE – STUDIO:

595 Lawrence Bender & Associates
596, 597 Norman Perman
598, 599 Moonink Inc.
600–603 Robert Miles Runyan & Associates

PUBLISHER / VERLEGER / EDITEUR:

595 Advanced Micro Devices, Inc.
596, 597 International Minerals & Chemical Corp.
600, 601 Technicolor, Inc.
602, 603 Larwin Realty & Mortgage Trust

Annual Reports

194

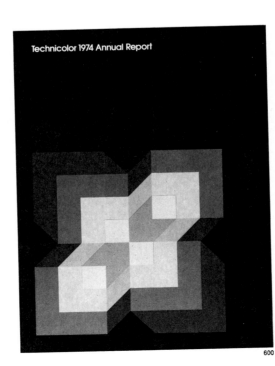

Technicolor 1974 Annual Report

600

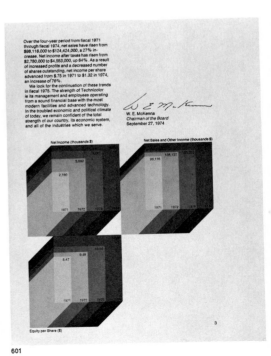

601

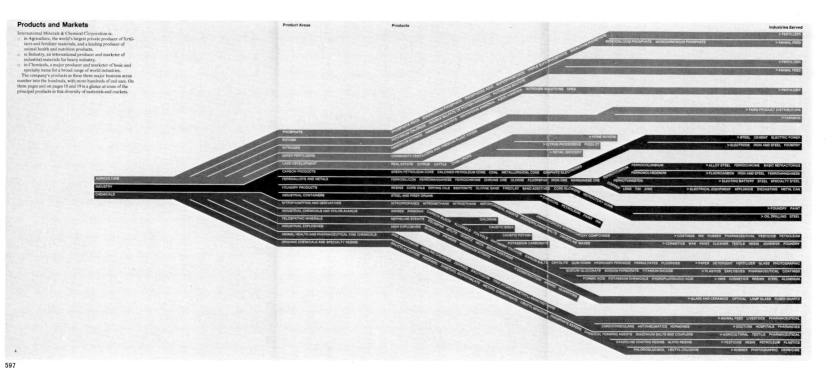

Products and Markets

International Minerals & Chemical Corporation is:
- in Agriculture, the world's largest private producer of fertilizers and fertilizer materials, and a leading producer of animal health and nutrition products.
- in Industry, an international producer and marketer of industrial materials for heavy industry.
- in Chemicals, a major producer and marketer of basic and specialty items for a broad range of world industries.

The company's products in these three major business areas number into the hundreds, with more hundreds of end uses. On these pages and on pages 18 and 19 is a glance at some of the principal products in this diversity of materials and markets.

Product Areas	Products	Industries Served

595 Cover of the 1975 annual report of Advanced Micro Devices, Inc. The design symbolizes product development and runs through the pages of the report. (USA)

596, 597 Cover of the 1975 annual report of International Minerals and Chemical Corporation (symbol in magenta, ochre and brown) and gatefold spread in the same colours representing products and markets. (USA)

598, 599 One of three fictitious annual reports used as promotion for the Beckett Paper Company: embossed cover showing Mother Goose and double spread with an illustration of one of the Three Bears. (USA)

600, 601 Cover and double spread from the 1974 annual report of Technicolor, Inc. Blocks in bright colours. (USA)

602, 603 Cover and page from the 1974 annual report of Larwin Realty and Mortgage Trust. Square and diagram in yellow, orange and red on brown. (USA)

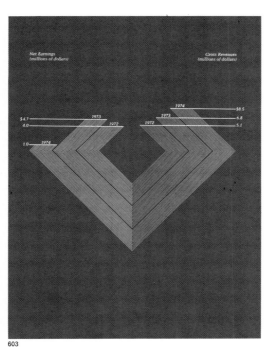

595 Umschlag des Jahresberichts für 1975 von Advanced Micro Devices, Inc. Die Graphik symbolisiert die Entwicklung in der Produktion und bildet ein konstantes Element des Berichtes. (USA)

596, 597 Umschlag des Jahresberichts 1975 der International Minerals and Chemical Corporation (Symbol in Magenta, Ocker und Braun) und Doppelseite mit Ausleger (in den gleichen Farben): Überblick über Produkte und Absatzmärkte. (USA)

598, 599 Einer der drei fiktiven Jahresberichte, die von einer Papierfabrik zur Eigenwerbung verwendet wurden. Blindgeprägter Umschlag, der Frau Holle zeigt, und Doppelseite mit einer Illustration zu den Drei Bären. (USA)

600, 601 Umschlag und Doppelseite aus dem Jahresbericht 1974 von Technicolor, Inc. In bunten Farben. (USA)

602, 603 Umschlag und Seite aus dem Jahresbericht 1974 von Larwin Realty and Mortage Trust. Quadrat und Diagramm in Gelb, Orange und Rot auf braunem Hintergrund. (USA)

595 Couverture du rapport annuel 1975 d'Advanced Micro Devices, Inc. Le graphisme symbolise le développement de la production et constitue un élément constant du rapport. (USA)

596, 597 Couverture du rapport annuel 1975 de l'International Minerals and Chemical Corporation (symbole en magenta, ocre et brun) et page double à repli (mêmes couleurs) représentant les produits et leurs débouchés. (USA)

598, 599 Un des trois rapports annuels fictifs utilisés en tant qu'élément autopromotionnel d'une papeterie: couverture gaufrée représentant la mère l'Oie et page double avec une illustration de l'un des Trois Ours. (USA)

600, 601 Couverture et page double du rapport annuel 1974 de Technicolor, Inc. Blocs en couleurs vives. (USA)

602, 603 Couverture et page du rapport annuel 1974 de Larwin Realty and Mortgage Trust. Carreau et diagramme en jaune, orange et rouge sur fond brun. (USA)

604

605

606

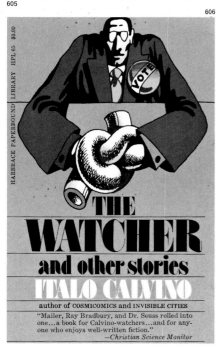

607

608

ARTIST / KÜNSTLER / ARTISTE:

604 Oskar Weiss
606 Stanislaw Zagorski
607 Edward Gorey
608, 609 Friso Henstra
610 Jan Buchholz/Reni Hinsch
611 Sidney Chafetz
612 Kjell Ivan Anderson

DESIGNER / GESTALTER / MAQUETTISTE:

604 Oskar Weiss
605 John McConnell
606 Stanislaw Zagorski
607 Edward Gorey
608, 609 Friso Henstra
610 Jan Buchholz/Reni Hinsch
611 Gerald Cinamon

ART DIRECTOR / DIRECTEUR ARTISTIQUE:

604 Oswald Dubacher
605 John McConnell
606 Harris Lewine
608, 609 Wim Mol
610 Jan Buchholz/Reni Hinsch
612 Ingvar Bylund

AGENCY / AGENTUR / AGENCE – STUDIO:

605 Pentagram

PUBLISHER / VERLEGER / EDITEUR:

604 Ex Libris Verlag AG
606, 611 Penguin Books
606 Harcourt, Brace, Jovanovich, Inc.
607 Diogenes Verlag AG
608, 609 Arbeiderspers N.V.
610 Fischer Taschenbuch Verlag
612 Liber Läromedel

604 Dust jacked for a novel by a Czech author. Green and mauve tie, black dots. (SWI)
605 Cover for a *Penguin* book on sociology. (GBR)
606 Cover for a *Harcourt, Brace* paperback novel. Shades of grey, black and pink. (USA)
607 Cover of an illustrated mystery story published by *Diogenes*. Black on grey stock. (SWI)
608 Colour cover for a translation of a Russian novel. (NLD)
609 Cover for a translation of stories by Hermann Hesse. Full colour. (NLD)
610 Complete cover for a paperback collection of ribald jokes. Pink bodies, red hair, tan title. (GER)
611 Cover for a *Penguin* book on Freud. (GBR).
612 Complete cover for a series of schoolbooks in English. Illustration in full colour. (SWE)

609

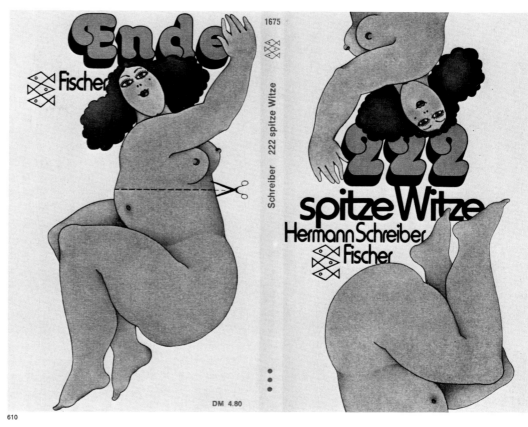

610

611

612

604 Schutzumschlag für eine Novelle eines tschechischen Autors; Kravatte grün und mauve, schwarze Punkte. (SWI)
605 Umschlag eines *Penguin*-Bandes über Soziologie. (GBR)
606 Umschlag für einen in Taschenbuchform erschienenen Roman. Grau-, Schwarz- und Rosatöne. (USA)
607 Umschlag für eine illustrierte Kriminalgeschichte, die bei *Diogenes* erschien. Schwarz auf grauem Papier. (SWI)
608 Für einen aus dem Russischen übersetzten Roman. (NLD)
609 Umschlag für die holländische Übersetzung von Hermann Hesses Erzählungen. Mehrfarbig. (NLD)
610 Geöffneter Umschlag für einen Band aus der Taschenbuchreihe «Spitze Witze». Rosa Körper, rote Haare, brauner Titel. (GER)
611 Umschlag für einen *Penguin*-Band über Freud. (GBR)
612 Geöffneter Umschlag für eine Schulbuch-Serie in Englisch. Mehrfarbige Illustrationen. (SWE)

604 Jaquette pour un roman d'un auteur tchèque. Cravate en vert et mauve, points noirs. (SWI)
605 Couverture d'un ouvrage sociologique *Penguin*. (GBR)
606 Couverture pour un roman paru dans une collection de poche. Tons gris, noirs et roses. (USA)
607 Couverture d'une histoire illustrée, publiée par les Editions Diogenes. Noir sur papier gris. (SWI)
608 Couverture pour la traduction d'un roman russe. (NLD)
609 Couverture pour la traduction hollandaise des nouvelles de Hermann Hesse. En polychromie. (NLD)
610 Pour un volume tiré d'une collection de poche consacrée aux paillardises. Corps roses, cheveux rouges, titre brun. (GER)
611 Couverture d'un livre de poche sur Freud. Noir-blanc. (GBR)
612 Couverture complète figurant dans une série de livres scolaires en anglais. Illustrations en couleurs. (SWE)

Book Covers
Buchumschläge
Couvertures de livres

als
die stad
eens
ommeviel...

613

614

615

613 "If the town once fell over..." Cover of a collection
of poems for the seventh centenary of Amsterdam. (NLD)
614, 615 Cover of a paperback story about a family. Bright
colours inside black house. (ITA)
616 Cover for a *Dutton* paperback anthology of Pre-
Raphaelite poetry. (USA)
617 Cover for a *Dutton* paperback autobiography of the folk
singer Woodie Guthrie. (USA)
618 Cover for a book of school stories published by *Simon
& Schuster*. Title white and black on red, green landscape,
characters in muted colours, ochre framing. (USA)
619 Cover for a *Fontana* paperback containing tales of
terror from Wales. (GBR)
620 Title page for a book of cat drawings (German edition)
by Ronald Searle. Ink and wash, pink cat. (GER)

613 «Wenn die Stadt eines Tages zusammenfällt...» Für
eine Gedichtsammlung zum 700. Gründungstag von Amsterdam. (NLD)
614, 615 Umschlag für einen Familienroman in Taschenbuchform. Leuchtende Farben in schwarzem Haus. (ITA)
616 Umschlag für eine in Taschenbuchform erschienene
Anthologie mit Präraffaeliten-Gedichten. (USA)
617 Umschlag der Autobiographie des Folksingers Woodie
Guthrie, als *Dutton*-Taschenbuch erschienen. (USA)
618 Umschlag eines Buches mit Schulgeschichten.
Schwarzweisser Titel auf Rot, grüne Landschaft, blassfar-
bene Figuren, Rahmen in Ocker. (USA)
619 Umschlag eines *Fontana*-Taschenbuches mit walisi-
schen Terrorgeschichten. (GBR)
620 Titelseite eines Werkes mit Katzenzeichnungen (deut-
sche Ausgabe) von Ronald Searle. Lavierte Tuschzeichnung,
rosa Katze. (GER)

613 «Si une fois la ville sera renversée...» Couverture d'une
collection de poèmes publiée lors du 7e centenaire de la
ville d'Amsterdam. (NLD)
614, 615 Couverture d'un roman de famille paru dans une
collection de poche. Couleurs vives. (ITA)
616 Couverture pour une anthologie de poésie prérapha-
élite. D'une collection de poche. (USA)
617 Couverture d'un livre de poche *Dutton*: autobiographie
du chanteur de folk music Woodie Guthrie. (USA)
618 Couverture d'un recueil d'histoires d'écoliers publié par
Simon & Schuster. Titre blanc et noir sur rouge, paysage vert,
personnages en tons mats, cadre ocre. (USA)
619 Couverture d'un livre de poche *Fontana*: recueil de
contes de terreur du pays de Galles. (GBR)
620 Frontispice d'un livre de dessins de chats (edition
allemande) de Ronald Searle. Dessin au lavis. (GER)

Book Covers
Buchumschläge
Couvertures de livres

618

616

617

619

620

ARTIST / KÜNSTLER / ARTISTE:

613 Mart Kempers
614, 615 Ferruccio Boca
616–618 Paul Davis
619 Justin Todd
620 Ronald Searle

DESIGNER / GESTALTER / MAQUETTISTE:

613 Mart Kempers

ART DIRECTOR / DIRECTEUR ARTISTIQUE:

614, 615 Bruno Binosi
616, 617 Cyril Nelson
618 Frank Metz

PUBLISHER / VERLEGER / EDITEUR:

613 Stadsdrukkerij Amsterdam
614, 615 Arnoldo Mondadori
616, 617 Dutton
618 Simon & Schuster, Inc.
619 Collins Publishers
620 Ehem. Verlag Kurt Desch Edition GmbH

621

ARTIST / KÜNSTLER / ARTISTE:

621, 622 Dieter Lange
623 William Biderbost
624 Wendell Minor
625 Stanislaw Zagorski
627 Simms Taback
628 Robert Byrd

DESIGNER / GESTALTER / MAQUETTISTE:

623 Lawrence Levy/William Biderbost
624 Wendell Minor
625 Stanislaw Zagorski
626 Zdenek Ziegler
627 Simms Taback
628 Robert Byrd

ART DIRECTOR / DIRECTEUR ARTISTIQUE:

623 Lawrence Levy
624 Char Lappan
625 Harris Lewine
626 Václav Rein
627 Carol Anthony
628 Robert Kraus

622

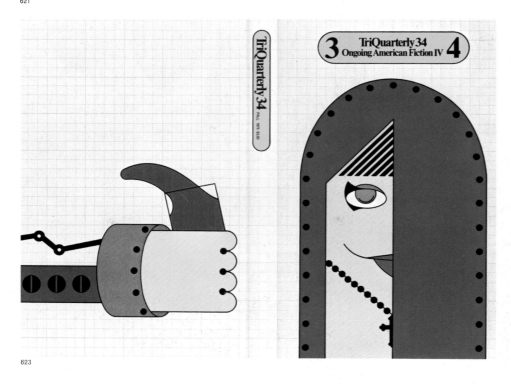

623

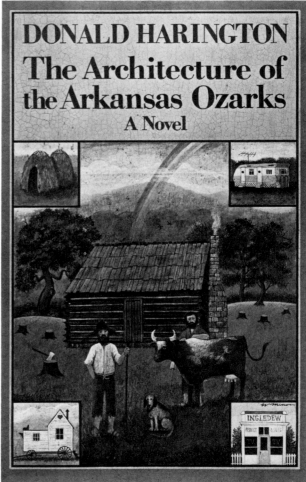

624

AGENCY / AGENTUR / AGENCE – STUDIO:

624 Wendell Minor Design
627 Simms Taback

PUBLISHER / VERLEGER / EDITEUR:

621, 622 Sauerländer Verlag
623 TriQuarterly
624 Little, Brown and Co.
625 Harcourt, Brace, Jovanovich, Inc.
626 Odeon
627 David McKay Company, Inc.
628 Windmill Publications Inc.

625

626

627

628

621, 622 Artwork and jacket of a book for girls. (SWI)
623 Complete cover of *TriQuarterly*, a journal in book form with new fiction. (USA)
624 Dust jacket of a novel about the Ozarks. Full colour, simulating a cracked oil painting. (USA)
625 Cover for an ''unwholesome'' book about the private life of Edward VII. (USA)
626 Complete dust jacket (predominantly green shades) for a translation of F. Forsyth's *The Day of the Jackal*. (POL)
627 Dust jacket for a humorous story about a cat. Bright colours on buff ground. (USA)
628 Complete dust jacket (full colour) for a children's book about a village of mice. (USA)

621, 622 Illustration und Umschlag eines Mädchenbuches. (SWI)
623 Geöffneter Umschlag von *TriQuarterly*, einer regelmässig erscheinenden Publikation mit neuen Erzählungen. (USA)
624 Umschlag eines Werkes über die Architektur der Bewohner der Ozark Mountains. Nachahmung eines Ölgemäldes. (USA)
625 Umschlag eines «boshaften» Buches über das Privatleben von Edward VII. (USA)
626 Schutzumschlag (vorwiegend in Grüntönen) für eine Übersetzung von F. Forsyths *Der Tag des Schakals*. (POL)
627 Schutzumschlag für eine humoristische Geschichte über Katzen. Leuchtende Farben auf beigem Grund. (USA)
628 Schutzumschlag in Farbe für ein Kinderbuch. Es erzählt die Geschichte einer von Mäusen bewohnten Stadt. (USA)

621, 622 Composition et jaquette d'un livre pour filles. (SWI)
623 Couverture complète de *TriQuarterly*, une série de publications consacrée au nouveau roman américain. (USA)
624 Jaquette d'un ouvrage consacré à l'architecture des Ozarks. Illustrations en couleurs, imitant une peinture à l'huile. (USA)
625 Couverture d'un livre «pernicieux» sur la vie privée du roi d'Angleterre Edouard VII. (USA)
626 Jaquette (prédominance de tons verts) pour la traduction d'un livre de F. Forsyth (Le jour du chacal). (POL)
627 Jaquette pour une histoire humoristique d'un chat. Couleurs vives sur fond chamois. (USA)
628 Jaquette (en couleurs) pour un livre d'enfant. Il raconte l'histoire d'une ville habitée par des souris. (USA)

629

631

630

ARTIST / KÜNSTLER / ARTISTE:

629, 630 Kveta Pacovská
631–633 Brad Holland
634 Santomaso
635 André François

DESIGNER / GESTALTER / MAQUETTISTE:

629, 630 Kveta Pacovská
631–633 Gloria Adelson

ART DIRECTOR / DIRECTEUR ARTISTIQUE:

631–633 Fran McCullough
635 Arthur Hubschmidt

AGENCY / AGENTUR / AGENCE – STUDIO:

635 SEREG, Société d'etudes et de
réalisations graphiques

PUBLISHER / VERLEGER / EDITEUR:

629, 630 Albatros
631–633 Harper & Row, Inc.
634 Alfieri
635 L'Ecole des loisirs

THE GEEK CRAIG NOVA
Drawings by BRAD HOLLAND

633

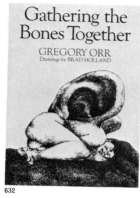

632

634

Book Covers
Buchumschläge
Couvertures de livres

635

203

636

ARTIST / KÜNSTLER / ARTISTE:

636 Joan Miró
637, 638 Etienne Delessert
639 Roberto Páez
640 Charles E. White, III
641 Hanspeter Wyss

DESIGNER / GESTALTER / MAQUETTISTE:

636 Jean Celestin
640 Kiyoshi Kanai

ART DIRECTOR / DIRECTEUR ARTISTIQUE:

636 Jean Celestin
639 Rodolfo Campodonico
640 Kiyoshi Kanai
641 Oswald Dubacher

AGENCY / AGENTUR / AGENCE – STUDIO:

640 Kiyoshi Kanai Associates

PUBLISHER / VERLEGER / EDITEUR:

636 Maeght Editeur/Ediciones Polígrafa
637, 638 Editions Gallimard
639 Editorial Hualen
640 Watson/Guptill Publications
641 Ex Libris Verlag AG

637

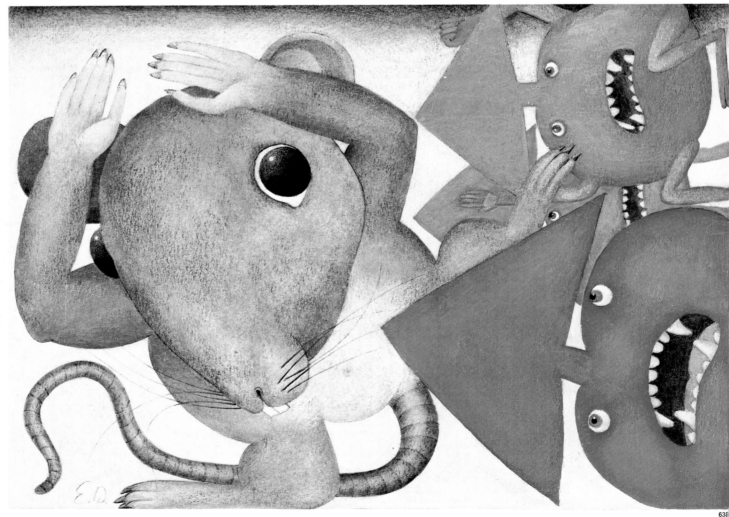

638

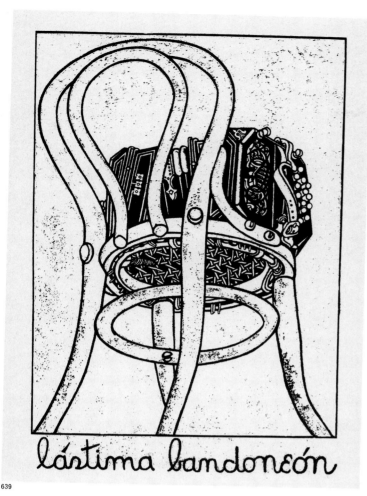

lástima bandoneón

639

MAURICE MESSÉGUÉ
DIE NATUR
HAT IMMER RECHT
Rezepte für Gesundheit und Schönheit durch die
geheimen Kräfte der Pflanzen

641

THE 54TH ART DIRECTORS ANNUAL
THE ONE SHOW

640

636 Large dust jacket (original lithograph) for a collection of lithographs by Joan Miró. (FRA)
637, 638 Cover for a book (The Mouse and the Poisons) about environmental pollution and a mouse. (FRA)
639 Large-format book cover (A Pity for the Accordion). Black and white drawing, red title. (ARG)
640 Cover for the 1975 annual of The One Show. Pale hues, blue title. (USA)
641 Cover for a book of plant recipes "for health and beauty" (Nature Is Always Right). Full colour, green title. (SWI)

636 Grossformatiger Schutzumschlag (Originallithographie) für ein Werk über Joan Mirós Lithographien. (FRA)
637, 638 Umschlag und Zeichnung für ein Buch (Die Maus und die Gifte), das von einer Maus und der Umweltverschmutzung handelt. (FRA)
639 Grossformatiger Buchumschlag (Schade für das Akkordeon). Zeichnung in Schwarzweiss, roter Titel. (ARG)
640 Umschlag eines jährlich erscheinenden Werkes über die Ausstellung The One Show. Matte Farben, blauer Titel. (USA)
641 Umschlag für ein Buch mit Pflanzenrezepten für Gesundheit und Schönheit. Mehrfarbig, grüner Titel. (SWI)

636 Jaquette grand format (lithographie originale) pour une collection de lithographies de Joan Miró. (FRA)
637, 638 Couverture complète et détail de la composition pour un livre de *Gallimard* sur un souris et la pollution de l'environnement. (FRA)
639 Couverture d'un livre grand format (Dommage pour l'accordéon). Dessin en noir et blanc, titre en rouge. (ARG)
640 Couverture du répertoire annuel 1975 de l'exposition The One Show. Tons atténués, titre en bleu. (USA)
641 Couverture d'un livre contenant des recettes végétales «pour la santé et la beauté» (La nature a toujours raison). En couleurs, titre vert. (SWI)

Book Covers
Buchumschläge
Couvertures de livres

4

Calendars

Trade Marks and Symbols

Letterheads

Packaging

Gramophone Record Covers

Kalender

Schutzmarken

Briefköpfe

Packungen

Schallplatten-Umschläge

Calendriers

Marques et emblèmes

En-têtes

Emballages

Pochettes de disques

642

643

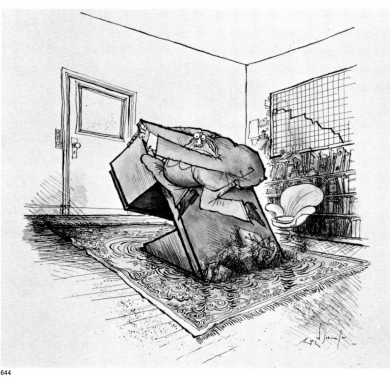

644

646

645

647

Calendars/Kalender/Calendriers

ARTIST / KÜNSTLER / ARTISTE:

642–645 Ronald Searle
646, 647 Ad van Hoof
648 Heinz Edelmann
649, 650 Fernando Maza

DESIGNER / GESTALTER / MAQUETTISTE:

646, 647 Marie Louise Mannaerts

ART DIRECTOR / DIRECTEUR ARTISTIQUE:

649, 650 Giorgio Soavi

642–645 Three of the colour illustrations and one complete sheet of the 1976 *Voko* calendar portraying the twelve office deities—here the reception goddess, the stress god and the sales god. (GER)
646, 647 Colour illustration and complete sheet of the 1976 calendar issued by the printers Eindhovensche Durkkerij. It depicts games—here patience. (NLD)
648 Cover of a local calendar issued by the district of Heinsberg. (GER)
649, 650 Two of the gouaches by Fernando Maza—on the subject of types—used as colour spreads in an *Olivetti* appointments calendar. (ITA)

642–645 Drei der mehrfarbigen Illustrationen und ein komplettes Blatt aus dem *Voko*-Kalender 1976. Es werden darin die zwölf Büro-Gottheiten vorgestellt: Empfangsgöttin, Stressgott und Verkaufsgott. (GER)
646, 647 Mehrfarbige Illustration und Blatt aus dem Kalender 1976 einer Druckerei. Jedes Blatt ist einem Spiel gewidmet; hier Patience. (NLD)
648 Titelblatt eines Kalenders mit Bildern der Region Heinsberg. (GER)
649, 650 Zwei der Gouachen von Fernando Maza zum Thema Buchstaben. Diese wurden als doppelseitige Illustrationen in der *Olivetti*-Agenda für 1976 verwendet. (ITA)

642–645 Trois illustrations en couleurs et feuille complète figurant dans le calendrier *Voko* pour 1976. Il présente les douze divinités du bureau: ici la déesse de la réception, le dieu du stress et le dieu-vendeur. (GER)
646, 647 Illustration en couleurs et feuille complète du calendrier 1976 de l'imprimerie Eindhovensche Drukkerij. Il présente des jeux – ici le patience. (NLD)
648 D'un calendrier avec des prises de vues de la région Heinsberg. (GER)
649, 650 Deux gouaches de Fernando Maza (toutes consacrées au sujet des caractères) d'un agenda d'*Olivetti* pour l'année 1976. (ITA)

648

649

650

651, 652 Complete wall calendar and detail of the monument-alphabet. The calendar was issued by the *Galerie Push* in Paris. (FRA)
653–656 Four of the monthly sheets from a *Pepsi-Cola* concertina-folding calendar using motifs from the world of showmanship. Full colour on yellow ground with a red headline. (USA)

651, 652 Vollständiger Wandkalender und Detail des Monumenten-Alphabets. Dieser Kalender wurde von der *Galerie Push* in Paris herausgegeben. (FRA)
653–656 Vier Monatsblätter aus einem leporello-gefalteten Kalender von *Pepsi-Cola,* mit Bildern aus dem Showbusiness. Mehrfarbige Illustrationen auf gelbem Hintergrund mit rotem Titel. (USA)

651, 652 Calendrier mural et détail des monuments alphabétiques. Ce calendrier a été publié par la *Galerie Push* à Paris. (FRA)
653–656 Quatre feuilles mensuelles figurant dans un calendrier en accordéon de *Pepsi-Cola* avec des motifs tirés du showbusiness. Illustrations en couleurs sur fond jaune avec titre en rouge. (USA)

651

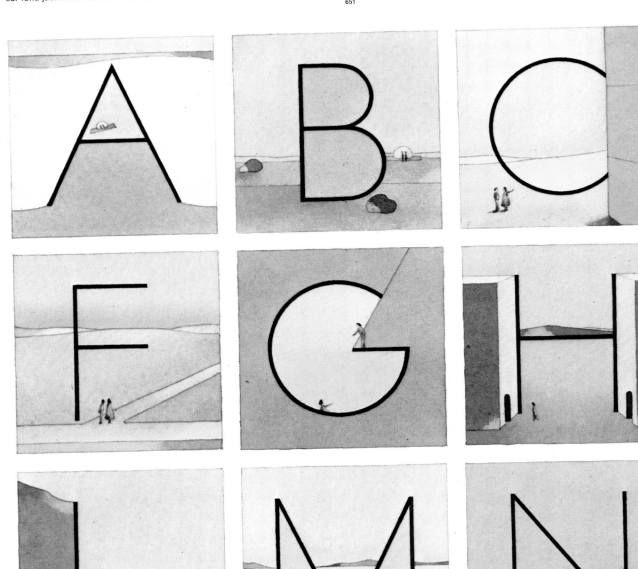

652

GOODBUZZIN
MAY 1975
T F S S M T W T F S S M T W T F S S M T W T F S S M T W T F S
1 2 3 4 5 6 7 8 9 10 11 12 13 14 15 16 17 18 19 20 21 22 23 24 25 26 27 28 29 30 31

653

COOLTALKIN
FEBRUARY 1975
S M T W T F S S M T W T F S S M T W T F S S M T W T F
1 2 3 4 5 6 7 8 9 10 11 12 13 14 15 16 17 18 19 20 21 22 23 24 25 26 27 28

654

HIGHWALKIN
SEPTEMBER 1975
M T W T F S S M T W T F S S M T W T F S S M T W T F S S M T
1 2 3 4 5 6 7 8 9 10 11 12 13 14 15 16 17 18 19 20 21 22 23 24 25 26 27 28 29 30

655

WHIZFIZZIN
JUNE 1975
S M T W T F S S M T W T F S S M T W T F S S M T W T F S S M
1 2 3 4 5 6 7 8 9 10 11 12 13 14 15 16 17 18 19 20 21 22 23 24 25 26 27 28 29 30

656

ARTIST / KÜNSTLER / ARTISTE:

651, 652 Georges Lemoine

DESIGNER / GESTALTER / MAQUETTISTE:

651, 652 Georges Lemoine
653–656 Seymour Chwast/Milton Glaser

ART DIRECTOR / DIRECTEUR ARTISTIQUE:

651, 652 Georges Lemoine
653–656 Judy Smith

AGENCY / AGENTUR / AGENCE – STUDIO:

653–656 Boase Massimi Pollitt/
Push Pin Studios, Inc.

657

658

659

660

657 Black-and-white spread from a calendar issued by *Rolling Stone* magazine. It lists events of the week and birthdays of prominent people on the right; the illustration on the left combines some of these features, here for instance Ho Chi Minh and a Texas festival. (USA)
658 Desk calendar in high-gloss acrylic for Plastofilm Industries, Inc. (USA)
659–661 Pages in black and one colour and complete spread from a Bicentennial calendar for teachers issued by *The New York Times*. The illustrations relate to events listed on the left—here Hannah Dustin kills nine Indians and Benedict Arnold sells his honour. (USA)
662, 663 Two calendars issued by the *Fokker* works. On one movable aeroplanes indicate the day of the week, date and month; on the other, with an aeroplane printed on cellophane, the position of the horizon changes when the date is adjusted. (GER)
664, 665 Complete sheet and details of the two-colour designs for the first eight months, in a calendar issued by a design studio. (ITA)

657 Schwarzweisse Doppelseite aus einem Kalender der Zeitschrift *Rolling Stone*. Die rechte Seite enthält Veranstaltungen und Geburtstage prominenter Persönlichkeiten; die Illustrationen links kombinieren jeweils einige Angaben – hier Ho Chi Minh und ein Festival in Texas. (USA)
658 Pultkalender aus glänzendem Acryl von Plastofilm Industries, Inc. (USA)
659–661 Seiten (schwarz und eine Farbe) und Doppelseite aus einem anlässlich der 200-Jahr-feier herausgegebenen Kalender für Lehrer. Illustrationen zu den auf der linken Seite angeführten Gegebenheiten – Hannah Dustin tötet neun Indianer, Benedict Arnold verkauft seine Ehre. (USA)
662, 663 Zwei Kalender der Flugzeugwerke *Fokker*. Auf dem einen zeigen bewegliche Flugzeuge den Wochentag, das Datum und den Monat an; beim anderen, mit einem auf Cellophan gedruckten Flugzeug, verändert sich der Horizont mit jedem Tag. (GER)
664, 665 Vollständiges Kalenderblatt und Details der zweifarbigen Illustrationen für die ersten acht Monate. Aus dem Kalender eines Design-Studios. (ITA)

657 Page double en noir et blanc d'un calendrier publié par le magazine *Rolling Stone*. Une page indique les manifestations de la semaine ainsi que les anniversaires de personnages importants, l'autre combine quelques événements, p. ex. Ho Chi Minh et un festival texane. (USA)
658 Agenda en acrylique brillant d'une fabrique de matières plastiques. (USA)
659–661 Pages (noir et une couleur) et page double d'un calendrier bicentenaire pour les profs, publié par le *New York Times*. Les illustrations se réfèrent aux événements indiqués à gauche – Hannah Dustin tue neuf Indiens, Benedict Arnold vend son honneur. (USA)
662, 663 Deux calendriers publiés par l'usine d'aviation *Fokker*. Sur l'un d'eux des avions mobiles indiquent le jour de la semaine, la date et le mois; sur l'autre, avec un avion imprimé sur une feuille de cellophane, la position de l'horizon change lorsqu'on ajuste la date. (GER)
664, 665 Feuille d'un calendrier et détails des illustrations (en deux couleurs) qui y figurent. Elles se rapportent aux premiers huit mois de l'année. D'un studio de design. (ITA)

661

664

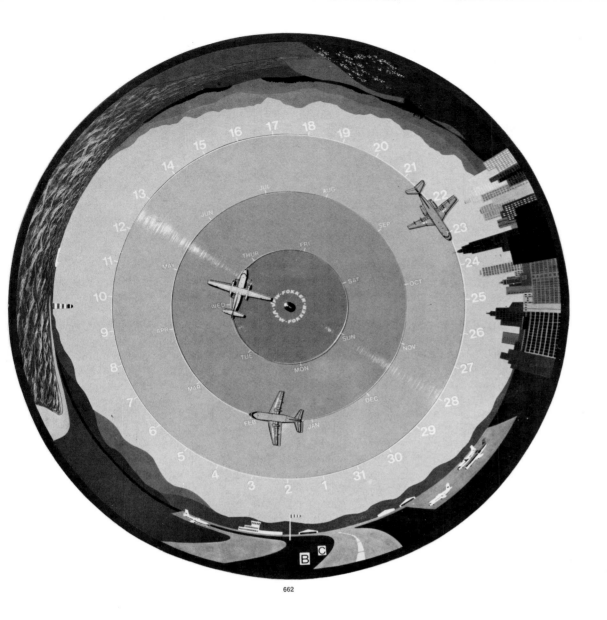

662

663

Calendars / Kalender
Calendriers

ARTIST / KÜNSTLER / ARTISTE:

657 Patrick O. Chapin
659–661 Diana Bryan

DESIGNER / GESTALTER / MAQUETTISTE:

657 Bob Kingsbury
658 Thomas H. Rossman
659–661 Emil T. Micha
662 Dietrich Ralle
663 Fritz Haase
664, 665 Giorgio Davanzo

ART DIRECTOR / DIRECTEUR ARTISTIQUE:

657 Bob Kingsbury
658 James V. Neill
659–661 Andrew Kner
662, 663 Fritz Haase
664, 665 Giorgio Davanzo

AGENCY / AGENTUR / AGENCE – STUDIO:

658 Source, Inc.
662, 663 Haase & Knels
664, 665 Publistudio

665

666

667

666, 667 Opening of a spirally bound riddle calendar for children published by Charles Scribner's Sons, New York, and detail of one of the full-colour riddle sheets. (USA)
668, 669 Cover and double spread from a sports calendar issued by ABC Television. Blue and white with red vignettes on cover. (USA)
670–674 Four of the colour pages (Fig. 670 in roughly actual size) and a double spread with date and note page from a desk agenda for 1976 issued by Sharp S/A, makers of television sets, computers and other types of electronic equipment. (BRA)

666, 667 Geöffneter spiralgebundener Rätselkalender für Kinder und Detail eines der Rätselblätter. Der Kalender wurde von Charles Scribner's Sons in New York herausgegeben. (USA)
668, 669 Umschlag und Doppelseite aus einem von der Fernsehstation ABC herausgegebenen Sportkalender mit sportlichen Ereignissen des ersten Halbjahres 1975. Blau und weiss mit roten Vignetten. (USA)
670–674 Vier der mehrfarbigen Seiten (Abb. 670 ungefähr in Originalgrösse) und Doppelseite mit Kalender und Notizseite aus einer von Sharp S/A herausgegebenen Agenda für 1976. Diese Firma fabriziert Fernsehapparate, Computer und elektronische Apparate. (BRA)

666, 667 Page complète d'un calendrier à reliure spirale pour enfants publié par Charles Scribner's Sons, New York, et détail d'une page couleur contenant des devinettes. (USA)
668, 669 Couverture et page double d'un calendrier publié par la station TV ABC. Il est consacré aux événements sportifs de la première moitié de l'année 1975. Bleu et blanc avec vignettes rouges. (USA)
670–674 Quatre pages couleur (fig. 670 approx. en grandeur nature) et page double avec dates et agenda figurant dans un calendrier de bureau pour 1976. Celui-ci a été publié par un fabricant d'appareils de télévision, d'ordinateurs et d'appareils électroniques. (BRA)

668

669

ARTIST / KÜNSTLER / ARTISTE:

666, 667 Reynold Ruffins
670–674 Zélio Alves Pinto

DESIGNER / GESTALTER / MAQUETTISTE:

666, 667 Reynold Ruffins
668, 669 Mark Johnson
670–674 Zélio Alves Pinto

ART DIRECTOR / DIRECTEUR ARTISTIQUE:

666, 667 Allen Benjamin
668, 669 Mark Johnson

AGENCY / AGENTUR / AGENCE – STUDIO:

670–674 Praxis Propaganda Ltda.

671

673

674

675

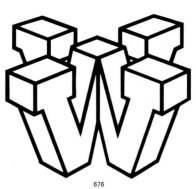

676

680

684

688

689

216

677

678

679

681

682

683

685

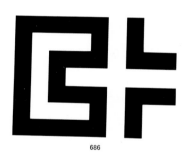

686

687

675 Bicentennial logo for the Printing Industries of Metropolitan New York. (USA)
676 Logo for *Woodpecker* do-it-yourself furniture kits. (USA)
677 Emblem for International Women's Year for the UN. It combines a dove, the equals sign and the female symbol. (USA)
678 Trade mark for Alpine Villa Development Company, Sun Valley, Idaho. (USA)
679 Emblem for the Nassauer Hof Hotel in Wiesbaden. (GER)
680 Trade mark for Airport Marina Hotels. Pale blue. (USA)
681 Trade mark for Long Equipment Co., heating plant. (USA)
682 Symbol for the Ardsley/Suffern Blood Bank. (USA)
683 Trade mark for Ventilasjonsbehov A/S, Oslo, a company active in the ventilation branch. (NOR)
684 Logo for a Leadership and Training Institute. (USA)
685 Trade mark for Le Colombier family homes, Corporation de Salaberry, Inc. (CAN)
686 Symbol for a Children's Hospital medical centre. (USA)
687 Symbol for Audio Archives, Chicago. (USA)
688 Emblem for a waterworks (Sociedad General de Aguas de Barcelona S. A.). (SPA)
689 Symbol (F in film) for an international film Festival of Festivals. (CAN)

675 Anlässlich der 200-Jahrfeier eingeführte Schutzmarke von Printing Industries of Metropolitan New York. (USA)
676 Schutzmarke für *Woodpecker*-Do-it-yourself-Möbel. (USA)
677 Symbol für das von der UNO proklamierte Internationale Jahr der Frau. Kombination von Taube, Gleichheitszeichen und dem weiblichen Symbol. (USA)
678 Schutzmarke einer Immobiliengesellschaft. (USA)
679 Symbol des Hotels Nassauer Hof in Wiesbaden. (GER)
680 Schutzmarke der Airport Marina Hotels. Hellblau. (USA)
681 Schutzmarke eines Herstellers von Heizkörpern. (USA)
682 Symbol der Blut-Bank der *Ciba-Geigy* in Ardsley. (USA)
683 Schutzmarke der Ventilasjonsbehov A/S, Oslo, einer auf dem Gebiet von Ventilationsinstallationen tätigen Firma. (NOR)
684 Logo des Leadership and Training Institute. (USA)
685 Schutzmarke der Familienheime Le Colombier. (CAN)
686 Symbol der medizinischen Abteilung einer Kinderklinik in Boston. (USA)
687 Symbol der Audio Archives, Chicago. (USA)
688 Symbol der städtischen Wasserversorgung (Sociedad General de Aguas de Barcelona S. A.). (SPA)
689 Symbol (F durch Filmstreifen gebildet) für ein internationales Film-Festival der Festivals. (CAN)

675 Logo de Printing Industries of Metropolitan New York, introduit à l'occasion du Bicentenaire. (USA)
676 Logo pour les boîtes *Woodpecker* contenant des éléments pour des meubles à assembler. (USA)
677 Symbole de l'ONU pour l'Année Internationale de la Femme. Le design combine la colombe, le signe d'égalité et le symbole de la femme. (USA)
678 Marque d'une société immobilière à Sun Valley. (USA)
679 Symbole de l'Hôtel Nassauer Hof à Wiesbaden. (GER)
680 Marque des Airport Marina Hotels. Bleu pâle. (USA)
681 Marque d'une fabrique d'installations de chauffage. (USA)
682 Symbole de la banque du sang de *Ciba-Geigy*. (USA)
683 Marque d'une entreprise spécialisée dans la fabrication d'installations de ventilation. (NOR)
684 Logo du Leadership and Training Institute. (USA)
685 Marque pour les maisons de famille Le Colombier. (CAN)
686 Symbole du centre médical d'un hôpital pour enfants à Boston. (USA)
687 Symbole pour Audio Archives à Chicago. (USA)
688 Marque pour les services des eaux de Barcelone. (SPA)
689 Symbole (F constitué par la pellicule) pour un festival international des festivals du film. (CAN)

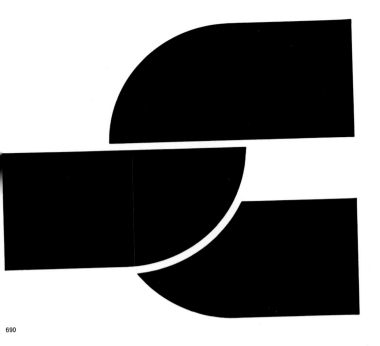

690

692

695

CABANHA SANTA BÁRBARA

691

698

693

694

701

702

696

697

703

699

700

704

Trade Marks / Schutzmarken
Marques et emblèmes

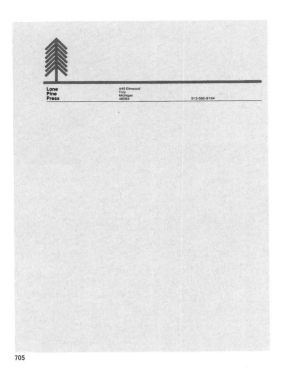

705

706

707

The Anthurium Association of Hawaii • P.O. Box 429 • Mountain View, Hawaii 96771 • Tel: (808) 968-6228 Cable: ANTHURIUM

709

710

711

ARTIST / KÜNSTLER / ARTISTE:

707 Bill Aller
712–714 Donna Brown

DESIGNER / GESTALTER / MAQUETTISTE:

705 Katherine McCoy
706 Camilla Masciardi
707 Peter Schaefer
708 Ivan Chermayeff/Stephan Geissbühler
709 Joe Lambert/Sharon Aki
711 Jim Lienhart
715 Marcello Minale/Alex Maranzano
716, 717 Michael Gross

ART DIRECTOR / DIRECTEUR ARTISTIQUE:

705 Katherine McCoy
706 Franco Bassi
707 Andrew Kner
708 Ivan Chermayeff/Stephan Geissbühler
709 Sharon Aki
711 Jim Lienhart
712–714 Alan Fletcher
715 Marcello Minale/Brian Tattersfield
716, 717 David Kaestle

AGENCY / AGENTUR / AGENCE – STUDIO:

705 McCoy & McCoy Associates
708 Chermayeff & Geismar Assoc.
709 Aki, Lubalin, Inc.
712–714 Pentagram
715 Minale, Tattersfield, Provinciali Ltd.
716, 717 Pellegrini, Kaestle & Gross, Inc.

705 Letterhead for a printer, Lone Pine Press. Green pine. (USA)
706 Letterhead for a Hotel in Monte Carlo. Buff frame. (MON)
707 Letterhead for the mail subscription department of *The New York Times*. Brown wrapper. (USA)
708 Stationery for a Neighbourhood Conservation Conference. Typographically crowded conference topics. (USA)
709 Letterhead with red symbol for a flower association. (USA)
710 Letterhead for White Owl Conservation Awards. (CAN)
711 Letterhead for Von Photography, Chicago. (USA)
712–714 Letterhead and two postcards as personal stationery for Kenneth Grange, who has moved. Drawings in colour. (GBR)
715 Range of business stationery for R. Fox Limited, an exhibition contractor. Letters in bright colours. (GBR)
716, 717 Stationery for Henson Assoc., Inc. Green "ha!" (USA)

705 Briefkopf einer Druckerei. Grüne Tanne. (USA)
706 Briefbogen eines Hotels in Monte Carlo. (MON)
707 Briefkopf der Abonnement-Versandabteilung der *New York Times*. Braunes Streifband. (USA)
708 Briefpapier für eine Konferenz zur Erhaltung der städtischen Umgebung, mit Angabe der Konferenzthemen. (USA)
709 Briefkopf (rotes Symbol) für einen Blumenverein. (USA)
710 Briefkopf für White Owl Conservation Awards. (CAN)
711 Briefpapier für Von Photography, Chicago. (USA)
712–714 Briefbogen und Postkarten für den kürzlich umgezogenen Kenneth Grange. Farbige Zeichnungen. (GBR)
715 Geschäftspapier eines Ausstellungsorganisators. Buchstaben in leuchtenden Farben. (GBR)
716, 717 Briefbogen für Henson Assoc. Grünes «ha!» (USA)

705 En-tête pour une imprimerie. Sapin vert. (USA)
706 En-tête pour un hôtel à Monte Carlo. (MON)
707 En-tête pour le département d'expédition du service d'abonnement du *New York Times*. Bande brune. (USA)
708 Papier à lettre pour une conférence consacrée à la conservation de l'environnement, avec sujets traités. (USA)
709 En-tête d'une association de floristes. (USA)
710 En-tête en vert pour White Owl Conservation Awards. (CAN)
711 En-tête pour Von Photography, Chicago. (USA)
712–714 Papier à lettre et deux cartes postales pour la correspondance privée de Kenneth Grange. Dessins en couleurs. (GBR)
715 Gamme des imprimés d'un contractant d'expositions. Lettres en couleurs vives. (GBR)
716, 717 Imprimés pour Henson Assoc., Inc., «ha!» vert. (USA)

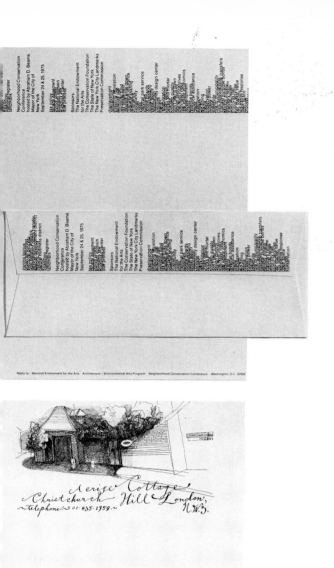

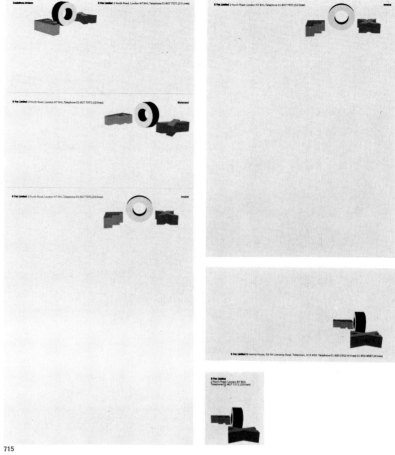

718

719

ARTIST / KÜNSTLER / ARTISTE:

718 Kroehl Design Gruppe
719 Melabee M. Miller
720 Lorraine Epstein
721 Roger Bezombes
722 Paolo Buttafava
723 David Epstein
724 Tandy Belew/Primo Angeli

DESIGNER / GESTALTER / MAQUETTISTE:

718 Kroehl Design Gruppe
719 Paul Hanson/Kenneth Cooke
720, 723 David Epstein
721 Roger Bezombes
722 Paolo Buttafava
724 Primo Angeli
725 Anspach Grossman Portugal Inc.
726 Richard Walukanis

ART DIRECTOR / DIRECTEUR ARTISTIQUE:

718 Heinz Kroehl/Peter Offenberg
719 Robert P. Gersin
720 David Epstein
721 Jean-François Feige
722 Paolo Buttafava
723 Ellen Grean
724 Primo Angeli/Roger Shelly
725 Eugene J. Grossman
726 Richard Walukanis

AGENCY / AGENTUR / AGENCE – STUDIO:

718 Kroehl Design Gruppe
719 Robert P. Gersin Associates
720, 723 Dave Epstein, Inc.
721 Artuel
722 Studio Paolo Buttafava
724 Steedman, Cooper & Busse
725 Anspach Grossman Portugal Inc.

720

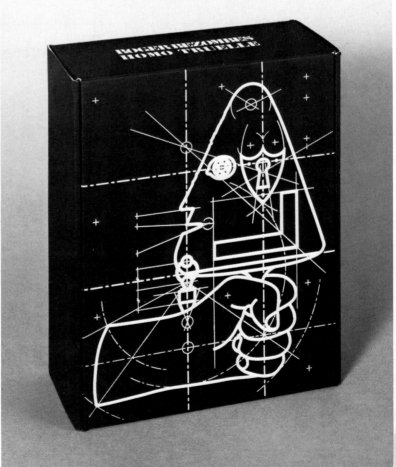

721

722

723

724

725

718 Sprinkler containers for lawn and flower fertilizers. (GER)
719 Boxes containing sheets of band music for the US Bicentennial, as a gift from the *J. C. Penney* department stores. (USA)
720 Set-up box for mailing *Roche* pharmaceutial samples to doctors on request. The allusion of the drawings is to ancient Egyptian symbols of life. (USA)
721 Box containing an artefact made by a French artist, the *Homo Truelle* (Trowel Man). White drawing on black. (FRA)
722 Folding box for a pie tin. Design in flat colours. (ITA)
723 Merchandising aid for Cotton Incorporated, New York. Lettering in blue, arch of lower O in blue, green and yellow. (USA)
724 Paper bags for French bread freshly baked by *Boudin Bakeries* in San Francisco. Brown, red. yellow, blue and green. (USA)
725 Packages for sausages made by Swift & Co., Chicago. (USA)
726 Cloth carrier bag as a promotional gift from *Fortune* magazine. (USA)

718 Streudosen für Rasen- und Blumendünger. Grün und weiss. (GER)
719 Schachteln mit Orchestermusiknoten, die vom Warenhaus *J. C. Penney* zum Anlass der 200-Jahrfeierlichkeiten als Geschenk abgegeben wurden. (USA)
720 Schachtel für pharmazeutische Mustersendungen von *Roche,* die von Ärzten angefordert werden. Die Zeichnungen zeigen alte ägyptische Lebenssymbole. (USA)
721 Schachtel, die einen *Homo Truelle* (Spaten-Mann) enthält, der von einem französischen Künstler geschaffen wurde. Weisse Zeichnung auf schwarzem Grund. (FRA)
722 Faltschachtel für ein Kuchenblech. Flach aufgetragene Farben. (ITA)
723 Werbegeschenk der Cotton Incorporated, New York. Schrift in Blau, Bogen des unteren O in Blau, Grün und Gelb. (USA)
724 Papiersäcke für frischgebackene Pariserbrote der Bäckerei *Boudin* in San Francisco. Braun, rot, gelb, blau und grün. (USA)
725 Verpackungen für Würste von Swift & Co., Chicago. (USA)
726 Tragtasche, die von der Zeitschrift *Fortune* als Werbegeschenk abgegeben wurde. (USA)

718 Epandeurs d'engrais spéciaux pour le gazon et les fleurs. Vert et blanc. (GER)
719 Boîtes avec des feuilles de musique d'orchestre pour le Bicentenaire. Cadeau de la chaîne magasins *J. C. Penney.* (USA)
720 Boîte-présentoir pour des échantillons de produits pharmaceutiques de *Roche* distribués au corps médical. Les dessins font allusion aux anciens symboles égyptiens de la vie. (USA)
721 Boîte contenant un artefact, l'*Homo Truelle,* créé par un artiste français. Dessin blanc sur fond noir. (FRA)
722 Boîte pliante pour une tôle à tarte. Design en couleurs à plat. (ITA)
723 Boîte pour la promotion de vente de Cotton Incorporated, New York. Caractères en bleu, arche de l'O d'en bas en bleu, vert et jaune. (USA)
724 Sacs en papier pour du pain français de la boulangerie *Boudin* à San Francisco. Brun, rouge, jaune, bleu et vert. (USA)
725 Emballages pour des saucissons de Swift & Co., Chicago. (USA)
726 Sac en étoffe distribué par le magazine *Fortune* en tant que cadeau promotionnel. (USA)

726

727

728

729

730

731

732

727 Bottle styling for *Pastene* Californian chianti. (USA)
728 Bottle styling for a rosé wine from the vineyards of the Canton of Geneva. Gold and black, with red in coat-of-arms. (SWI)
729 Label for a red wine from Cavas Bach SA. (MEX)
730 Bottle styling for a white wine bottled by Vin-Union, Geneva. Lettering in black and gold. (SWI)
731 Bottle styling for *Buchanan's* scotch whisky. (GBR)
732 Bottle styling for an American bourbon whisky marketed in Germany. Front of label black on tan, red title. (USA)
733 Folding boxes for packs of 12 and 36 colour pens of various types in a wide range of colours made by *Edding*. (GER)
734 Carton, bottle and label for a *Suntory* brandy. Black bottle. (JPN)
735 Folding cartons for *Haig* scotch whisky sold in Japan. (JPN)

727 Flaschengestaltung für den kalifornischen Chianti *Pastene*. (USA)
728 Flasche für einen Rosé, der im Kanton Genf angebaut wird. Gold und schwarz, rote Farbtöne im Wappen. (SWI)
729 Etikette für einen Rotwein der Cavas Bach SA. (MEX)
730 Flaschengestaltung für einen Weisswein, auf Flaschen gezogen durch die Vin-Union in Genf. Schrift in Schwarz und Gold. (SWI)
731 Flaschengestaltung für einen schottischen Whisky. (GBR)
732 Flasche für einen in der Bundesrepublik verkauften amerikanischen Bourbon. Vorderseite der Etikette in Schwarz und Braun, Name in Rot. (USA)
733 Faltschachteln für 12er oder 36er Packungen der *Edding*-Filzschreiber, die in einer grossen Auswahl von Farben erhältlich sind. (GER)
734 Karton, Flasche und Etikette für einen Cognac. Schwarze Flasche. (JPN)
735 Faltschachteln für den in Japan verkauften *Haig* Whisky. (JPN)

727 Bouteille pour le chianti californien *Pastene*. (USA)
728 Bouteille pour un *Pinot Gris* provenant des vignobles du Canton de Genève. Or et noir, écusson avec des tons rouges. (SWI)
729 Etiquette pour un vin rouge de Cavas Bach SA. (MEX)
730 Bouteille pour un vin blanc mis en bouteille par la Vin-Union à Genève. Typo en noir et or. (SWI)
731 Bouteille pour le whisky écossais *Buchanan*. (GBR)
732 Bouteille pour un whisky bourbon américain, en vente en Allemagne. Etiquette en noir sur brun atténué, nom en rouge. (USA)
733 Boîte pliante pour des cartons contenant 12 ou 36 stylos feutre de différentes couleurs et qualités, fabriqués par *Edding*. (GER)
734 Carton, bouteille et étiquette pour une eau-de-vie. Bouteille noire. (JPN)
735 Boîtes pliantes pour le whisky écossais *Haig*, en vente au Japon. (JPN)

733

Packaging / Packungen / Emballages

ARTIST / KÜNSTLER / ARTISTE:	DESIGNER / GESTALTER / MAQUETTISTE:	ART DIRECTOR / DIRECTEUR ARTISTIQUE:	AGENCY / AGENTUR / AGENCE – STUDIO:
727 Tom Courtos	727 Tom Courtos	727 Tom Courtos	727 Lois/Chajet Design Group
728, 730 Ernest Witzig	729 Graham Edwards	728, 730 Michel Logoz	728, 730 Roth & Sauter
729 Ruben Padova	731 Dick Steel	729 Graham Edwards	729 Laboratorio de Diseño Carton y Papel
	732 John McConnell	732 John McConnell	de Mexico SA
	733 J. Otto	734 Nobuyoshi Itoh	731 THM Design Consultants Ltd.
	734 Nobuyoshi Itoh	735 Michio Yamata	732 Pentagram/Young & Rubicam Ltd
	735 Michio Yamato		733 Jürgen Burkhart/Studio 2

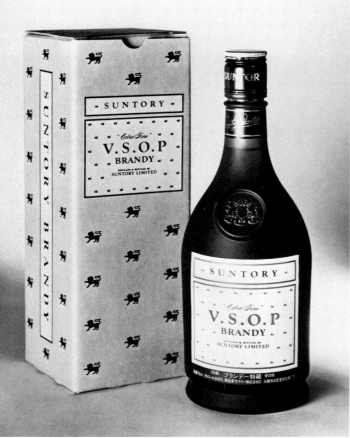

734

735

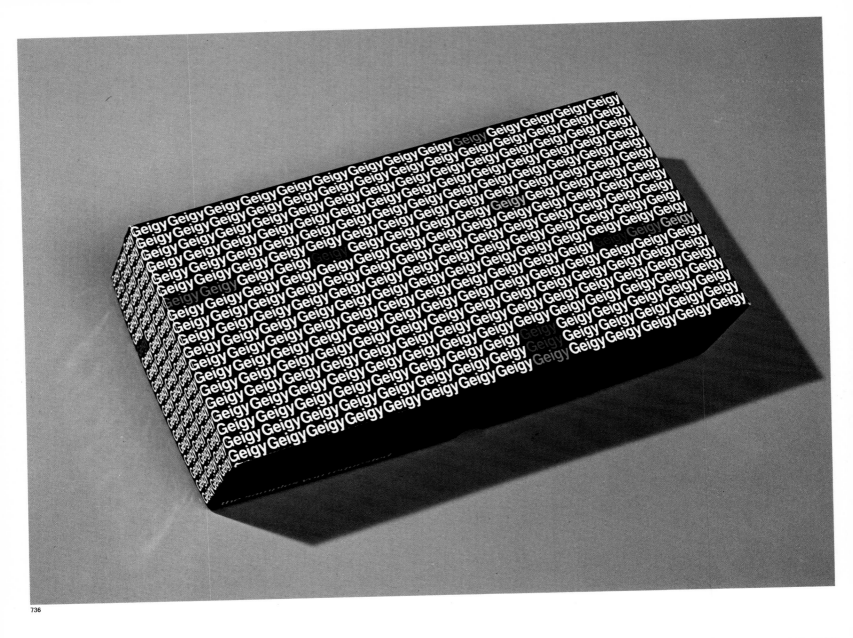

736

737

738

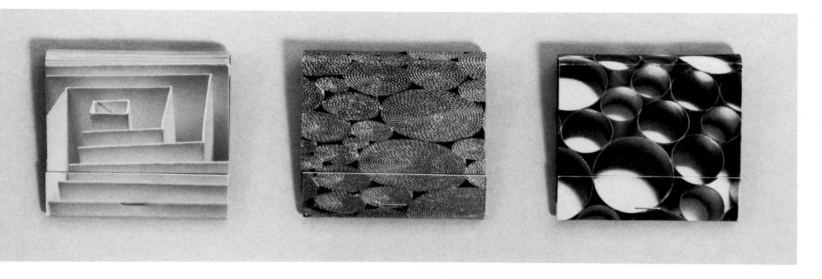

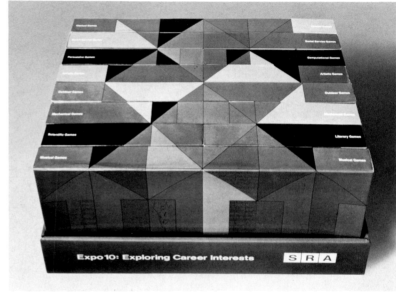

741

Set-up box for samples of *Geigy* pharmaceuticals sent to doctors. (USA)
Packages for a stimulant for the circulation. (GER)
Boxes in full colour for puppet kits based on folk tales, issued by the Society for Visual Education, Inc. (USA)
Match books for the Container Corporation of America, Inc., showing various forms of paper board. (USA)
Kit on the subject of "Communities in Nature", issued by the Society for Visual Education, Full colour. (USA)
Kit for games designed to allow children to explore career interests, issued by Science Research Associates. (USA)

Schachtel für den Versand von Arzneimittel-Mustern an Ärzte. (USA)
Packungen für ein Durchblutungs-Präparat. (GER)
Schachteln, die Figuren zu verschiedenen Volksmärchen und -sagen enthalten. Diese wurden einer amerikanischen Gesellschaft für visuelle Erziehung herausgegeben. (USA)
Streichholzbriefchen aus einer Kollektion, von der Container Corporation of America zu Geenkzwecken herausgegeben. Sie zeigen Papier und Karton in verschiedenen Formen. (USA)
Schachteln mit Spielen zum Thema «Gemeinschaften in der Natur». Diese Spiele wurden von amerikanischen Gesellschaft für visuelle Erziehung herausgegeben. (USA)
Sammelpackung für verschiedene Spiele, deren Themen sich auf die Berufswahl beziehen. (USA)

Boîte-présentoir pour des échantillons de produits pharmaceutiques *Geigy* distribués au corps dical. (USA)
Emballages pour un vasodilateur. (GER)
Boîtes pour des sets de marionnettes basés sur des contes populaires diffusés par la Society Visual Education. En couleurs vives. (USA)
Collection de pochettes d'allumettes distribuées en guise de cadeau par la Container Corpoion of America. Pochettes décorées de dessins structurels de cartons. (USA)
Set intitulé «Communautés naturelles», diffusé par la Society for Visual Education, Inc. En ychromie. (USA)
Set de jeux d'orientation professionnelle diffusé par Science Research Associates. (USA)

ARTIST / KÜNSTLER / ARTISTE:

737 Kroehl Design Gruppe
738 David Lawrence/Ute Jansen/A. Clark
740 David Lawrence

DESIGNER / GESTALTER / MAQUETTISTE:

736 Bob Paganucci
737 Kroehl Design Gruppe
738 Ute Jansen
740 David Lawrence
741 Bruce Daniels

ART DIRECTOR / DIRECTEUR ARTISTIQUE:

736 Bob Paganucci
737 Heinz Kroehl/Peter Offenberg
738, 740, 741 David Lawrence
739 Wilburn O. Bonnell III

AGENCY / AGENTUR / AGENCE – STUDIO:

736 Geigy Pharmaceuticals
737 Kroehl Design Gruppe
738, 740, 741 David Lawrence Design

Packaging / Packungen / Emballages

742

743

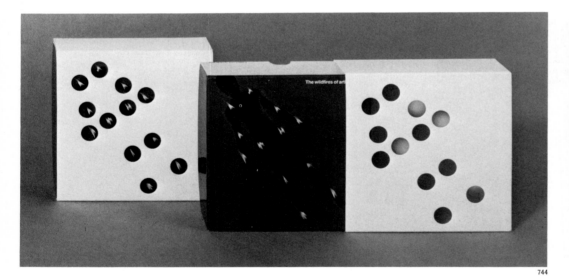

744

745

746

747

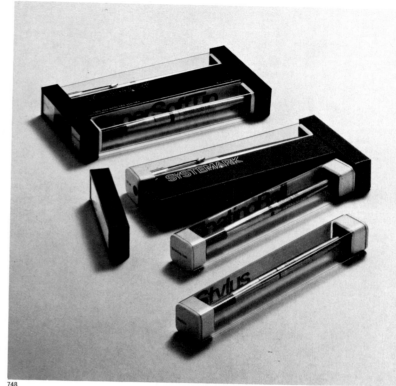

748

749

742 Container for a *Gainsborough* foam bath for men. (GER)
743 Container and carton for a medicine against acne made by *Pharmacraft*. (USA)
744 Packaging for a doctor's sample of a *Ciba-Geigy* drug which claims to combat the "wildfires of arthritic pain". The flames at the joints of the blue figure on the lid of the set-up box appear through the perforations of the sleeve. (USA)
745 Set-up boxes for samples of *Roche* pharmaceuticals sent to doctors. In two and three shades of blue respectively. (CAN)
746 Container for a *Spa* foam bath sold in boutiques. (USA)
747 Wrapping paper and scent bottle for the Hôtel du Cap d'Antibes. (FRA)
748 Modular packages for *Parker* pens and pencils. (USA)
749 Range of packaging for *Blu Max* cosmetics for men. (ITA)
750 Folding box acting as a dispenser for *Kleenex* facial tissues. Special design in the spirit of the US Bicentennial. (USA)

742 Flasche für ein Schaumbad für Männer. (GER)
743 Dose und Verpackung für ein Mittel von *Pharmacraft* gegen Akne. (USA)
744 Verpackung für Ärztemuster der *Ciba-Geigy*. Dieses Mittel soll die stechenden Schmerzen bei Arthritis lindern. Die Flammen an den Gelenken der blauen Figur, die sich auf der Einstecklasche der Schachtel befindet, werden durch die Perforation des Schubers sichtbar. (USA)
745 Schachtel für den Versand von *Roche*-Arzneimittelmustern an Ärzte. Je nach Schachtel in zwei oder drei Blautönen. (CAN)
746 Flacon für ein in Boutiquen verkauftes Schaumbad. (USA)
747 Einwickelpapier und Parfumflasche des Hotels du Cap d'Antibes. (FRA)
748 Standardverpackung für *Parker*-Füllfederhalter und -Drehbleistifte. (USA)
749 Verpackungsreihe für *Blu Max*-Kosmetikartikel für Herren. (ITA)
750 Faltschachtel für *Kleenex*-Gesichtstücher. Die Illustration wurde speziell aus Anlass der 200-Jahrfeier entworfen. (USA)

742 Récipient pour un bain de mousse pour messieurs. (GER)
743 Récipient et carton pour un produit pharmaceutique pour le traitement de l'acné. (USA)
744 Boîte pour un échantillon *Ciba-Geigy* distribué au corps médical. Ce produit est prétendu adoucir les douleurs cuisantes de l'arthrite. Les flammes aux articulations de la figure bleue sur le couvercle se font voir à traves les perforations de la manche. (USA)
745 Boîte-présentoir pour les échantillons pharmaceutiques de *Roche* diffusés au corps médical. Chaque boîte en deux ou trois tons bleus. (CAN)
746 Récipient pour un bain de mousse en vente dans des boutiques. (USA)
747 Papier d'emballage et flacon de parfum pour l'Hôtel du Cap d'Antibes. (FRA)
748 Emballages modulaires pour les stylos et portemines *Parker*. (USA)
749 Gamme d'emballages pour les produits cosmétiques *Blu Max* pour messieurs. (ITA)
750 Boîte pliante pour les tissus faciaux *Kleenex*. Le design a été créé spécialement pour l'occasion du Bicentenaire. (USA)

750

Packaging / Packungen / Emballages

751

752

753

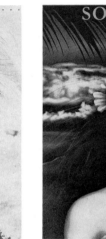

754

755

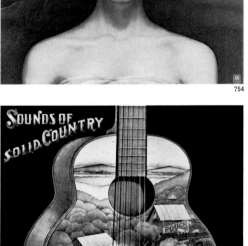

756

757

758

759

760

761

762

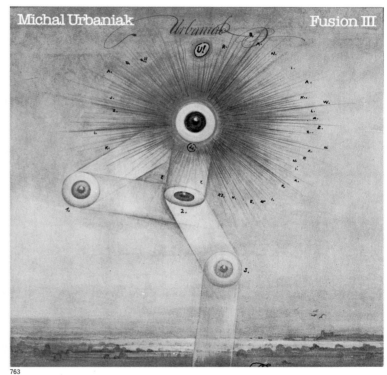

763

Record Covers
Schallplattenhüllen
Pochettes de disque

764

765

766

767

768

769

770

ARTIST / KÜNSTLER / ARTISTE:

764 Richard Hess/Henrietta Condak
765 Seymour Chwast/Eloise Vega/John Berg
766 Bernard Bonhomme
767, 770, 771 Holger Matthies
768 Oskar Weiss
769 Manfred Vormstein
772 Maurice Sendak/Chuck Beeson

ART DIRECTOR / DIRECTEUR ARTISTIQUE:

764 John Berg/Henrietta Condak
765 John Berg
766 Alain Marouani
767, 770 Lutz Bode
769 Manfred Vormstein
771 Holger Matthies
772 Lou Adler

PUBLISHER / VERLEGER / EDITEUR:

764, 765 CBS Records
766 Barclay
767, 770 Polydor International GmbH
768 Helvetas
769 Ariola-Eurodisc GmbH
771 Teldec
772 A & M Records, Inc.

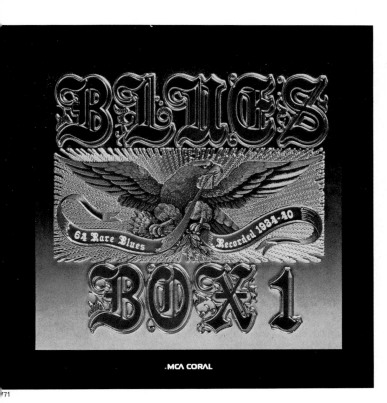

771

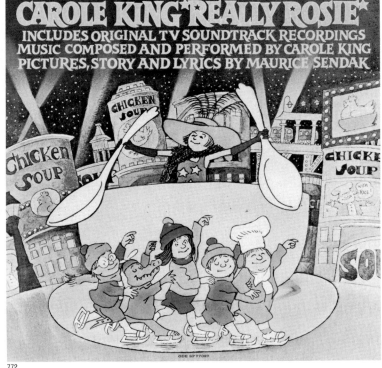

772

Record Covers
Schallplattenhüllen
Pochettes de disque

ARTIST / KÜNSTLER / ARTISTE:

773 Etienne Delessert
775 Kálmán Molnár
776, 777 Manfred Vormstein
778 Dave Willardson
779 Nick Fasciano
780 Martin Springett
781 Geoff Hocking
782 Richard Hess

DESIGNER / GESTALTER / MAQUETTISTE:

775 Kálmán Molnár
776, 777 Manfred Vormstein
778 Mike Salisbury
779 John Berg/Nick Fasciano
781 Geoff Hocking
782 Henrietta Condak

773

774

775

776

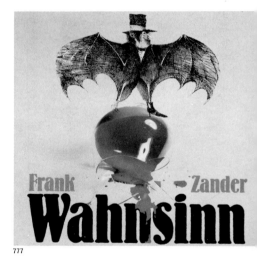

777

ART DIRECTOR / DIRECTEUR ARTISTIQUE:

775 Zupán Péterné
776, 777 Manfred Vormstein
778 Craig Braun
779 John Berg
780 Roslav Szaybo
781 Terry Beard
782 Henrietta Condak

AGENCY / AGENTUR / AGENCE – STUDIO:

778 Craig Braun Inc.

PUBLISHER / VERLEGER / EDITEUR:

774 Barclay
775 Budavox Telecommunication Foreign Trading Co. Ltd.
776, 777 Ariola-Eurodisc GmbH
778 United Artists Records, Inc.
779, 780, 782 CBS Records
781 Music for Pleasure Ltd.

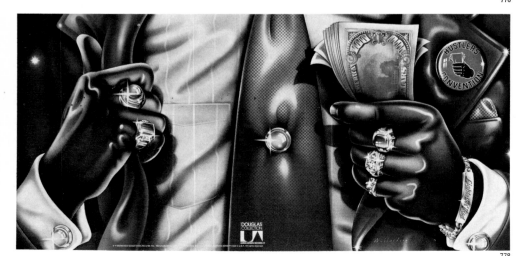

778

234

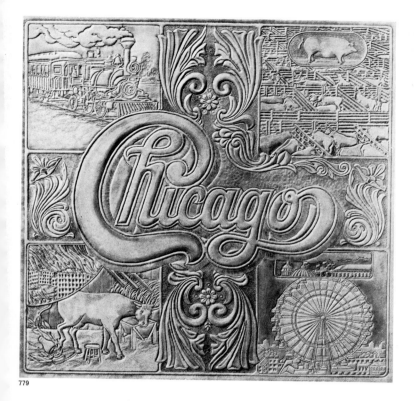

779

780

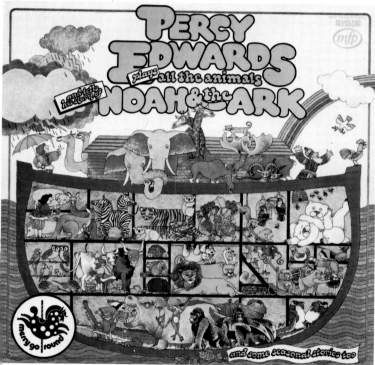

781

782

773 Record covers for songs written and sung by Henri Dès. Shades of brown on pale green background, red heart. (SWI)
774 Complete cover in full colour for a recording of songs by Jimi Hendrix. (FRA)
775 Cover for a record used as a gift by the *Budavox* telecommunications company. (HUN)
776, 777 Detail and complete cover for a record entitled "Madness". (GER)
778 Complete cover in airbrush technique for a *United Artists* record. (USA)
779 Embossed cover for a *Columbia* recording of a group called Chicago. (USA)
780 Record cover for songs by Ian Hunter. Full colour. (USA)
781 Cover for a "sound picture" of the animals in the Ark. Full colour. (GBR)
782 Cover for a recording of Copland's *The Red Pony*. The full-colour artwork capturing some of the scenes from the piece is in oils on canvas. (USA)

773 Pochette pour un enregistrement de chansons, composées et chantées par Henri Dès. Tons bruns sur fond vert clair, cœur rouge. (SWI)
774 Pochette pour un enregistrement de songs de Jimi Hendrix. Polychromie. (FRA)
775 Disque-cadeau distribué par la compagnie de télécommunications *Budavox*. (HUN)
776, 777 Détail et pochette complète pour un disque intitulé «Folie». (GER)
778 Pochette – exécutée à l'aide d'un aérographe – d'un disque de *United Artists*. (USA)
779 Pochette gaufrée pour un enregistrement du groupe Chicago. (USA)
780 Pochette pour un enregistrement de songs de Ian Hunter. En polychromie. (USA)
781 Pochette pour une «image musicale» des animaux de l'Arche de Noé. (GBR)
782 Pochette pour un enregistrement de *The Red Pony* de Copland. L'illustration – huile sur toile – reprend quelques scènes de la pièce. (USA)

773 Schallplattenhülle für Lieder, die von Henri Dès komponiert und gesungen werden. Braune auf hellgrünem Hintergrund, rotes Herz. (SWI)
774 Geöffnete Plattenhülle für Songs von Jimi Hendrix. Mehrfarbig. (FRA)
775 Platte, die von der Fernsprechgesellschaft *Budavox* als Geschenk verteilt wurde. (HUN)
776, 777 Detail und vollständiger Umschlag für eine Platte von Frank Zander. (GER)
778 Geöffnete Plattenhülle – in Spritztechnik – für eine Aufnahme von *United Artists*. (USA)
779 Blindgeprägte Plattenhülle für Aufnahmen der Gruppe Chicago. (USA)
780 Schallplattenhülle für Songs von Ian Hunter. Mehrfarbig. (USA)
781 Hülle für eine musikalische Erzählung über die Tiere der Arche Noah. Mehrfarbig. (GBR)
782 Plattenhülle für eine Aufnahme von Coplands *The Red Pony*. Die Illustration, in Öl auf Leinwand, gibt einige Szenen des Stücks wieder. (USA)

Paper/Papier: Papierfabrik Biberist – Biber GS SK3, blade coated, pure white, 120 gm² and Biber Offset SK3, pure white, machine-finished, 140 gm²/Biber GS SK3, hochweiss, satiniert, 120 gm² und Biber-Offset SK3, hochweiss, maschinenglatt, 140 gm²

Printed by/gedruckt von: J.E. Wolfensberger AG, Zurich (Colour pages/Farbseiten), Merkur AG, Langenthal (black and white/schwarzweiss)

Cover/Einband: Buchbinderei Schumacher AG, Bern/Schmitten Glossy lamination/Glanzfoliierung: Durolit AG, Pfäffikon SZ